ALAN F. PARKINSON

Ulster loyalism and the British media

FOUR COURTS PRESS

This book was set in 10.5 on 12 point Ehrhardt
by Woodcote Typesetters for
FOUR COURTS PRESS LTD
Fumbally Court, Fumbally Lane, Dublin, Ireland
Email: info@four-courts-press.ie
and in North America for
FOUR COURTS PRESS
c/o ISBS, 5804 NE Hassalo Street, Portland, OR 97213.

A catalogue record for this title
is available from the British Library.

ISBN 1-85182-367-X cased
1-85182-392-1 paperback

Printed in Ireland by ColourBooks Ltd, Dublin.

Contents

Preface

This book is an edited and updated version of a doctoral thesis which was completed in 1996. I am particularly indebted to my supervisor at Swansea University, Professor George Boyce, for his wise counsel and thoughtfulness throughout my six years of research. The suggestions of George's colleague at Swansea, Professor Richard Taylor, and Professor Paul Bew at Queen's University Belfast, were also much appreciated. Many people gave generously of their time and assistance in the conducting of the survey in 1995. These include Sally Mitchell, Frank Shields and the Sociology 'A' level class at St Francis Xavier Sixth Form College in Balham, London, for participating in a 'pilot' survey, Dr Jennifer Dewhurst for distributing survey forms in Lancashire, Ivor Hobson for carrying out a similar task in Glasgow, David Dickson and Dr Stuart Parker for assisting with the research in Surrey and Berkshire respectively, Beryl Sanders for helping me with the survey at Guildhall University, London, Eric Mundy for distributing forms in Devon and, most especially, those who participated in the survey in the afore-mentioned areas.

Despite considerable initial difficulties, I was fortunate to receive help from a number of people working in television. These included Jane Arrowsmith and Roger Bolton, then of Thames Television, for allowing me access to Thames TV records and sparing the time to talk about 'Death on the Rock' and other Thames programmes relating to Northern Ireland. I am also grateful to Ann Woolf of London Weekend Television, Cathy Campbell and Grant McKee of Yorkshire TV, the news research department at Channel Four, Carol Deakins of the BBC TV News and Current Affairs Department and Neil Somerville at the BBC Library and Archives Centre in Reading for assisting me in my research into 'Panorama' coverage of the Irish conflict. Although I was unable to gain direct access to the archives of the Conservative Party, I did receive assistance from Victoria Janetta, Labour Party librarian, Jim Wilson and Gavin Adams of the Ulster Unionist Party, Ian Paisley Junior of the DUP and J.W. George Patton, Executive Officer of the Orange Order. Staff in several libraries helped me in my research. These included staff at the British Newspaper Library, in Colindale, the Public Record Office at Kew, the Linenhall and Central libraries in Belfast, Swansea University library and Surbiton, Kingston and Ewell libraries in Surrey. Chris Costa had the onerous task of typing out my doctoral thesis and again came to the rescue during its editing in preparation for publication.

I would like to thank Martin Fanning, Ronan Gallagher and Michael Adams at Four Courts Press for their interest in my work and their professionalism during its publication phase. I am deeply indebted to Janet, Nick and Katherine for their perseverance over the last seven years and especially to my younger son, Thomas, for his assistance in the collation of the survey findings.

Finally I would like to express my gratitude to my father John for unfailingly remembering to forward cuttings from the Belfast papers. This book is dedicated to him and to my late mother.

CHAPTER ONE

Introduction

> In Northern Ireland the Protestants proudly proclaim their loyalty to England and the Crown, and are regarded as vulgar aliens. The Catholics, who have, after all, bred the IRA and vote regularly for secession from Britain, are, by contrast, seen as lovable rascals, no less a part of the nation than the Scots or the Welsh – and better company. The Prods (of whom I am one) are used to being shunned. Nobody likes us. We are regarded for the most part as bloody-minded scum, lost down one of history's blind alleys. The English are not touched by our devotion. Rather, they think that we ourselves are 'touched'. Proper Paddies, in fact. Vile is how they see us, just like the Boers, and when we pledge our loyalty, they shy away, embarrassed, as though we had just broken wind.[1]

In this book I attempt to draw attention to the way in which the poor quality of presentation of the loyalist case, emanating from both unionist politicians and media agencies, has been most influential in creating the predominantly hostile reaction of mainland public opinion, and unionists' increasing political marginalisation in Great Britain. I briefly examine the nature of loyalism, the content of unionist propaganda and the effect of the unionists' message on British political policy, but the main focus is on media representations of 'loyalism' and their influence on British public opinion.

What is striking about those few researches which have concentrated specifically on loyalism, is their limited scope. Though some of the weightier tomes delve into the manifestations of unionists' 'loyalty', they fail to investigate how the nature of Unionist propaganda and the 'messages' which the national media transmitted to the British viewing and reading public have reinforced existing misconceptions about loyalism.[2]

1 Walter Ellis, writing in the *Sunday Times*, 26 June 1994. 2 Although journalists and academics have been more reticent in writing about mainstream loyalism than they have about Irish nationalism or republicanism, a number of eloquent contributions have surfaced, notably those of David W Miller, Sarah Nelson, Steve Bruce, Arthur Aughey and Norman Porter. Miller's 1978 work, *Queen's Rebels: Ulster Loyalism in Historical Perspective*, was instrumental in encouraging others to reconsider the aimless, knee-jerk interpretations of loyalism and instead stressed the 'conditional' and 'reciprocal' nature of Unionists' loyalty to Britain. Sarah Nelson, in her 1984 book, *Ulster's Uncertain Defenders; Loyalists and the Northern Ireland Conflict*, developed Miller's siege mentality thesis, and though she highlighted a number of inherent contradictions within loyalism, she also endeavoured to present a multi-dimensional view of the loyalist identity. The more recent works of Steve Bruce, Arthur Aughey and Norman Porter have, each in their own way, extended the debate on the essence of loyalism. Steve Bruce's

This is where my book differs from previous research. Whilst it briefly retraces much-furrowed ground, such as the debate over the nature of loyalism, its main emphasis is on how the 'loyalist' case has been reported in the British media during the present conflict. I was only too aware of the tendency of previous research to concentrate on the censorship issue in general and the republican case in particular, and I wanted to make a contribution to the literature of an area which has, if anything, been under-researched. In any case, this subject reflects my interest in the history of the unionist community in Northern Ireland. In a previous project I had been intrigued by the contrast between the sympathy which was displayed for the unionist case during the Edwardian period and the comparative contempt with which it was regarded by people in Great Britain during the current Troubles and I was interested in investigating the reasons behind this stark contrast.[3]

Where academics and journalists have made some attempt to address specific areas of my subject (for instance, in the analysis of what constitutes 'loyalism'), I have commented critically on their analyses, but I have also endeavoured to utilise several intriguing primary sources previously not referred to in such discussion. Therefore, I have quoted extensively from a variety of unionist policy documents (mainly those from the Unionist Party), which illustrate loyalists' viewpoints on a number of issues.[4] In general, there has been a conspicuous lack of literature in my main area, namely media interpretations of 'loyalism'. Consequently, I was faced with a sources challenge. Although I enjoyed a certain degree of success in researching this subject, I also encountered a number of problems. Fortunately I already had a fairly extensive collection of national press cuttings and was able to supplement these after researching at the Newspaper Library at Colindale. It was clear from the start that an enormous amount has been written about Northern Ireland and even though a comparatively small proportion has been devoted to analysing the loyalist viewpoint, it would have been an impossible task to monitor every news entry. My choice, therefore, was either to select several important events over the thirty year period under ques-

1994 book, *The Edge of the Union – the Ulster Loyalist Political Vision*, concentrated on Paisleyism and loyalist militarism and emphasised the fundamental impact of religio-political influences on Protestants as well as stressing their differing interpretations of their own ethnicity. In his 1989, book, *Under Siege: Ulster Unionism and the Anglo-Irish Agreement*, Arthur Aughey played down the importance of determinants such as 'conditional' loyalty and ethnicity, preferring the explanation that unionism should be placed within the context of a united British state in which equality of treatment for all it citizens would be of paramount importance. Norman Porter's 1996 book, *Rethinking Unionism – An Alternative Vision for Northern Ireland*, elucidates the case for loyalists to reject 'liberal' and 'cultural' unionism and instead urges them to embrace a broader, cross-community 'civic' unionism. 3 See my MA dissertation, 'Ulster will fight and Ulster will be right – The Presentation of the Anti-Home Rule Case in Great Britain 1912–1914', University of Westminster, 1989. 4 I was also fortunate in having access to a plethora of primary sources pertaining to the Conservative, and particularly, the Labour Parties. A more detailed assessment of the inter-relationship between British political parties and unionism can be found in my doctoral thesis, 'Loyal Rebels Without a Cause? The Presentation and Reception of the Loyalist Case in Great Britain 1968–1996', University of Swansea, 1996.

tion and observe how the same two or three papers or TV programmes handled these events, or else to widen and vary the range of sources taken for a reduced number of incidents or talking-points and at the same time investigate recurring themes in a range of media outlets. I chose this latter approach which is graphically illustrated by the methods adopted in the case study on the Enniskillen bombing. As I had some difficulty in getting a precise breakdown in TV programmes with a Northern Ireland input (in any case, the size and cost of this venture was prohibitive), I decided to avoid adopting a full-scale analysis of the content of news bulletins and focus instead on observing, in the main, instances of investigative, in-depth coverage of the loyalist position (this is the approach taken in the media chapter). Another important challenge posed by this project was the gauging of mainland opinion on a number of aspects, or characteristics, of 'loyalism'. Whilst several opinion polls have contributed much to the understanding of British attitudes to Northern Ireland, very little has been carried out which improves understanding of British attitudes to the Protestant predicament. I therefore designed and conducted a small-scale survey in six main centres throughout Great Britain, which endeavoured to extricate information and attitudes from people on the British mainland to several of the images of loyalism developed elsewhere in this work.

There are essentially two free-standing but inter-related sections in this book. In the following chapter I attempt to unravel what constitutes 'loyalism' in the Northern Ireland context, and I examine the political 'messages' emanating from Unionists' propaganda material. In doing so, I shall discuss the influence of such 'messages' on determining the policies of successive British administrations, as well as their degree of success in winning support at grassroots level. The final section of this chapter adopts a case study approach and investigates how existing political and media perceptions of the Unionist case mitigated against loyalist exploitation of British moral indignation at republican terrorism in the wake of the Enniskillen bombing in 1987. The media element of this case study acts as a 'bridge' between the two chapters. In the media chapter I look at how the loyalist case has been covered by the British press and television over the last thirty years, examining in particular instances where loyalists have dominated the media 'agenda' and the predominant images which have become associated with unionism. Special attention will be paid to investigating analytical treatment of loyalist 'stories' and to assessing how these media perceptions have influenced the formation of public opinion in Great Britain. I turn first to the nature of 'loyalism' and the British response to its political message.

CHAPTER TWO

Loyalism, its political message and the British response

A QUESTION OF LOYALTY

Then rally Ulster's loyal sons,
And proud your banners wave,
With heart and voice make it your choice,
Our blood-bought rights to save,
Our brethren across the sea,
Will join the glad refrain,
Then in God's name your watchword raise,
The Union We'll Maintain[1]

'Loyalism'. To the outside observer, the very use of the word, in the Ulster context, is a misnomer. In contrast with their improving knowledge of the nationalist community, the British public remain perplexed by Ulster's Protestants and this confusion has led to the formation of a number of negative responses, including frustration, apathy, disdain and anger. This obvious lack of sympathy on the British mainland for the loyalist cause is directly related to their confusion over what they perceive to be the rather shady manifestations of such loyalism. What causes this confusion? Ulster's Unionists have little doubt. To them, it is a combination of a nationalist 'conspiracy' in which unionists have been constantly misrepresented as 'oppressors' and 'reactionaries' and British bad faith and equivocation, particularly on the issue of the union, which have produced this bewilderment.[2] Other explanations of this confusion abound. Clearly the long-standing inarticulation of unionist politicians has not assisted the loyalists in putting across their case. Although unionists are not as naive on the importance of promoting themselves in a favourable light as they were back in 1969, they are still the clear losers in Northern Ireland's propaganda 'war'. British ignorance of the situation in Northern Ireland can be partly explained by the region's geographical remoteness which accounts for the fact that most of the 'receiving audience' have never been to the province.[3] Nor does the sheer complexity of Ulster Unionism help the beleaguered British observer. The proliferation in the number of loyalist paramilitary groups and the splinters within Unionism increase the confusion of the

1 *The Crimson Song Book* (Belfast 1975), quoted in G. Bell, *The Protestants of Ulster* (London 1975), p. 10. 2 A. Aughey, *Under Siege*, op. cit., p. 1. 3 Liz Curtis, in emphasising that the British public are 'almost entirely dependent' on their media for knowledge of the Irish situation, argues that the logical corollary of this 'dependence' is that the national media's coverage of events in Northern Ireland must be of a high quality. See Liz Curtis, *Ireland – The Propaganda War* (London, 1983), p. 2.

ordinary English onlooker. Therefore when a Devon dairy-farmer or City stockbroker see TV pictures of Ian Paisley leading sinister groups of men up an Antrim hill on a dark winter evening, or Orangemen strutting their defiance every 12th of July, not only do they reinforce existing misconceptions, but empathy with Ulster's 'loyalists', when they are the 'victims', is hindered. This could either be in the physical sense (such as the IRA's 'genocide' policy against Protestants in border areas) or on the political front (which explains unionist failure to capitalise on their gaining of the 'moral high ground' over issues such as the Anglo-Irish Agreement).

In this section I look not only at the main characteristics of loyalism but also at the images which surround it. Negative images of loyalism, including bigotry, ambivalence, egotism, triumphalism, intransigence and their siege mentality are also observed here, as they have tended to predominate national coverage of loyalism and have resulted in its stereotyping. The reasons for the pre-dominance of negative images, the lack of analytical coverage of the loyalist position in particular and loyalists' own poor presentational skills are looked at in detail in the third chapter. Apart from analysing some of the negative characteristics of loyalism, I shall look at other, more positive features of loyalism and briefly observe changes in interpretations of unionism.

Contradiction in terms?

It is the apparently contradictory nature of Ulster 'loyalism' which bemuses the English. Ulster Unionists defied a massive parliamentary majority on the Anglo-Irish Agreement in 1985 just as they had ignored the wishes of an albeit smaller majority between 1912 and 1914. Their political leaders pledge fealty to the Crown, yet refuse to attend Royal weddings.[4] They bemoan their own political marginalisation, yet they denied certain democratic rights to the Catholic minority in the 1960s. Sarah Nelson identified a number of apparent contradictions in the manifestation of Ulster Protestants' 'loyalty' to Britain.[5] She observed that loyalists were perceived to be 'loyal to Britain, yet ready to disobey her; they reject clerical tyranny, yet oppose secularism; they proclaim an ideology of freedom and equality, except for Roman Catholics; they revere law and order, then break the law'.[6]

A more detailed examination of the political nuances of Ulster Unionism and the basic philosophies of Northern Ireland's Protestants, would however, make their 'loyalty' appear less contradictory. Part of this misunderstanding is due to the negative nature of unionism. Unionist emphasis has, over the years, been more on what they are against, rather than what they promote. Richard Rose, in his pertinent 1968 study, *Governing without Consensus*, concluded that Protestants were a lot more clear about what they were not, rather than what they were.[7]

4 The Reverend Ian Paisley refused to attend the wedding of Prince Charles and Lady Diana Spencer in 1981, because Catholic priests had been invited to participate in the ceremony. 5 Nelson, *Ulster's Uncertain Defenders*, op. cit., p. 9. 6 Ibid. 7 R. Rose, *Governing without Consensus* (London 1971).

Despite this uncertainty over their identity, Rose argued that Ulster's Protestants had a tendency to express strong feelings about this identity (whatever it might be), a pattern influenced by the perennial unionist insecurity over their physical well-being.[8] Consequently unionist demands are restricted to maintaining a constitutional status quo and a simple desire for self-determination, rather than the attainment of greater political goals such as the annexation of neighbouring territory, or even a desire for a social or economic reform 'package'. The 'single object' nature of Ulster Unionism restricts not only its appeal but also gives it this limited, negative image.

An illogical and nihilistic creed?

Critics of Ulster loyalism have not been slow to point a finger at their nihilistic tendency. The complexities of loyalism, its seemingly contradictory political demands delivered by fiery clerics entrenched in a sectarian time-warp, assisted by ranks of dour, marching Orangemen, prompted Geoffrey Bell into dismissing Ulster loyalism as 'the voice of unreason, the voice of illogicality'.[9] A less simplistic interpretation of loyalism was profered by Michael MacDonald. In describing Ulster loyalism as 'ambivalent', MacDonald acknowledges the far from straightforward nature of the phenomenon. In his explanation of this ambivalence MacDonald points out that Protestants 'depend on a benefactor whom they cannot fully trust'.[10] This ambivalence and the resultant loyalist sense of 'betrayal' reached its zenith in 1972 when Ulster Unionists' perceived 'friends', Ted Heath's Conservative government, prorogued Stormont. This 'unreciprocated' loyalty, MacDonald argues, helps to explain how Ulster Protestants have developed 'a fervent but unsteady commitment to Britain'. [11] The results of this ambivalence over what constitutes 'loyalism' are quite profound. The confusion which the mainland public have in attempting to decipher the complexities of political loyalism has led to their tendency not to take unionists seriously and to reduce the loyalist position to one of easily understood stereotypes. Ulster loyalists' identification with the Crown, as distinct from Parliament, also distances them from the rest of British society, particularly at a time when there has been increasing public disquiet over the monarchy.

Bigots in bowler hats?

Perhaps the most prominent of loyalism's negative characteristics is the perceived bigotry of Ulster's loyalists, epitomised collectively by the Orangemen and individually by Ian Paisley. The intolerance of Protestants, reflected in their historical and cultural traditions and treatment of Catholics was, particularly in the early phase of the Troubles, taken for granted. It remains, for many Englishmen,

8 39% of Protestants interviewed in the Rose survey regarded themselves as British. 32% emphasised their Ulster identity, whilst 20% believed themselves to be Irish. 9 G. Bell, *The Protestants of Ulster* (London 1976), p. 9. 10 M. MacDonald, *Children of Wrath – Political Violence in Northern Ireland* (Cambridge 1986), p. 124. 11 Ibid.

the most enduring image of Ulster loyalism. Arthur Aughey pinpoints this quintessentially antiquated and irrelevant reputation of unionism. To most British observers, unionism, the political ideology of the vast majority of Protestants, appears as 'the self-justification of an exclusive set of bigots whose guardians of the faith delight in whipping up their demented enthusiasm'.[12] According to Aughey, loyalism normally manifests itself to the British public 'as nothing other than a primitive local cult given to rituals of a barbaric nature'.[13]

As has already been noted, it is a religious pressure group, the Orange Order, which personifies, for a British and indeed, international, audience, this 'bigotry'. Yet apart from the early years of the Troubles when Orange parades provided curiosity value for English audiences, and later when violence was anticipated at parades (such as Portadown in 1986, Belfast's Ormeau Road in 1991, 1995 and 1996 and Drumcree in 1995, 1996 and 1997) national coverage of Orange marches has been almost cursory in its treatment.[14] Even the Tercentenary of the Boyne celebrations received scant coverage on the BBC, with only a marginal increase in the attention paid to the 1990 Twelfth and the special Tercentenary parade in September. The media has made much of the 'provocative' nature of Orange parades. Yet historical evidence suggests that, although constituting a significant contributory factor in sparking off sectarian violence, they are by no means the sole reason for such tension. Indeed, Patrick Buckland has argued that Orange processions were 'a precipitatory factor' in only 6 out of 15 major riots between 1813 and 1914.[15]

The most recent criticism of such parades is that Orangemen's insistence on marching along 'traditional' routes which pass through nationalist areas constitutes not only a threat to public order, but also, and more fundamentally, to the much-vaunted peace process. Although one journalist despaired of the lack of tabloid interest in what was occurring at Drumcree in July 1996, several broadsheets and television commentators interpreted the government's reversal of their decision to ban an Orange parade proceeding through a nationalist housing estate, as offering renewed evidence of loyalist 'triumphalism'.[16] Suggesting that the government had made an error of judgement in allowing the Drumcree parade to eventually proceed, David Dimbleby argued that the peace process might prove to be the victim of such 'triumphalism' and, in an interview with the Prime

12 A. Aughey, *Under Siege*, op. cit., p. 5. 13 Ibid. 14 Referring to the presence of eleven *Guardian* reporters in Northern Ireland during July 1970, Simon Winchester admitted that few of them 'could begin to understand what it was that welded these people together in such a gaudy community': *In Holy Terror – Reporting the Ulster Troubles* (London 1974). 15 P. Buckland, *Ulster Unionism and the Origins of Northern Ireland 1886–1922* (Dublin 1973), p. 37. 16 Roy Greenslade's *Observer* headline on 14 July 1996 was 'Tunnel-vision tabloids push tribal thuggery off front page'. However, the occasional sympathetic journalist had started querying this notion of 'triumphalism' years before the events at Drumcree. C.C. O'Brien suggested in the *Times*, 7 July 1990, that, whilst the manifestations of Orange rejoicing appear triumphalistic, the rationale behind them reflects a status quo philosophy and he described the Orange celebrations as 'a ritualised expression of defiance, by a besieged people, to the besiegers who outnumber them, in the whole island of Ireland'.

Minister, he stressed the 'perception that the majority population always gets its own way' in Northern Ireland.[17] Other critics of loyalism maintained that the 'boneheadness' of unionist leaders and their refusal to compromise 'confirmed the political bankruptcy of unionism'.[18] The *Economist* leader went on;

> If the current crop of unionist leaders cannot achieve, or even propose, a compromise about a short stretch of road in Portadown, what chance is there that they can bring themselves, or their followers, to accept a broad political compromise that would also be acceptable to moderate nationalists.[19]

Other papers referred to 'the naked sectarian hatred' displayed by Orangemen in County Armagh, and even those journals which expressed some understanding of the loyalist predicament didn't attempt to deny 'the reality of Orange bigotry let alone defend it'.[20] However, Geoffrey Wheatcroft went on in his *Express* article to explain unionist dissension, sneering at the 'modish commentators' who accused loyalists of exhibiting 'paranoia'.[21] Wheatcroft suggested that the same accusations might have been made of 'a German Jew 60 years ago'.[22] The *Sunday Telegraph* also adopted the 'embattled minority' interpretation of events, rather than the 'triumphalist' one.[23] The paper argued that 'the discontent of the past few days reflects not only the legacy of the Province's sectarian past but the quite specific sense of betrayal which has been nurtured among unionists during the peace process'.[24]

I hope that subsequent analysis will illustrate more clearly that British politicians and journalists have misconceived the nature of loyalism, and by concentrating specifically, and nearly exclusively, on the negative aspects of the phenomenon, have initiated a labelling process, from which loyalists find themselves ensnared. As Griselda Cann noted in her commentary for Rod Stoneman's film, 'Ireland - the Silent Voices', it is the intricate, complicated nature of loyalism which confuses the external audience.[25] Therefore, the problem is simplified into 'a struggle between the IRA and the British government' and the majority Protestant population is 'either ignored or reduced to superficial stereotypes'.[26] In other words, they are dismissed as 'bigots in bowler hats'.[27] Thus, a complex concept such as loyalism, instead of being carefully analysed, is usually observed within the confines of familiar, simplistic or stereotypical images and hastily dismissed.[28]

17 BBC1, *Panorama*, 15 July 1996. Other references to loyalist ascendancy included Mary Holland's *Observer* report (14 July 1996), which suggested that 'two years of peace hopes lie trampled in the dust of triumphalist Orange marches' and an *Independent* report (12 July 1996) which described Ulster's Catholics as being 'white niggers' who had been 'stunned by the Orange victory'. 18 *Economist*, 13 July 1996. 19 Ibid. 20 *Daily Mirror*, 10 July 1996 and *Daily Express*, 13 July 1996. 21 Ibid. 22 Ibid. 23 *Sunday Telegraph*, 14 July 1996. 24 Ibid. 25 Channel Four, *Ireland: The Silent Voices*, 1983. 26 Ibid. 27 Ibid. 28 The odd programme did question this stereotype of Orangeism. In *The Peep of Day* (BBC Radio 4, 10 May 1995) Fintan O'Toole observed that Orangemen 'march not just to remember the past but to win control of the present'. In any case, it would be wrong to place all the blame for this stereotyping on the media. A weakness in effectively articulating the Orange case, a slowness to

A privileged caste

It is argued that the internalised nature of Unionist thinking has accentuated the problems caused by Unionist privilege and selfishness, firmly casting them in the mould of simplistic dupes of an imperial master. Many critics have maintained that it was the privileged nature of loyalism - the vestige of colonial power lavished on a regional parliament with all the trappings of imperial authority, a built-in constitutional guarantee and seemingly limitless economic support - that lies at the heart of such 'loyalty'. In other words, Unionist self-centredness is stronger than Unionist principle. MacDonald argues:

> ... for Protestants loyalty to Britain is inseparable from loyalty to themselves. British support is the condition of all those traditions that defines what it means to be Protestant.[29]

Yet this notion of loyalist self-centredness fails to explain unionists' devotion to the British nation during times of crisis (such a theory tends to ignore the enormous blood sacrifice of Ulstermen at battlefields such as the Somme) or the depth of genuine feeling amongst Protestants for the Royal Family. The notion of a privileged caste, a west Britain version of the Varnas, does not quite stand up. Even before the current Troubles started and the degree of British involvement reluctantly increased, the extent of Protestant control over their own, let alone Catholic, destiny lay ultimately in disinterested English hands. Despite the considerable degree of regional autonomy over security policy and local government, Westminster still had the powers to control taxation and, of course, would have been the omnipotent authority in bringing Stormont to heel. Test cases of Unionist power in the early days of the state (such as the Unionist Government's decision to remove proportional representation and their reconsideration of a move towards integrated schooling, both in the 1920s) fell due to Westminster indifference. Any resultant vestige of 'power' and 'privilege' certainly didn't filter down to the Protestant working class on the Shankill Road and in any case, since direct rule was established in 1972, the privileged caste theory is, today, a 'non-starter'.

Unionist control over their own destiny has been destroyed and any existing privilege eroded.[30] This notion that, in its essence, the Northern Ireland conflict is 'imperialistic' in its nature hinges around these notions of colonialism and privilege. Thus MacDonald and others argue that the vast majority of senior positions in industry, commerce and government were held by Protestants, who were also more likely to occupy skilled manual positions. Consequently it was

develop the cultural side of their movement and the apparently outdated religious nature of their organisation, have also contributed to the formation of this stereotype. 29 M. MacDonald, op. cit., p. 137. Also, Frank Wright in 'Protestant Ideology and Politics in Ulster', *European Journal of Sociology*, 1973, 213–80, p. 272 suggested that the allegiance of Protestants to Britain depended on the sovereign power leaving the province to its own devices. 30 A Aughey, op. cit., p. 21.

crucial that unionists continued to propagate notions of 'disloyalty' amongst the Catholic population and to deny them certain rights.

However, there are several flaws to the settler colonialism thesis which MacDonald sees as a crystallization of the whole Ulster problem. Firstly, settler colonialism is dependent on a policy of encouragement from the colonial power. Britain has rarely expressed a desire to 'exploit' Northern Ireland in a colonial sense. Indeed, the creation of the state was construed as a way of passing power to the 'natives', and the half century of 'Stormont' rule was devoid of any real British interest in the affairs of Northern Ireland. Again their inactivity should not be confused with benign, passive support for the 'settlers', but rather should be seen as a further example of avoiding the 'latest nasty news story from Ireland'. Like the office boss who delegates the unpleasant task of disciplining a miscreant filing-clerk to his deputy, successive Westminster governments passed on the awesome responsibility of running a troublesome region to its local leaders. Therefore the bulk of support for modern unionism has its roots in the indigenous Ulster population: it is not a movement with real support from the centre of colonialism. Indeed, the opposite has frequently been the case, with Ulster's loyalists proving to be a constant source of deep embarrassment to British 'mainlanders'. Not only is the settler colonialism thesis susceptible on a number of counts but in stressing certain factors (such as the Protestant 'psyche'), the danger is in ignoring other, more significant, aspects of Protestant consciousness such as national identity, religious affiliation, cultural traditions, and the oft-ignored influence of Troubles 'life experiences' on attitude formation.[31]

Besieged?

Although initially regarded as symptomatic of the paranoia and bleak future associated with the product of such 'settler colonialism', the concept of siege mentality has been modified over the last fifteen years.[32] The notion of loyalists possessing the attitudes of 'frontier defenders' increased as the Troubles endured and, along with a political agenda dominated by the nationalist perspective, such loyalist fears were increasingly regarded in a less dismissive light. At times of crisis for the loyalist community the political and military 'successes' of Catholics appeared to threaten Protestant interests. It was at that point, Padraig O'Malley argued, when 'Protestant perspectives polarise, the hard line becomes the only line and Paisleyism comes to the fore'.[33] Media interest in and interpretation of the fears behind loyalists' siege mentality has grown both in terms of scope and sophistication.[34] There has been a noticeable increase in the willingness of the

31 The belief that Ulster Protestants have, as a result of colonialisation, been 'duped' is popular amongst Britain's 'liberal aristocracy', who despaired of its lack of modernity. In acknowledging that loyalism 'lacked creditibility in the modern age', Arthur Aughey argues that 'unionist principles appear as the flotsam and jetsam of political thought which has foundered in history' (in A. Aughey, *Under Siege*, op. cit., p. 137). 32 For a detailed account of the siege mentality thesis, see D.W. Miller, *Queen's Rebels*, op. cit. 33 P. O'Malley, *The Uncivil War: Ireland today* (Belfast 1983), p. 182. 34 The portrayal of loyalists as the 'losers' in the Irish conflict is considered in greater detail in the media chapter.

national media to acknowledge that these loyalist fears of isolation are genuine. Loyalists, particularly since control over their destiny has gradually slipped out of their hands, earnestly believe that they have, against their wishes, become physically, psychologically and increasingly spiritually detached from their nation. Unlike their Catholic counterparts, who enjoy sympathy throughout Ireland, within the ranks of the political left in Britain and particularly amongst the huge Irish community in America, support for the loyalist cause is minimal and unionists feel friendless, deserted and betrayed, both by the political actions of their governments and by a general public whose apathy and indifference they greatly resent.

Status ambiguity?

Loyalists have also suffered confusion over their political and ethnic identity. Although their leaders constantly stress their majority status within the province, unionists have been increasingly aware of their 'minority' status, both in the 'Irish island' and 'British national' senses. This 'status ambiguity' of loyalists has resulted in the Protestant identity being labelled a 'surrogate' one, the equivalent of the Scots' 'phoney Gaelic or Tartan culture'.[35] The 'artificiality' of loyalist political doctrine and cultural traditions has been taken for granted by the liberal intelligentsia in Britain and by republicans, many of whom appeared to regard doctrines and traditions as the sole prerogative of Irish nationalists. The upsurge of Protestant cultural awareness challenges Osmond's restricted view of loyalist culture.

Internal and external pressures, combined with problems of identity, not surprisingly, have produced a community lacking in confidence. This does not coincide with the prevailing impression of a 'master' race of Ulster Protestants, but the political inarticulation of the loyalist community, compounded by its reticence to speak out when they feel all are against them, is very real.[36] Although they tend to unite in extreme crisis (such as in the wake of especially horrific terrorist attacks like Bloody Friday in 1972 and the 1987 Enniskillen bombing), and in their political reaction to the increased threat of Irish unity, (for instance their response to the Anglo-Irish Agreement in 1985) they are still inclined to lack the cohesive, self-contained character of working-class Catholic communities such as west Belfast or Derry's Bogside.[37] Thus the isolation of Protestants, the inarticulation of their political representatives, and the comparative lack of cohesion in their community, has prompted much endeavour to find the 'true' loyalist identity. What Muinzer has described as 'a double identity crisis' has encouraged writers to explore relationships in contemporary unionism.[38] For Ulster Protestants, it was the anxiety and perplexity provoked by such confusion about the present, which prompted them into re-examining their past. By the

35 J. Osmond, *The Divided Kingdom* (London, 1988), p. 117. 36 S. Nelson, *Ulster's Uncertain Defenders*, op. cit., p. 13. 37 This owes much to the divided nature of the Protestant churches in Ireland and to the Catholic Church's greater propensity for active involvement in its community. 38 P. Muinzer's essay, quoted in J. Osmond, op. cit., p. 97

mid 1970s Protestant disillusionment was at its peak. Michael Hall, assessing the effects of English 'betrayal' at this time, wrote:

> The frequent crises were only proving what a sham the cherished British connection was, when it was only too apparent that the two sides distrusted and disliked each other intensely. Paradoxically, it was to be in their history, within which the Protestant had seemingly been trapped, that they were to find a way forward.[39]

'The way forward' was a reference to the pivotal inter-relationship between identity and political direction. Previous adherence to the 'settler phobia' thesis – that loyalists' paranoia was a natural consequence of the fact that they were not the indigenous people of Ulster – was challenged by Ian Adamson who questioned the Gaelic legacy, describing much of it as 'a myth' and arguing that the Cruthin, originally from Scotland, had been the original inhabitants of Ulster some eight thousand years ago.[40] In other words, the 17th-century Scottish plantation was simply a return to their 'homeland'. A. Buckley developed this thesis, arguing that it challenged the primacy of Irish nationalism. Buckley argued:

> ... the historical 'lynchpin' of Irish nationalism, the Plantation of Ireland, is transformed from a conquest by an oppressive people into a conquest by a people who had been forcefully expelled.[41]

The break-up of monolithic unionism

One of the most important but frequently understated repercussions of the Northern Irish conflict has been the disintegration of the Unionist Party in the early phase of violence and its perennial attempts to conceal its ever-growing cracks. The exposure of these fissures within unionism towards the end of the 1960s was in stark contrast with Unionism's unity during the Edwardian period. Increasingly threatened by the likely prospect of Home Rule, Unionists responded to the challenge. The Ulster Unionist Council (UUC) was set up in 1905, Carson was elected parliamentary leader in 1910 and a paramilitary group, the Ulster Volunteer Force (UVF), was more and more to the fore as the crisis deepened. As has been noted elsewhere, Ireland's unionist minority enjoyed the support of Bonar Law's Conservative Party and there was great backing for their cause on the British mainland.[42]

When the Northern Ireland state was created in the early 1920s Unionists' concern with maintaining the status quo (reflected in draconian legislation such as the Special Powers Act) at the expense of broadening the base of unionism's

39 M. Hall, *Ulster – the Hidden History* (Belfast 1986). 40 I. Adamson, *The Identity of Ulster* (Belfast 1982). 41 Quoted in J. Osmond, op. cit., p. 104. 42 Over 5000 anti-Home Rule meetings were held in English between September 1911 and July 1914 and 3800 meetings were staged in Scotland. Over 2 million signatures were collected for the British Covenant and nearly 7 million Unionist leaflets and posters were distributed in Great Britain, whilst over a quarter million English voters in over 200 constituencies were canvassed on the home rule issue.

appeal, necessitated that the Unionist Party was a united one, not subject to internal friction. This was largely achieved in the unimaginative premierships of Craig (1921–40), Andrews (1940–3) and Brooke (1943–63). Brooke's nephew and successor, Captain Terence O'Neill, combined a policy of industrial investment and economic development with the offer of comparatively minor, if symbolically profound, concessions to the Catholic grassroots.[43] Unionists were perturbed over O'Neill's willingness to reform areas such as local government, and much of their disdain had a class-based explanation. As they were the group most threatened economically by change and also on account of the 'messenger's' (O'Neill's) aloofness, working-class and lower-middle class loyalists were amongst the most vociferous opponents of reform. Consequently, for the first time since Carson's heyday, serious cracks began to appear in the Unionist hegemony. Frank Wright wrote of the disillusionment of ordinary Protestant voters:

> From the start ... the 'loyalism' of O'Neill's unionism was very decidedly identified with the protestant middle class. In general, the working class Protestants who favoured O'Neill's reforms and accepted the legitimacy of the Civil Rights demands tended to be those very people least likely to be Unionist party members.[44]

O'Neill, constantly menaced by divisions from within his own parliamentary backbenches and an increasingly confident Civil Rights movement, called a 'Crossroads' election February 1969, when he asked the electorate, 'What kind of Ulster do you want?' O'Neill's ultimate failure (he resigned two months later when it became apparent that he had insufficient support amongst Unionist followers) was not just on account of his inability to convince his own supporters that his strategy was 'the correct one to safeguard the Union', but also because the Catholic minority was not convinced about Unionist sincerity over their involvement in the affairs of government.[45]

This disenchantment with O'Neill's reforming policies was to have great repercussions for the unionist movement, long after O'Neill departed office. The votes of many working- and lower-middle class Protestants, taken for granted for so long by 'Big House' Unionism, could no longer be ignored and many Protestant opponents of political reform transferred their allegiances to the emerging DUP and Vanguard parties, with their own particular brand of appeal and uncompromising messages. Although its political life was to be quite short, the Van-

43 Generous Government grants and a persuasive Minister of Development, Brian Faulkner, were responsible for the region's economic growth in the 1960s. Faulkner told a gathering of Leeds industrialists in 1966: 'We want you to learn that here is a community proud to be British and leading a productive life. Our farms and factories are as much part of the economic muscle of the country as the mills of Yorkshire. We export linen and whiskey, ships and missiles, optical lenses and oil drills, playing a full part in the economic struggle for prosperity which is vital to every citizen in Britain' (quoted in B. Faulkner, *Memoirs of a Statesman*, London 1978, p. 37). 44 F. Wright, Protestant Ideology and Politics, op. cit. 45 J. Harbinson, *The Ulster Unionist Party 1882–1973* (Belfast 1973).

guard Unionist Progressive Party (VUPP) made considerable inroads into the Unionist Party's Protestant working-class support during the first half of the 1970s. Established in February 1972, VUPP was increasingly attractive to such groups because of its belligerent attacks on Stormont's inability to cope with the worsening situation and by its foreboding denunciation of impending Westminster intervention. Following the establishment of direct rule in March 1972, the party highlighted what they perceived to be the inconsistencies of British politicians. VUPP argued:

> The criterion of consent, used to condemn Stormont, condemns with still greater force the system that has supplanted it ... Jackboot government deserves only one response from free men – resistance.[46]

The DUP derived its support from similar sources. However, its peculiar combination of 'conservative populism', reflected in its hardline security demands and insistence on a return to devolved government, and the party's religious fundamentalism, personified in the charismatic appeal of its leader, ensured its political longevity.[47] In its 1995 paper, *Formula for Political Progress* the DUP advocated the establishment of a elected convention which 'would provide a forum for active politicians in which every party would be represented according to its strength'.[48] The party was equally vociferous in its condemnation of republican paramilitarism and was more likely to stress the sectarian nature of many IRA attacks, than other unionist groups. Listing a catalogue of attacks specifically aimed at Protestants on mini buses, in Orange halls, Canine Club meetings in hotels and gospel hall congregations, the DUP concluded:

> This bloody butchery has been unashamedly carried out by the IRA, defended by Sinn Fein, supported by many in the Roman Catholic community, and the organisation which perpetuated it still has its headquarters in Dublin, was originally financed and is now sheltered by the Government of the Irish Republic.[49]

Although the Unionist Party was to suffer many such defections to the DUP and VUPP, others stayed on within the party, where they continued to oppose reforming premiers such as Chichester-Clark and Faulkner. The latter's decision to accept the terms of Sunningdale and the opportunity to lead a power-sharing administration led to further friction between the Unionist Party's 'traditional' wing and Faulkner's moderate, power-sharing group. Even when this latter group, the Unionist Party of Northern Ireland (UPNI), folded in 1981, moderate, conciliatory unionists did not necessarily return to the Unionist Party's fold, with many opting to join the Union-supporting Alliance Party. The schism between

46 *Ulster – A Nation*, Vanguard Publications, April 1972. 47 S. Wichert, *Northern Ireland since 1945*, London 1991, p. 140. 48 DUP, *Formula for Political Progress*, February 1995. 49 DUP, *The Unionist Case – The Forum Report Answered*, 1984.

left and right within the party was not really to heal. Therefore, although the party was to hold together in the 1980s and 1990s, largely due to James Molyneaux's imperturbable leadership, divisions were apparent over policy direction in the early 1980s (over the integration issue) and towards the end of Molyneaux's leadership.

THE TRUE ESSENCE OF LOYALISM

The political nature of loyalism

Clearly at the heart of loyalists' political philosophy has been their opposition to Irish unity. Although problems arise in attempting to determine the nature of their 'loyalty', particularly in their attempts to subvert the will of the British Parliament, and in the short-lived, but highly significant, outpouring of Ulster nationalism in the 1970s, loyalists' awareness of what they were 'against', has always been explicit. Whilst unionists were proud of their 'Irishness' in Carson's period, their opposition to Irish unity was as strong then as in the 1990s when loyalists are more inclined to proclaim their 'Britishness'.

It would be incorrect to argue that unionists have failed to change their political perspectives over 25 years but their intransigent image and apparent unwillingness to compromise does suggest to outsiders that this might well be the case. Unionists have long since dropped their insistence on the return of a Stormont-style system of devolved government to Northern Ireland and have advocated a number of changes in the form of government for the Province which would also entice members of the minority community. These have included giving nationalists the opportunity to chair select committees, the creation of PR-elected assemblies and a Bill of Rights.[50] Indeed, the party went as far as advocating 'a partnership-based Assembly', albeit on 'an interim basis', with membership, chairs and vice chairs being allocated pro-rata with the number of seats won by each party.[51] Whilst David Trimble met the Irish premier in 1995 and Ulster Unionists are receptive to the idea of cross-border economic bodies, the party's condemnation of the Framework Document illustrates its continuing opposition to Dublin having a substantial say in Ulster's affairs.

Yet these concessions do not camouflage Unionism's broadly one-sided political message over the years. There was a tendency for many Ulster Unionists to hide behind the constitutional issue and to refrain from initiating a social and economic reform programme. As John Harbinson wrote in his history of the Unionist Party, they (Unionists) 'put no distinct principle or programme before the people'.[52] When their political autonomy was displaced and their constitutional security seriously threatened, Ulster Unionists retreated further into their one-issue 'trenches'. As the 'Irish' dimension became even more central to unionist thinking, there was a shift in the emphasis, which gradually moved away

50 UUP, *Blueprint for Stability*, 28 February 1994. 51 UUP, *A Practical Approach to Problem-solving in Northern Ireland*, 21 February 1995, p. 5. 52 J. Harbinson, op. cit., p. 166

from an emotional desire to 'belong' to the British nation, towards a demand that their citizenship should be equal in value to that enjoyed by other British citizens. In demanding a speedy return of strong local government to the province, Unionists reiterated their desire for 'equality' of citizenship. In *The Way Forward* they stressed 'the universal desire' of people in Northern Ireland for a return of devolved government and suggested that the Government's reluctance to 're-store this degree of democracy' as being indicative of 'its unwillingness to treat citizens in Northern Ireland on an equal footing with those in the rest of the United Kingdom'.[53]

Unionist attitudes to the question of Northern Ireland's integration within the United Kingdom have also developed over the period of the Troubles. From the late 1970s under the influence of Enoch Powell and Airey Neave, the balance swung away from the devolutionists to the integrationists.[54] The pendulum was to swing back in the devolutionists' favour following the closer liaison between the Dublin and London governments (though even then, devolutionists were rarely prepared to demand the restoration of 'Stormont'-style institutions).[55]

Unionism's failure to disseminate its political message has been attributed to shortcomings of its leaders in the field of public relations, most notably James Molyneaux. Molyneaux was leader of the Unionist Party from 1979 to 1995 and though relatively successful in maintaining party unity, he was considered a poor television communicator.[56] Molyneaux tended to prioritise the task of pressurising unionists' erstwhile 'friends', the Conservatives, although towards the end of his leadership, he followed the advice of papers like the *Times* and improved the channels of communication between Glengall Street and Tony Blair's 'new' Labour Party.[57] Molyneaux's successor, David Trimble, was acknowledged to be a superior communicator, but the media's response to his appointment as leader in September 1995, was a guarded one. Several papers interpreted Trimble's victory in the context of the IRA ceasefire and 'peace' talks, with the *Independent on Sunday* describing his election as 'a considerable upset for Irish peace hopes', whilst *Newsnight*, in describing it as 'a victory for the Orange card', perceived it as a list to the right for unionism.[58] On the other hand, papers on the right be-

53 UUP, *The Way Forward*, April 1984. 54 Many were convinced by what they considered to be the 'logic' of the integrationist case. Arthur Aughey has neatly described the essence of this as 'being when – and only when – Northern Ireland is governed in the same way as the rest of the United Kingdom, will the conditions for peace and reconciliation ever exist' (A. Aughey, op. cit., p. 134). 55 This is not to suggest that the unionist 'family' suddenly became 'united' on the devolution/integration debate. Apart from the obvious differences between the staunchly pro-devolution DUP and the UUP, there were also signs of different interpretations held by Westminster Unionists and those at local level. 56 One should not underestimate the former achievement. Ann Purdy has noted Molyneaux's ability to 'hold together a party which was practically dead in the mid 1970s and which still tends to enjoy its internal wranglings being washed in public'; in A Purdy, *Molyneaux – The Long View* (Antrim, 1989), p. viii. 57 The *Times* (29 March 1995) observed: 'Having declared his Government neutral on the future of the union, Mr Major should not be surprised if the Unionists are now asking whether his opponents have something better to offer.' 58 *Independent on Sunday*, 10 September 1995, and BBC2, *Newsnight*, 18 September, 1995.

lieved that Trimble's success reflected dissension amongst the party faithful and was a populist move. The *Daily Telegraph* noted that Trimble's win 'constituted a revolt by the grassroots against the way the party has been run and led over the past few years'.[59]

The security war

Detestation of the aims, and especially the methods of militant republicans, has for a long time been a fundamental part of the unionist 'thought' process. However, the prolonged nature of the IRA's current 'war' against the British has ensured that a determination to resist their demands has, if anything, hardened during the current conflict. It certainly has resulted in a vigorous non-stop condemnation of what unionists have regarded as the lack of will of successive British governments in combating terrorism. Addressing the Bow Group in 1972, Brian Faulkner suggested that is was the differing degree of experience of terrorist violence which explained the very different public reactions to it. He told the meeting:

> The British Government, however good their intentions might be ... have not got our will to win. For Mr Heath, Mr Wilson and Mr Thorpe, the affairs of Northern Ireland are a matter of political science ... for us in Ulster, it is a matter of life and death.[60]

Unionist anger with Westminster's unwillingness to consider the pursuit of more strident measures, including internment and more frequent employment of SAS teams, again illustrates the important of differing experiences and their effect on attitude formation. Thus, liberal opinion in Great Britain constantly sided with the rights of the individual in Northern Ireland, whilst unionists tended to stress the wider rights of 'the Ulster society to live in peace'.[61] Describing the death of an ex-RUC reservist, 'the latest victim of the IRA genocide campaign against the border Protestant community', the Unionist Party maintained:

> The lack of selective internment which could take these people (IRA) out of circulation, to everyone's benefit, means that they can carry on murdering. One recent American visitor to our Province condemned internment, saying that 'the sanctity of the individual must be protected at all times'. The fact is that without internment, the sanctity of innocent life is extremely hard and often impossible to protect in Northern Ireland.[62]

Loyalists have taken republican actions as a yardstick for their own responses, which have normally been the opposite. Republicans have been an easy and frequent target for Unionist propagandists, whose anger at the relative political success of Sinn Fein/PIRA has been compounded by what they regard as 'the re-

59 *Daily Telegraph*, 9 September 1995. 60 B. Faulkner, op. cit., p. 161. 61 UUII Issue 2, winter 1988/9. 62 Ibid.

warding of terrorism'.[63] Although this feeling is shared by a large number of Protestants and is one which has hardened as the conflict deepened, it is a position which has not been fully appreciated by the British public, media or political representatives. This is best illustrated by loyalist responses to the 1994 ceasefire. In contrast with the mainland perception that accommodation and willingness to negotiate with ex-terrorists should be offered in order not to stall the all-important peace process, unionists were adamant that terrorists should, at the very least, be excluded from participating in negotiations until they had agreed to a decommissioning of weapons. This is evident in the Unionist Party's repudiation of the government's attempt to use the ceasefire as a weapon with which to blackmail loyalists. The party maintained:

> Ulster Unionists will not allow themselves to be subjected to this type of blatant humiliation and innuendo or to be intimidated into working to a strictly Nationalist agenda just because IRA/Sinn Fein are able to exercise a veto on democracy through the barrel of a rifle.[64]

The economic factor

The argument that Irish unity would harm Ulster's prosperity, was at the centre of unionist political thinking before 1914.[65] It was also pivotal to unionist thinking at the start of the Troubles, and remains, to a degree, a factor in unionist deliberation. Indeed, in a conference on post-ceasefire loyalist options, John Taylor argued that citizens of the Irish Republic would find the financial task of maintaining economic standards in the north an impossible one.

> What Gerry Adams and the people of his ilk must begin to understand is that homes and schools and hospitals and the better way of life cannot come about simply by waving a green flag. Economics ignores sentiment, tradition and national rhetoric ... If we were in a united Ireland those 3.50 million people (in south) ... would each have to sign a cheque for £1,000 per annum and send it up here to maintain even our *present* standard of living in the province, never mind address the other major economic and social issues which beset us.[66]

Yet the economic dimension has not been such a significant factor in unionist debate in recent years.[67] This may be due to the narrowing in economic success

63 Ulster Unionist Party anti-IRA literature is analysed in the section on Unionist propaganda. 64 Ulster Unionist Party, *A Practical Approach to Problem-Solving in Northern Ireland*, 21 February 1995. 65 The pivotal importance of the economic argument during Carson's period as Unionist leader is illustrated by its central place in the Solemn League and Covenant (1912), in which unionists expressed their view that 'Home Rule would be disastrous to the well-being of Ulster as well as of the whole of Ireland' (quoted in P. Buckland, *Irish Unionism 1885–1923*, Belfast, 1973, p. 224). 66 *Beyond the Fife Drum – a report of a Conference held on Belfast's Shankill Road* (October, 1994), Island Pamphlets, 1995. 67 The economic dimension was not a major feature in recent Unionist Party pamphlets such as *Framed* and *Practical Approach*.

differentials between the north and the south, on account both of the violence in the north (and the resulting decision of several international companies to transfer their investment to southern Ireland and elsewhere) and economic recession which crippled a number of the province's leading industries (particularly the textile industry). Consequently, the contrast which had existed between the industrial area of Greater Belfast and most of the rest of Ireland, before the conflict, is not now so prominent.

Ethnic identity

Loyalists have frequently been criticised for their uncertainty and confusion in this area. This has prompted much unionist introspection and has also led loyalists, more recently, to query the quality of their British citizenship.[68] Younger loyalists tend to lay greater emphasis on their 'Britishness' than previous generations.[69] Steve Bruce considers this increasing awareness of their respective ethnic identity to be at the heart of the conflict, although he also conceded that religious factors (especially evangelicalism) to be also important.[70] One possible ramification of the tendency of mainland Britons to lump together people born in Northern Ireland and the Irish Republic is that ethnic differences between the groups have been understated and frequently misunderstood in Great Britain.[71]

Unionists have shown increased urgency in demanding equality of citizenship within the United Kingdom. This call for a 'union partnership' necessitated the larger partner (Great Britain) recognising its reciprocal duty to praise the value of the union, as distinct from merely honouring its responsibility for governing the province. A Unionist Party councillor, Reg Empey, reflected this growing unionist disquiet with governmental reluctance to acknowledge fraternal feelings towards loyalists. In an UUII article, 'Climate of Submission', Empey criticised Ulster Secretary Patrick Mayhew's belief that Britain's role in Northern Ireland was that of a 'facilitator' and suggested that in adopting the role of 'referee' and by refusing to side with the constitutional status quo in the province, Mayhew and his colleagues were assisting the terrorists.

> Here we have a senior Cabinet minister in charge of a department of State, that has no particular policy to pursue. No mention of defending the integ-

68 Sceptics of Ulster Protestant claims to 'Britishness' point to their failing the 'rugby test' by supporting the all-Ireland team against England. Although is to some extent true, it ignores the fact that Protestant support for Northern Irish sides is always greater than for purely 'Irish' teams. Indeed, when these 'Irish' teams only represent the Republic, as was the case with the 1994 Irish World Cup soccer team, loyalist support tends to be minimal. **69** Older generations of unionists proclaim their 'Irishness' with pride, arguing that it goes alongside their British identity. Younger unionists are less likely to stress their 'Irishness' than in the past. **70** S. Bruce, *The Edge of the Union*, op. cit., p. 30. **71** This also explains the failure of the British media to communicate Protestant fears of 'ethnic cleansing'. Conor Cruise O'Brien is an exception. Writing in the *Daily Mail* on 29 August 1992, he compared the killing of Protestants in south Fermanagh with ethnic cleansing in Serbia, suggesting that the IRA's killing of individuals from Protestant families and the subsequent exodus of their relatives, was 'ethnic cleansing of a creeping variety'.

rity of the kingdom not even a personal expression of what the constitutional position of Northern Ireland should be. This attitude is not new and is one of the principal causes of instability in the province.[72]

Loyal to the Crown?

When asked to define their 'loyalty', unionists have frequently pointed out that it is the monarchy and not parliament to which they profess their allegiance. There is no doubting, even in a period of growing disquiet over the future of the Royal Family, that it remains popular amongst the unionist community of Northern Ireland. Thus, even the comparatively unpopular Prince Charles received 'a rapturous welcome from flag-waving loyalists' during his 1995 visit to Belfast's Shankill Road, the first regal tour of that bastion of loyalism since 1941.[73] What lies behind this deep affinity to the monarchy? It can be argued that unionists, in refusing to accept Westminster sovereignty over their constitutional status, pledge their fealty to an institution which is symbolic of the British nation, but which, for loyalists, also has the convenient safeguard of being politically impotent. Loyalists' outpourings of affection for the monarchy might reflect their lack of trust and confidence in other British institutions, such as Westminster, the BBC and Fleet Street, which have, from the loyalist perspective, combined to produce unfavourable representations of their case. This is not to imply that the Royal Family has offered loyalists encouragement and support. In comparison with King George V, who, like most of the British establishment of his day, sympathised with the unionists' predicament in the period before the Great War, the modern Royal Family has maintained a 'neutral' stance on the constitutional issue during the whole conflict. Whilst they clearly sympathised with the victims of violence, they steered clear of becoming embroiled on the question of the union, only lending their support to those voices of reconciliation (such as Gordon Wilson) and in their concern for security force victims of the terrorist violence.[74] The apparent lack of reciprocation between the Royal Family and Northern Ireland's loyalist community is provided by the low level of interest shown by the more senior members of the Royal Family, compared to that extended to other regions of the United Kingdom.[75]

Religious differences

Despite the national media's gross over-simplification that the Irish war was a purely 'religious' one and its accompanying dismissal of increasingly secular trends in the north, it is important to note that religious adherence is still closely related to political affiliation in Northern Ireland. As far as loyalists are concerned, not only are the vast majority of unionists Protestant, but they also express their community cohesion in their rejection of an all-Ireland 'catholic' state. In the

72 R. Empey, UUII, *Climate of Submission*, issue 10 February 1993. 73 *Times*, 24 June 1995. 74 Prince Andrew was Colonel-in-Chief of the UDR and later, the RIR. 75 The Queen only visited the Province twice during the long conflict (during her Silver Jubilee in 1977 and for a short visit in June 1991).

past, the links between the paramilitary, religious and political agencies of unionism were that much stronger and more apparent. In the late 20th century the Unionist movement was divided, politically and religiously, with most Protestants firmly opposed to the activities of loyalist paramilitary groups. With the decline in Protestant adherence to literal translation of theological messages – despite the emphasis which Steve Bruce places on it, evangelical Protestantism only attracts a minority of Protestants – the religious potency of the loyalist message is not as strong today.[76] Regardless of the Orange Order maintaining its support, there is a growing demand for reconsideration of the link between loyalism's most vigorous religio-political pressure group and the UUP.

Whilst Unionists may no longer live in trepidation of Catholic religious practices and personnel, they are still suspicious of the Church's hold on social and moral, as well as political policy, within the Republic.[77] They believe that the Catholic Church and Irish political parties have been disingenuous about loyalist accusations over such Church 'intrusion' into political, as well as moral, affairs.[78] They argue that, despite the protestations of the Irish Catholic Church, it has special position within the Irish state's political system, which consequently means that its clergy do not have to adopt a higher, more 'official' profile.[79]

To summarise, I have endeavoured to stress that 'loyalism' is not merely a political phenomenon, but has also significant social, economic and cultural characteristics, which are inter-related to its political infrastructure. Nor is it static and it has developed throughout the Troubles, particularly at moments of crisis, such as the mid-1970s and the early 1990s, when loyalists searched in desperation for their political and cultural identity. Yet some aspects of loyalism, such as Protestant antipathy towards unity, have not really altered over time and many loyalists still appear to be less sure of what they're for, as distinct from what they're against. However, it would be wrong, and foolish, to merely dismiss them. Rather what is required is an examination of what constitutes 'loyalism' and how this is presented in the British media. The former aspect was briefly investigated in this introductory section, with the confusion over what constitutes 'loyalism' leading to is unpopular reception in Great Britain.[80]

Characteristics and images of loyalism were explored, with changes in interpretation observed. Negative images or characteristics, of course, tend to dominate, with the contradictory, intolerant, egoistic, settler colonialist, fifth column nature of loyalism obscuring other, more positive, features, or alternative diagnoses, of the loyalist predicament. These include the longstanding fear of Irish unity, as well as loyalist allegiance to the monarchy, but also encompass the de-

76 See S. Bruce, *God Save Ulster! The Religion and Politics of Paisleyism* (Oxford, 1986). 77 Loyalists have frequently pointed out the reluctance of the Irish state to change their essentially ultra-conservative attitude to 'moral' issues, including divorce, contraception and abortion. 78 See Peter Smith, UUP, *Opportunity Lost – A Unionist view of the Report of the Forum for a New Ireland* 12 November 1984, p. 11. 79 R. McCartney made such a point in *Priests, Politicians and Pluralists,* Unionist Review 2, February 1984, arguing that since the Catholic Church in Ireland was 'in such a position of entrenched power', it was able 'to dictate policy to the state'. 80 I was made fully aware of this during my survey research, where a number of respondents equated 'loyalism' with purely terrorist activities.

cline in importance of the economic and religious factors behind unionist resistance, as well as the rise of comparatively new ones such as ethnic separateness and abhorrence of political terrorism.

SPREADING THE WORD – THE DILEMMA OF UNIONIST PROPAGANDISTS

Unionists freely admit they lost the propaganda 'war' to their nationalist opponents early in the conflict and never managed to recover from their loss. Despite the occasionally effective pamphlet or overseas counter-republican initiative (such as the visit of unionists to America during the H Block crisis of 1981 and later trips to the States which coincided with those of Gerry Adams), there was an absence of a carefully-orchestrated propaganda campaign aimed specifically at the Great British market until the Ulster Unionist Information Institute (UUII) was established in 1988.[81] This was in stark contrast with the anti-Home Rule campaign at the start of the century when an energetic crusade was mounted on the British mainland.[82]

Disseminating propaganda material outside your own society is, obviously, always going to prove to be a more difficult task than 'winning the minds' of your own community.[83] This has been particularly the experience of the loyalist community in Northern Ireland, which, whilst conceding it has 'lost' the propaganda 'war' in Britain and overseas to its opponents, has, been periodically successful in utilising the 'hate' propaganda techniques perfected by the British during World War One.[84] However, they have been noticeably less successful in 'delivering' their own political case to the British mainland and, already handicapped by their own inadequacies in this sphere and their damaging stereotyping during the early years of the conflict, they have tended to rely on wordy, detailed pamphlets which were more geared to the needs of the local, rather than the national, audience. One explanation of this propaganda failure was Ulster Unionists' firm belief in the moral supremacy of their case. This notion that they were 'so right', that they didn't have to 'sell' either themselves or their case, was held by Unionists for many years. With built-in control of their state and an uncritical overseer in London, Ulster Unionists did not feel pressurised into justifying their political be-

81 I return to the UUII's propaganda contribution later in this section. It was not until the middle of 1996 that a London-based publicity department was established. This new organisation, the Unionist Information Office, picked up unwanted headlines on account of its manager, Patricia Campbell, suing the party for alleged discrimination; reported in the *Times*, 27 July 1996. 82 Arguably Ulster Unionists have been more aware of the need to state their case in America than they have been in Great Britain. 83 Several definitions of 'propaganda' have been offered by academics. Perhaps the most widely-regarded is Jacques Ellul's belief that 'the aim of modern propaganda is no longer to modify ideas but to provoke action'; quoted in J. Ellul, *Propaganda – The Formation of Men's Attitudes* (New York, 1973), p. 25. 84 Unionists were occasionally successful in their targeting of easily recognisable 'common foes', such as Bernadette Devlin, Gerry Adams and the IRA. This theme is examined in greater detail later in the section.

liefs or policies. Another reason for unionist antipathy towards propaganda was their conviction that the media was so much against them that theirs was a lost cause. This was particularly the case during the early part of the Troubles when, after many decades of virtually ignoring the province, external media agencies appeared to Ulster Unionists to be very sympathetic to the nationalist position. Unionists developed a belief that, due to a combination of the complex nature of the situation in Northern Ireland and the very essence of the tabloid press, most of the media's interest, tended to focus on sensational aspects of the Irish 'story'. In recent years, Ulster Unionists have appreciated more fully the need to promote their case and point out that 'a considerable quantity of material is delivered from the Unionist Party Headquarters at regular intervals'.[85] Unionist public relations teams, as in the past, distinguish between propaganda specifically for the 'home' market (with its emphasis on denigrating political opponents, particularly the DUP) and 'external' literature (which underplays internal divisions), 'designed for the attention of individuals and institutions, both on the mainland and abroad'.[86] Targeted groups include politicians and their parties, members of legislative bodies throughout the world, students' organisations, and Great Britain-based pressure groups including the Monday Club, the Friends of the Union and the Tory Action Group.[87]

Although Ulster Unionists became more adept at compiling propaganda literature for the 'external' market, their publications lacked the cohesion and consistency which were associated with a purpose-built 'propaganda' department. This was not to be rectified until 1988 when Martin Smyth founded the Ulster Unionist Information Institute (UUII), a group run from Unionist Party headquarters in Belfast. The emergence of the UUII is evidence of Unionists' acceptance that they had failed to make adequate inroads into reversing nationalists' success in the area of propaganda. The purpose of their news-sheet is 'to inform and update people throughout the United Kingdom and the wider world of the views of Ulster Unionists'.[88] The news sheet features the research of specific Unionist Party groups, such as the legal committee's 'simple guide' to the complex subject of extradition, and has acted as a vehicle for leading Unionists such as Smyth, James Molyneaux, Enoch Powell, Ken Maginnis and John Taylor to air their views on a variety of issues, normally coinciding with their own portfolios or specific areas of expertise. The style of the sheets – they concentrated on reproducing lengthy extracts from speeches of Unionist Party personalities – was not designed to appeal to the non-committed reader. Thus James Molyneaux's 1988 Party Conference address was quoted in depth, Ken Maginnis's *Independent* article, 'Britain's failure to understand the IRA', was quoted in its entirety, whilst David Trimble's parliamentary maiden speech and a selective review of papers critical of the Duisburg Conference, were all basic 'fodder' for the committed reader.[89] Although certain features in the news sheets included the pre-

85 Gavin Adams, Unionist Party researcher, in a letter, 4 September 1990. 86 Ibid. 87 Ibid. 88 *Ulster Unionist Information Institute Newsletter*, issue 1, Autumn 1988. 89 These articles can be found in *UUII Newsletter*, issues 1–5, covering the period between Autumn 1988 and Summer 1990.

dictable loyalist moans of 'treachery', criticism of the Tories' security policy, the perceived ambivalence of the SDLP, the evils of the Anglo-Irish Agreement and a considerable degree of gloating over the 'trouncing of the Tories' in the Upper Bann by-election, other, less likely subjects, such as 'the unfair employment prospects' for many Protestants were also included.[90]

Other contributors reiterated loyalist disdain with British miscomprehension of the Ulster problem. Ken Maginnis, in his article, 'Britain's failure to understand the IRA', argued that twenty years into the conflict, 'there is still little indication that Britain has been able to interpret the problem properly, let alone define its objectives for a solution'.[91] Maginnis probed deeper than many Ulster Unionists in his quest to explain this British misunderstanding of the Irish problem. He maintained that, with a legacy of imperial guilt, British mainlanders exhibited 'self-consciousness' as far as Northern Ireland was concerned.[92] At the heart of this 'self-consciousness' lay 'a sense of guilt, well fuelled by Republican propaganda about an Irish debt to be paid'.[93] Maginnis argued that the practicalities of this made the repaying of such 'debts' difficult. British authorities eased their consciences and deflected external pressure by their tendency to 'transfer the guilt to Ulster Unionists'.[94] According to Ken Maginnis, such a psychological rationale had contributed to Britain's 'apologetic and dilatory approach to 20 years of violence'.[95]

Even old 'friends' of the loyalist cause were not safe from attack in Unionist literature. Conservative policy in the province was especially prone to criticism in the post-Hillsborough period. At the heart of Ulster Unionist disillusionment with the Tory analysis of Northern Ireland was their decision to focus on political initiatives when constitutional guarantees and stronger security policies had, from their viewpoint, a greater call on Cabinet prioritisation. Thus, James Molyneaux lamented:

> ... the Government has formally expressed ambiguity about Ulster's constitutional position, an ambiguity which fuels the engine of IRA/Sinn Fein violence. Firm constitutional guarantees will succeed where political solutions have failed, and where futile political initiatives result in yet more savagery.[96]

Despite fraternal links (which, in any case, operated in recent years, on a strictly informal and low-key basis) tension between Ulster Unionists and Tories has continued to increase in the post-Hillsborough period and particularly since the late 1980s when the Conservatives started to organise in the province. Unionists' rejoicing in the 'humiliating defeat' of the Conservative candidate in the 1990 Upper Bann by-election was based not just on their disillusionment with the policy of a government which 'is perceived by the majority British community in Ulster as being anti-Unionist and as wishing to nudge Northern Ireland out of the United Kingdom by stages', but also their anger at the Tory 'teams of

90 Ibid. 91 K. Maginnis, 'Britain's Failure to understand the IRA', UUII Issue 1, Autumn 1988. 92 Ibid. 93 Ibid. 94 Ibid. 95 Ibid. 96 James Molyneaux's speech to the 1989 AGM of the UUC, quoted in UUII *Newsletter* Issue 3, Summer 1989.

Hooray Henries' which had been 'flown into Upper Bann ... to support offensive policy lies'.[97]

The status quo nature of their political aspirations and the restricted range of subjects for publicity purposes meant that Unionist Party propaganda focused largely on the 'evil' attributes of 'enemy' figures ranging from Civil Rights and political leaders to representatives of Sinn Fein and the IRA. Much of the early Unionist Party propaganda was directed towards demythising the claims perpetuated about the Northern Ireland state by the Civil Rights movement in general and Bernadette Devlin in particular. The concentration on 'hate' propaganda relating to one personality or subject, popular outside the province in 1969, is significant. Unionists realised that the Ulster problem, too complex for 'external' audiences to fully comprehend, could be understood in terms of stereotypes, and they resorted to aping their opponents' caricature of their own political leaders by concentrating on the colourful personality of Bernadette Devlin. The latter was initially portrayed sympathetically by the British media as a modern Joan of Arc, with even right wing sections of the press presenting the young MP for Mid Ulster in a favourable light.[98] Unionist propagandists capitalised on Devlin's fall from grace following her involvement in the Derry riots of August 1969. In an influential party booklet, *Ulster – the Facts*, the image of Devlin the 'wrecker', breaking up paving stones for use by rioters – 'Young Lady with a £60 a week job' – was juxtaposed with that of an injured Derry policeman – 'Young Man with a £20 a week job'.[99] Unionists exploited her clear participation in the Bogside riots – 'the highlight of her career as a public figure' – claiming it illustrated her unreliability as a public representative and showed one who was rather more interested in street politics than parliamentary debate.[100]

The main target of Unionist Party 'hate' propaganda since the early 1970s has, of course, been republican terrorist groups, most notably the IRA. Perhaps the Unionists' most memorable propaganda triumph occurred when the Stormont Government's Information Service concentrated their attack on the grotesque nature of the Provisionals' bombing campaign. The result was the 1972 booklet, *The Terror and the Tears*, the popularity of which was to take even Unionists by surprise.[101] Brian Faulkner, Prime Minister of Northern Ireland at the time, later noted that the demand for it was 'overwhelming as Ulster folk circulated thousands of copies to friends and relatives across the globe'.[102] *Terror and Tears* was successful because of its lack of political dogma. The theme of the twelve page

97 J. Taylor, 'Tories Trounced', UUII Newsletter, Issue 5, Summer 1990. 98 Even David Langdon in *Punch* was enthusiastic. His cartoon depicted her arrival in Parliament where, in the midst of an admiring, predominantly male, audience one front-bencher turns round to a colleague and comments. 'It'll look a bit strange in Hansard – the Honourable Member for Mid Ulster, bracket, long low wolf whistles, bracket'; quoted in J. Darby, *Dressed to Kill – Cartoonists and the Northern Ireland Conflict* (Belfast, 1983), p. 34. 99 Ulster Unionist Party, *Ulster – the Facts* (undated, believed to have been written in 1970). 100 Ibid. 101 Unionist Research Department, *The Terror and the Tears*, 1972. 102 B. Faulkner, *Memoirs of a Statesman*, op. cit., p. 145. 103 A follow-up to the original version was even more widely distributed. See Unionist Research Department, *Continuing the Terror and The Tears – more facts about the inhumanity of the IRA*, undated (believed to be late 1972).

booklet was 'the inhumanity of the IRA', which they illustrated in graphic, pictorial fashion.[103] Innocent victims of the violence - children, women and pensioners – were selected. One section, labelled 'D Day IRA style – suffer little children', concentrated on child victims of the violence.[104] A photograph showed a wounded girl sobbing as the coffin of her UDR father was removed for burial, whilst another showed an ambulanceman removing the body of an infant killed in a 1971 IRA attack on a funeral showroom on Belfast's Shankill Road.[105] The caption at the foot of the photo encapsulated loyalist thinking;

> If there is power in the sobs of children and the tears of husbands and fathers, then the cause espoused by the terrorist is on the point of death. Its followers now are but walking dead animated husks, soulless and mindless, disowned by any creature capable of pity and compassion.[106]

A double-page section of the booklet stressed the detrimental effect the terrorist campaign was having on what should have been 'normal' life. Other photographs depicted everyday activities such as people shopping, dustmen and bus drivers at work, people drinking coffee in downtown cafes and related them to specific terrorist attacks, such as the killing of workers and shoppers in Belfast's Oxford Street and Abercorn Restaurant.

Unionist criticism of the IRA was a major feature of their propaganda and continued even into the post-ceasefire period. Although the choice of targets for such literature widened as the Troubles developed, the excesses of the Provisionals ensured their place at the top of loyalist 'hate' propaganda. Whilst the tone of such literature was always virulent, its nature was to change in the 1980s and beyond, as the political dimension of the Republican campaign grew stronger. Consequently Unionist Party attacks on 'political' Republicanism increased, and the Unionists adjusted their position to a claim that Protestants were more likely to suffer from terrorism than Catholics. In a 1990 UUII news-sheet interpreting terrorism statistics covering a five-year period, Ken Maginnis claimed that between the signing of the Anglo-Irish Agreement and the start of 1990, 217 of the 287 killings had been committed by republicans (and only 66 by loyalist terrorists), with nearly twice as many Protestants as Catholics dying from such attacks (188:99 respectively).[107]

Although the Unionist Party's political literature was more aggressive in its treatment of Republican terrorism, other popular quarries for periodic attack were those agencies which also threatened to bring Irish unity closer, whether they were the SDLP, the Irish, or even British governments.[108] Whether it was

104 Ibid. **105** Ibid. **106** Ibid. The headline was, 'Next time you go into a cafe ... think of the girls maimed for life.' **107** K. Maginnis, UUC Information sheet, 1990. The period quoted was that between 15 November 1985 and 6 January 1990. Obviously Ulster Unionists were selective in their choice of specific periods and decided to ignore the 1991–4 period, when loyalist violence increased markedly, eventually overtaking the level of republican violence. **108** They felt that 'an enormous barrier of accumulative falsehoods' placed a smokescreen over the whole issue of Irish unity and even as late as 1980 the party was stressing the importance of

the Council of Ireland in 1974, the Thatcher-Haughey summits of 1980–1, the Forum Report (1984), the Anglo-Irish Agreement (1985), the Downing Street Declaration (1993) or the Framework Document (1995), Ulster Unionists' perennial fear was the impending threat of Irish unification. Loyalist propaganda directed against the SDLP tended to be, on the whole, less virulent than that directed against the London and Dublin governments, though there were a number of notable exceptions. This was primarily the case because the SDLP were not perceived to be in control of either the political or military agenda (as say, Sinn Fein in the post-ceasefire period). This was not always so. Before the politicisation of the republican movement, the 'infant' SDLP adopted a more radical approach to the problem in the North.[109] With the implementation of direct rule in March 1972, Ulster Unionists turned their attention to British and Irish administrations, only returning to denounce the SDLP position when it shifted from its espousal of power-sharing in the late 1970s to an increasing emphasis on the unity issue. Whenever the SDLP did appear to be setting the political pace the Unionist Party responded. Such a case was the publication of the 1984 Report from the John Hume-inspired New Ireland Forum. With its proposals of Irish unity, federalism and joint authority, the Report demanded an Ulster Unionist response. In *The Way Forward*, Ulster Unionists rejected joint sovereignty and castigated the SDLP for their refusal to seriously consider devolution, claiming that British insistence on the principle of 'widespread consent' had given the party 'an absolute veto on the Assembly's progress'.[110] For a time the SDLP had to endure the venom not only of the Ulster Unionists but that of the DUP and Mrs Thatcher who had, in her 'treble no' speech, denounced the Report. However, with all the constitutional parties and both governments accepting the broad terms of the Hillsborough Agreement in the following year, Unionist propagandists again turned their sights to republican paramilitaries and the governments in London and Dublin.[111] Yet the demarcation lines of 'decency' between constitutional nationalism and militant republicanism were occasionally to blur, particularly following the Hume-Adams talks which preceded the IRA ceasefire in 1994 and which led to insinuations of a 'pan-nationalist front' agenda dominating the Irish question. Unionists' obsession with being forced into a united Ireland against their will still dominates their political literature. A 1995 critique of the Framework Document highlighted its Irish dimension and interpreted the Document as 'a case to take us out of the United Kingdom into an all Ireland'.[112]

The general acceptance of Ulster Unionists' inability to project their case is

'putting the record straight on a number of subjects' relating to N. Ireland; quoted in a UUC leaflet, *Northern Ireland – the Truth* March 1980. **109** The party's withdrawal from Stormont in July 1971 and its subsequent orchestration of a civil disobedience campaign appeared to confirm loyalist fears about the 'irresponsibility' of many in the nationalist community. **110** UUP, *The Way Forward* op. cit. **111** This is not to understate the strength of Unionist feeling on the subject of SDLP 'ambivalance' towards terrorism. Many believed that the IRA was doing the SDLP's job for them and a Unionist document suggested that SDLP criticism of the IRA was ' a very hollow affair', quoted in UUII, *Hollow Criticism*, Issue 2, Winter 1988/89. **112** UUII, *Framed – A Critical Analysis of the Framework Document* 1995.

illustrated by an article, 'Selling the Unionists' in the *Independent on Sunday.*[113] This 1995 article started with the premise that loyalists were 'the image-maker's nightmare' and asked six advertising agencies how they would counteract the 'negativism' of unionism which 'seems to be losing them a PR battle with the Republicans'.[114] The agencies believed that the existing unionist image as 'dour, stubborn, bigoted, inarticulate (though excessively noisy) and tribal' was a 'caricature' and that the Unionists had a genuine case which can be powerful, even moving'.[115]

The article justified its claim that unionists had a case by maintaining:

> They are the majority community in Northern Ireland, an entity that has existed longer than about half the world's sovereign states ... What if they (Unionist leaders) set out, using all the artifices of modern politics, to win the hearts and minds of the British public? Would it – could it – change the character of the debate?[116]

Two of the agencies contrasted the unionists' failure to project their right for self-determination with those of Nelson Mandela and black South Africans.[117] Saatchi and Saatchi depicted Ian Paisley as a black man and its poster asked, 'What would it take for us to be recognised as a repressed minority?'[118] Another agency, TBWA, exploited the theme of a 'bullying foreign power '(the Republic of Ireland) trying to annex Ulster. Drawing a clear parallel with the question of Britain's national sovereignty in an increasingly dominant EEC, the poster showed a map of Ireland with the caption, ' These days we're all in danger of being controlled by foreigners. But ours aren't from Brussels'.[119] Agencies' reactions to dealing with the 'Paisley factor' and its harmful effect on the loyalist image, were varied. One agency shifted attention away from the politicians, placing the emphasis on the voters who elected them whilst another stressed the DUP leader's popularity, suggesting that as he represented the voice of the majority, his message should be listened to more carefully.

Unionists admitted losing the propaganda battle early in the conflict and despite the occasional propaganda success, have struggled in the intervening quarter of a century to make an impressive presentation of their case to the British public. Interestingly, Ulster Unionists were more successful when they adopted 'hate' propaganda techniques in their attack of the 'enemy', rather than providing a detailed justification of their own case. Therefore, Ulster Unionist 'mudslinging', directed against Bernadette Devlin and the IRA in particular, was successful in the early stages of the conflict, but later Unionist Party propaganda material, despite organisational improvements, tended to be over-wordy and inappropriate for the 'external' market. It was generally accepted that unionists had extreme difficulty in presenting their case and that these problems were so

113 *Independent on Sunday* 19 March 1995. 114 Ibid. 115 Ibid. 116 Ibid. 117 These two agencies were Holder Wilson Pearce and Bailey and Saatchi and Saatchi. 118 *Independent on Sunday*, op. cit. 119 Barker and Ralston asked 'Maybe it's because he (Paisley) speaks for 90% of the population that his voice seems so loud.'

deep-rooted that one paper even employed advertising agencies in an attempt to put their message across more clearly. This image problem of loyalists was partly due to miscomprehension of their political position, but was also a result of Ulster Unionists' initially slow awareness of the power of propaganda and the underdeveloped public relations skills of their representatives. Despite the undoubted validity of their argument and the opportunity of capturing the moral high ground at the expense of republican terrorists, unionists were rarely able to capitalise on anti-IRA sentiment in Britain largely because of the way they had themselves been stereotyped in the national media. Unionist propaganda, too, was not sophisticated enough, nor was it likely to reach many of the 'undecided' in Britain in their endeavours to challenge these misrepresentations.

THE LEPERS OF BRITISH POLITICS?

The shortcomings in the area of propaganda referred to above were compounded by a growing realisation on the part of unionists that they were bereft of political 'friends' in Great Britain. Perhaps the biggest blow to unionist sensitivities was their perception that one-time companions, the Conservatives, increasingly distanced themselves from Ulster Unionism as the Troubles developed. The prevalence of a bipartisan approach to Northern Ireland's problems hardly eased such sensitive feelings. Suspicious of Labour's nationalist aspirations, unionists despaired of the Tories' increased tendency to lean towards 'neutrality' over the union issue. As a result, their sense of isolation steadily deepened.

It was this shift in the thinking of Conservatives which demoralised Ulster Unionists. Near the beginning of the century the Conservative leader Bonar Law had conceded he could imagine 'no length of resistance to which Ulster will go' in which he would 'not be ready to support them' and in which they would 'not be supported by the overwhelming majority of British people'.[120] Bonar Law realised that the plight of Ulster's Unionists was a vote-winning issue with the British public which, in an age of class deference, pride in Empire and national unity, was more likely to respond to the Unionist cause than in the last years of the century.[121] In contrast, John Major's Conservative Party had, during the intervening eighty years, become increasingly separate from the Unionist Party. Unionists became responsible for running their own administration and Conservatives, whilst periodically expressing their 'loyalty' to the union, appeared to be disinterested in the province's political affairs. When they became embroiled in the events of the early 1970s, the situation had changed. Britain's Empire and her leading world role had all but gone, the religious fervour which many mainland Britons had shared with Ulster Protestants during the Edwardian period

120 Bonar Law, speaking at Blenheim Palace; reported in the *Times*, 29 July 1912. 121 The British Covenant, patronised by the signature of several leading figures of the day, including Kipling, Elgar and Roberts, obtained over two million signatures between 1912 and 1914.

was much less apparent in a secular society and the national sense of 'British' unity had eroded during the intervening decades along both class and regional lines. Indeed, the main reaction of many Tories to the riots on the streets of Belfast and Derry was one of deep embarrassment. Although many were to remain loyal, initially at least, to the principle of maintaining the union, they were to quickly revise their thinking regarding the nature of that relationship and as the conflict developed, antipathy to the unionist cause also deepened. Therefore, only a small, if vociferous, rump of Tory backbenchers supported Unionist Party demands in the 1990s, whilst their government reiterated that they had 'no selfish, strategic or economic interest in Northern Ireland'.[122]

Whilst leading Tories were inclined to be dismissive of loyalists, they maintained their support of Unionist administrations until the IRA campaign necessitated Westminster, and not Stormont, control of security.[123] Hence the Conservatives, in their 1970 manifesto, lent their support for both the existing constitutional position and the reforming policy of the Unionist Government. The manifesto pledged:

> We reaffirm that no change will be made in the constitutional status of Northern Ireland without the free consent of the Parliament of Northern Ireland. We support the Northern Ireland government in its programme of legislation and executive action to ensure equal opportunities for all citizens in that part of the United Kingdom.[124]

From the early 1970s there was a distinctive and rapid transition in Conservative thinking from the above position to an increasingly critical tone adopted towards the Unionist Party and the suggestion of different political frameworks (most notably power-sharing and the Council of Ireland), against which traditional Unionism was to protest. This dilution of Tory support for the Ulster Unionist position and the subsequent change in their political approach were precipitated by the increase in IRA violence and the start of a loyalist 'backlash', as well as the hardening of the British desire to disentangle themselves from the Irish conflict. Therefore, there is a considerable difference in the tone of the next Conservative manifesto in which Conservatives claimed that their power-sharing experiment enjoyed 'majority' support. In this manifesto, the newly-formed Executive as described as 'a tender plant' and the progress that was being made in the province was 'a result of firm but fair Government action, which has succeeded against all the odds, in mobilising the silent majority of moderate opinion in Northern Ireland to assert itself against extremism of all kinds'.[125]

122 *Frameworks for the Future*, HMSO, 1995. 123 One sceptical 'high' Tory was Defence Secretary Peter Carrington who noted how he had been 'impressed most unfavourably with the bigotry – and insobriety – of a lot of the fairly senior people in Ulster politics'; in P. Carrington, *Reflect on Things Past – The Memoirs of Lord Carrington* (London, 1988), p. 249. 124 1970 Conservative Manifesto, *A Better Tomorrow*. 125 Feb. 1974 Conservative Manifesto, *Firm Action for a Fair Britain*.

Ted Heath, highly influenced by Britain's imminent entry into the European Common Market and by the worsening security situation (the climax of which was Bloody Sunday), was probably more lukewarm on the question of the union than subsequent Tory leaders.[126] Heath was keen to exploit increasing unionist divisions, pressurising Faulkner during his brief period as Ulster premier and by his decision not to invite dissident unionists (who actually represented the majority of loyalist opinion) to Sunningdale in 1973. Indeed, in his endeavours to be even-handed, Ted Heath was even more cautious than John Major in being perceived as a 'persuader' for the union. In 1971 Heath argued:

> Many Catholics in Northern Ireland would like to see Northern Ireland unified with the South. That is understandable; it is legitimate that they should seek to further that aim by democratic and constitutional means. If at some future date the majority of people in Northern Ireland wants unification and express that desire in the appropriate constitutional manner, I do not believe that any British Government would stand in the way. But that is not what the majority want today.[127]

Heath's insistence that the Unionist government headed by Faulkner would have to forfeit control over security in the province led to the Unionist leader's resignation and the suspension of Stormont. The lack of an immediate 'Irish' political threat meant that the unionist response was less aggressive than their subsequent reactions to initiatives such as the Anglo-Irish Agreement. This is not to say that many failed to regard it as a 'victory' for the IRA. Michael MacDonald noted that many nationalists regarded direct rule as a halfway house on the road to a united Ireland:

> The Provisionals had thus won a double victory over the Unionists; they destroyed Unionism's most important political institution (Stormont) while at the same time estranging the Unionist Party from its closest political ally.[128]

One of the current conflict's greatest ironies has been the contradiction between Margaret Thatcher's espousal of unionism and her action of signing the Hillsborough Agreement. In her memoirs she stressed that 'any Conservative should in his bones be a Unionist too' and empathised with the unionist position.[129] She wrote:

> I knew that these people shared many of my own attitudes, derived from my staunchly Methodist background. The warmth was as genuine as it was usu-

126 Like the Brighton bombing was to prove to be the catalyst for Mrs Thatcher's conversion to Dublin involvement in deciding the future of Northern Ireland, so was Bloody Sunday the spark for Heath's action which precipitated Brian Faulkner's downfall. **127** Ted Heath, quoted in W. Flackes and S. Elliott, *Northern Ireland – A Political Directory 1968–1988* (Belfast 1989), p. 147. **128** M. MacDonald, *Children of Wrath*, op. cit. **129** M. Thatcher, *The Downing Street Years* (London 1993), p. 385.

> ally undemonstrative. Their patriotism was real and fervent, even if too narrow. They had often been taken for granted. From my visits to Northern Ireland, often after terrible tragedies, I came to have the greatest admiration in particular for the way in which the little Protestant communities would come together, looking after another one, after some terrible loss.[130]

This type of unionism, as Margaret Thatcher admitted, proved easier to sustain in opposition than it did in government. Her approach to Ireland had been strongly influenced by her close political ally and Shadow Northern Ireland Secretary Airey Neave who had, in the Conservatives' 1979 manifesto, laid stress on the primacy of Westminster in the governance of Northern Ireland. Thus, there was a move away from power-sharing and no mention was made of the 'Irish' dimension. The manifesto promised to 'maintain the union of Great Britain and Northern Ireland in accordance with the wish of the majority in the Province' and 'in the absence of devolved government', the Conservatives pledged to 'establish one or more elected regional councils with a wide range of powers over local services'.[131] The INLA's assassination of Airey Neave in 1979 virtually spelled the end of the integration option. Not only did subsequent Conservative manifestos praise the worthiness of the option of devolved, cross-community administration for the province in the early 1980s, but Tory leaders made clear their opposition to Northern Ireland's full integration within the United Kingdom. As the security situation worsened, Margaret Thatcher, influenced by her Cabinet Secretary Robert Armstrong and a closer relationship with her new Irish counterpart, Garret Fitzgerald, gradually came to the conclusion that in order to prevent republicans seizing the initiative from the SDLP, a political 'carrot' in the shape of an 'Irish' dimension would have to be considered. This 'carrot' was, of course, the Anglo-Irish Agreement which was 'novel' in 'its explicit acceptance of a role for the Irish government in the affairs of the north as a defender of the interests of the nationalist community'.[132] Like the UWC Strike (1974), the anti-Hillsborough campaign of the late 1980s provides a rare example of grassroots loyalism setting the political agenda in Northern Ireland. It too, was achieved without the support of the British media, but unlike the two-week work stoppage in 1974, loyalists failed to obtain their goal (the 'scrapping' of the Anglo-Irish Agreement). Despite their political mandate within Ulster and the spirited, even touching, espousal of patriotism exhibited by some of their leaders, there was little support in the British Press for the unionist case.[133] Although their anti-Hillsborough tactics, included the staging of mass protest meetings, in Belfast, petitions, en masse resignation of parliamentary seats (precipitating by-elections

130 Ibid. 131 *The 1979 Conservative Manifesto.* 132 P. Bew and G. Gillespie, *Northern Ireland – a Chronology of the Troubles 1968–93* (Dublin 1993), p. 189. 133 The UUP's Deputy leader, Harold, McCusker, told the Commons how he had found out about the Agreement. He said: 'I stood outside the gate of Hillsborough like a dog and asked them to put in my hand the document that sold away my birthright ... I felt desolate for this reason, as I stood in the cold in the square at Hillsborough everything I'd ever held dear turned to ashes in my mouth' (quoted in *Belfast News Letter* 28 November 1985).

in most of the Province), town-hall protests and harassment of off-duty RUC officers, earned considerable media attention, they were to gain few new friends in Great Britain. Their 'blinkered outlook' was condemned on the day the Hillsborough Agreement was signed and the unendearing image of their leaders was noted by an *Observer* journalist on the eve of the by-elections[134]. As their campaign unfolded, critics of Ulster Unionism were not slow in maximising these opportunities to denigrate their case. Writing in the *Sunday Mirror*, George Gale argued that by 'rejecting the Anglo-Irish Agreement and seeking to frustrate the will of Parliament and the British government', Ulster loyalists had 'released us from the obligation indefinitely to keep our troops in Ulster and indefinitely to uphold the (constitutional) guarantee'.[135]

The politics of neutrality which Thatcher had utilised in her endeavours to placate the Dublin government, were developed in the post-Hillsborough period of her premiership. Both in terms of her bad relationships with unionist leaders during their anti-Agreement campaign and the lack of support afforded by the party leadership to the fledgling Tory group in Northern Ireland, Thatcher ended her long spell as Conservative leader with the distance between her government and the unionists wider than it had been for many years. Despite the scale of this unionist protest, she did not make any concessions to them and defended the Agreement until she resigned as Tory leader in 1990. Yet years after her resignation as party leader, she was to reassess the Agreement, and, coming as close as she could to admitting she had made an error of judgement at Hillsborough, Lady Thatcher advocated a re-evaluation of the Agreement. She wrote in her memoirs:

> In dealing with Northern Ireland, successive governments have studiously refrained from security policies that might alienate the Irish Government and Irish nationalist opinion in Ulster in the hope of winning their support against the IRA. The Anglo-Irish Agreement was squarely in this tradition. But I discovered the results of this approach to be disappointing. Our concessions alienated the Unionists without gaining the level of security co-operation we had a right to expect. In the light of this experience it is surely time to consider an alternative approach.[136]

Both Margaret Thatcher and John Major shared the reputation of being 'unionists' who were paradoxically soft on the union. Yet there were some significant differences between their approaches in attempting to break the political dead-

134 *Evening Standard*, 15 November 1985 and the *Observer*, 5 January 1986. In the latter report Robert Taylor wrote: "The bull-horn oratory of Dr Ian Paisley and the pedantic constitutionalism of Mr Enoch Powell are not calculated to win friends or influence people this side of the Irish Sea'. 135 *Sunday Mirror*, 11 May 1986. The occasional criticism of the failure of the Irish government to curb terrorist acts from the Republic could be found in the Tory Press. The *Sun*, 5 November 1986, noted how loyalists had been 'driven to despair' by such attacks and implored the Prime Minister to 'tell the Irish (that) the agreement is dead'. 136 M. Thatcher, op. cit., p. 415.

lock in Northern Ireland. John Major's public image mirrored the 'politics of compromise' approach that was clearly required to deal with the complex Irish question and he also appeared to lend greater weight to the Irish question than his predecessor.[137] Therefore, Northern Ireland was given a higher profile on the Government's agenda. Major became Chair of the Northern Ireland Cabinet Committee, he was prepared to take the rare step of addressing the nation in a hastily-arranged broadcast to assuage fears surrounding the imminent Framework Document, and he also used unlikely venues to discuss the political situation in the province (these included the Lord Mayor of London's Banquet). The Tory press lauded Major's efforts to bring about a resolution of the conflict and developed the image of Major as a 'peace-maker'.[138]

How much was Major a 'friend' or an 'enemy' of Ulster Unionism? Unionists were in little doubt. They saw the Downing Street Declaration as an extension of the Hillsborough Agreement in that it clearly stated the 'neutral' approach to be adopted by the British goverment to the province's future constitutional status. Despite John Major's claim that this 'neutrality' was nothing new, it was a highly significant progression from Hillsborough.[139] Although Major and his government reiterated their intention of supporting the democratic right of the majority to determine their future, they also immediately proceeded to deny any interest in governing Northern Ireland. The pivotal clause in the Declaration was the fourth one. It said:

> The Prime Minister on behalf of the British Government reaffirms that they will uphold the democratic will of a greater number of the people of Northern Ireland on the issue of whether they prefer to support the Union or a sovereign united Ireland. On this basis, he reiterates on behalf of the British Government, that they have no selfish, strategic or economic interest in Northern Ireland.[140]

Although most sections of the British press were broadly in favour of the Declaration – even the right wing *Mail* described it as 'a blueprint for peace' – there was a recognition that the 'no strategic interest' clause was 'a hugely significant one' and that Major was treating Ulster 'as neutrally as if it were disputed between Mahommedans and Hindus'.[141]

In his foreword to the Framework Document Mr Major presented a rather ambiguous endorsement of the political union between Great Britain and Northern Ireland. The Conservative leader wrote:

137 Particularly as Major's premiership appeared to be disintegrating, Ulster seemed to be more and more 'a personal crusade' for the Tory Prime Minister; quoted in the *Sunday Times*, 5 February 1995. 138 Indeed, Major's fundamental importance to the future of the peace process was a rare instance of the Irish question actually taking precedence over internal disputes affecting the leadership of a leading political party in Britain. 139 *The Downing Street Declaration*, HMSO, 1993. 140 Ibid, p. 3. 141 *Daily Mail*, 15 February 1993 and the *Observer*, 19 December 1993.

> I cherish Northern Ireland as a part of the Northern Kingdom and it will remain so for as long as this reflects the democratic wish of a greater number of its people.[142]

The apparent contradiction between his 'cherishing' such a political union and his willingness to accept its removal without endeavouring to campaign on its behalf, indicated to loyalists that Conservatives were lukewarm on the issue of the Union and were content to merely maintain the status quo in the province until demographic changes resulted in a Catholic, and hence Nationalist, majority. They criticised the premier for not acting as a 'persuader' for the Union and maintained that Catholic issues were being prioritised at the expense of their own aspirations. Unionists referred to Major's recognition that 'there can be no going back to a system of government in Northern Ireland which has the allegiance of, and is operated by, only one section of the community', as well as the concession that 'the right of a section of the Northern Ireland community to aspire to a sovereign united Ireland, achieved by peaceful means and through agreement, is no less legitimate than the wish of a present majority to retain Northern Ireland's status within the United Kingdom'.[143] His 'neutral' stance on the question of the Union already evident in the Downing Street Declaration, made a mockery of the Tories' claim to be a 'unionist' party. Making no reference to the Republic's avowed intention to 'persuade' unionists to join them in an united Ireland, the Framework Document fuelled unionists' feelings of isolation.[144]

Parliament and public opinion reflected the overwhelming nature of support for Major's initiative. Labour leader Tony Blair argued 'the house of peace has stayed shut and locked in Northern Ireland for too many years' and that the Document provided 'the key to its door'.[145] A Gallup poll commissioned by the *Daily Telegraph* showed that 92% of the British public approved of the Document's recommendations and that over two thirds (68%) believed that unionists wouldn't be justified in refusing to attend all-party talks.[146] Some papers did express their reservations over Major's latest Irish initiative. The *Times*, which had 'leaked' the story on 1 February, had maintained that the Council of Ireland 'should act as a warning to those who believe that cross-border institutions can be estabished without provoking Unionist outrage'.[147] The *Daily Telegraph* suggested that 'Dublin's fingers seem to us further into this pie than Northern Ireland's Unionists should be expected to tolerate', whilst its sister paper, the *Sunday Telegraph*, maintained that if unionists accepted such a document they 'would reduce their people to a dying tribe like the Australian Aborigines, their quaint customs preserved, their grief at their loss of dignity and freedom assuaged by large sums of public money'.[148]

In addition to their concern over his apparent ambiguity towards the Union,

142 *Framework*, op. cit. 143 Ibid, p. 14. 144 Point two of the Document virtually repeated word-for-word the constitutional pledge given in the Downing Street Declaration. 145 *Independent*, 23 February 1995. 146 *Daily Telegraph*, 23 February 1995. 147 *Times*, 1 February 1995. 148 *Daily Telegraph*, 23 February 1995 and the *Sunday Telegraph*, 26 February 1995.

some loyalists were also perturbed by what they considered to be the uncharacteristic 'double-dealing' of the Conservative leader. They were especially irked by his admission of government officials participating in secret talks with Sinn Fein (he had initially denied this). Unionists were also embittered by his speech at the Lord Mayor's Banquet in London's Guildhall earlier that month when he suggested that if the IRA were prepared to stop its campaign, they could be allowed into the talks process. The premier further roused the ire of the Unionist leadership by appealing directly to their constituents. Concerned that the 'leaking' of the Framework Document could fuel loyalist anger and result in a devaluation of the peace process, Major assured both regional and national television audiences that the paper he and Irish premier John Bruton were in the process of preparing was only 'a consultative document' and reiterated his pledge that 'nothing is going to be imposed on Northern Ireland'.[149] He proceeded to assure his audience:

> Trust me – I need time to bring a lasting peace to Northern Ireland ... Judge our proposals as a whole. There is nothing you need fear. Tonight I ask for time. And I ask for trust. And I promise to pursue a lasting peace.[150]

Although most national papers were impressed by the statesmanlike quality of John Major's broadcast, a few voices of dissent challenged his political wisdom and even integrity. In a *Daily Mail* article, 'Ulster's Major lack of trust', Andrew Alexander sympathised with unionist reticence in placing confidence in the Prime Minister.

> Why should he (Major) be trusted by Northern Ireland? ... He once said it would turn his stomach to negotiate with terrorists. Yet his officials were conducting talks. Mayhew recently told Ulster Unionist leader James Molyneaux that he would be consulted on a framework document and said on January 1 that no such document existed. Yet the leaked one dates from November. However, to read much of the Press one would think it was the Ulster Unionists and their allies who were up to no good.[151]

Support for the unionist position was, particularly as the Troubles developed, to emanate from a small group of Conservatives. Although frontbench sympathy tended to evaporate, a number of maverick politicians and right wing groups were to campaign on behalf of unionist interests both from within the Conservative Party and on its fringe. Such a 'maverick' was Enoch Powell, a former Conservative minister who become MP for South Down in 1974. Powell achieved considerable success in influencing both the Unionist leadership and several Tory backbenchers on the significance of integrating Northern Ireland within the United Kingdom. To Powell, devolution was 'incompatible with the idea of a

149 BBC1, *Prime Ministerial Broadcast*, 1 February 1995. 150 Ibid. 151 *Daily Mail*, 3 February 1995.

unitary state' and as the potential consequence of such devolution was the dissolution of that nation, he was firmly opposed to it.[152]

A London-based pressure group, the Friends of the Union, which consisted mainly of Conservative MPs and businessmen, was founded in 1988 with the aim of 'increasing the knowledge and understanding throughout the United Kingdom of the need to maintain the Union'.[153] The group liaised with other Conservative fringe associations, including the Bow Group and Monday Club, providing a forum for meetings and the distribution of literature outlining alternatives to the Anglo-Irish Agreement and improvements in security which were the main interest of such groups.[154] Apart from expressing their sympathy with the suffering of Ulster loyalists, (both in terms of having to endure a prolonged terrorist campaign and their own political marginalisation) right wing groups have also expressed criticism of their 'parent' party, which, they concede, has perpetuated the misery of Ulster Unionists. Therefore far right rhetoric has a strong degree of solidarity with hapless loyalists. Monday Club chairperson, David Storey, speaking to the Ulster Unionist Women's Council in Belfast, stressed this bond between the far right and unionists:

> To be in Belfast is to express a great sense of national and political unity, of joining with our fellow citizens in a most noble cause, and of solidarity with those who are in the very front line in defending the integrity of the national territory ... Your cause is our cause! Your fight is our fight![155]

Despite the existence of some right wing support for the unionist cause, it would be inaccurate to suggest that there was significant backbench Tory support for loyalism.[156] Although several Conservatives were prepared to denounce IRA violence and the response of Irish governments to such terrorism, few Tories rebelled against their governments' Irish initiatives. Nor were the Tories' interest levels in Ireland any higher than those of their opponents.[157] Some concluded that fundamental changes in the relationships between the two parties had occurred. The *Times* believed that the death of a leading unionist, James Kilfedder, illustrated the ever-widening chasm between the Conservative Party

152 A. Aughey in B. Barton and P.J. Roche, *The Northern Ireland Question – Perspectives and Policies* (Aldershot, 1994), p. 133. 153 Friends of the Union, *Hope for Peace – an Alternative Anglo-Irish Agreement*, undated. 154 In claiming that unionists had been 'treated badly' by the Government, Ian Gow lambasted the Agreement's repercussions. He wrote: 'Instead of peace there has been strife. Instead of stability, turmoil. Instead of reconciliation, deeper sectarian suspicion' (quoted in Friends of the Union, *After the Agreement*, undated). 155 This speech , delivered in May 1988 by leading Monday Club member David Storey, was later published by the Monday Club alongside a photo of the Ballygawley coach bombing. 156 Indeed, more vociferous and sustained supported tended to come from extreme right wing groups such as the National Front and BNP, which perceived the Ulster situation as providing potential for the launch-pad for a fascist revolution. 157 Contrasting the lack of 'political will to give a total commitment' to Northern Ireland with the interest of his colleagues in Nicaragua and South Africa, Tory MP Geoffrey Dickens bewailed how 'we cannot get to grips with the remote problems of Northern Ireland': quoted in *Hansard*, 12 March 1990.

and Unionism. The *Times* leader suggested that any remaining links between the two parties were purely cosmetic.

> The symbolism of Sir James' death will not be lost on the dwindling number of older-fashioned Tories who cherish their party's Unionist past. In truth, the retreat of Conservatism from traditional Unionism is all but complete ... The rituals of fellowship between Conservative and Unionist are still being observed, but increasingly they are an expression of courtesy rather than a genuine mechanism of consultancy.[158]

Unionist expectations of their perceived political 'enemies', the Liberal and Labour parties, were inevitably lower and perhaps as a result, Labour administrations proved less hostile to loyalists than had been anticipated.[159] Even in its earliest stages the Labour Party had been sympathetic to the notion of Irish unity. In the early 1920s a Labour Party report had concluded that it was 'unequivocally prepared to allow Ireland to assume whatever form of self-determination the great mass of the Irish people desire'.[160] Yet Labour's front bench was to display little interest in Northern Ireland during the half century between partition and the start of the current conflict.[161] Despite considerable backbench and pressure group activity in the mid and late 1960s, Labour during this period showed no more concern for the affairs of Northern Ireland and the plight of its Catholics than the Tories had done.[162] However, Labour politicians derived considerable satisfaction in 'looking good' dealing with the events which were unfolding in Belfast and Derry. As Richard Crossman noted in his diary, Ulster had its political advantages:

> It has deflected attention from our own deficiencies and the mess of the pound. We have now got into something which we can hardly mismanage.[163]

Yet the deteriorating security situation and the obvious inability of the RUC to deal with the violence single-handedly, posed Labour a fundamental problem. Labour politicians were concerned about being perceived to assist the Unionist Government by becoming embroiled in a security quagmire from which they would find it difficult to extricate themselves. James Callaghan believed that it would be 'a grave mistake' to put British troops under the authority of the Unionist Government.

158 *Times*, 22 March 1995. 159 A brief analysis of the Liberal Party's response to the crisis in Northern Ireland and their close relationship with the province's Alliance Party, is provided in A. Parkinson (1996) 'Loyal Rebels Without a Cause', op. cit. 160 *Report of the Labour Commission to Ireland*, 1921. 161 Indeed, Laboured bolstered the union by passing the Ireland Act in 1949 which emphatically confirmed the province's constitutional status. 162 It was from this quarter that a civil rights pressure group, the Campaign for Democracy in Ulster (CDU) was formed in 1965 and the organisation was capable of harnessing the support of up to 100 Labour MPs. 163 *The Crossman Diaries*, entry for 7 May 1969, p. 478.

> Practically the whole of the Catholic population was by now thoroughly roused, and if the British Army were to appear to be an arm of the Ulster Unionist Government, the Catholics in their turn were likely to regard the troops with the same distaste as they regard their Government.[164]

Despite the personal unpopularity of Harold Wilson and Merlyn Rees with the unionist community, Labour in government did not turn out to be the 'red devils' unionists had feared. The Labour administration's failure to make an effective intervention during the 1974 UWC Strike convinced many loyalists that Labour had lost its will in Northern Ireland. However, Wilson angered loyalists with his 'spongers' speech in which he questioned the integrity of unionists' 'loyalism'. Although the premier's speech was designed for the wider British audience and might be perceived as an attempt to absolve his government from direct responsibility for the imminent collapse of the power-sharing Executive, it was an ill-advised intervention, and precipitated a significant increase in support for the strikers' position. It was the insinuation that pecuniary interests were pivotal to unionists' 'loyalty' which most offended the majority of the Province's population. A senior civil servant at the time later articulated the 'indignation' of Northern Ireland's Protestant community. Ken Bloomfield wrote:

> Listeners in Northern Ireland who had been risking their very lives daily in the face of an appalling terrorist threat, and who had continued to work in the face of great difficulties or been turned back from work when the forces of state had failed utterly to support them, listened with indignation as the prime minister of the United Kingdom classified them, alongside the thugs and hooligans of the UDA and UVF and the demi-constitutional politicians of the UUUC, as 'spongers'.[165]

Despite their political success – the downfall of the power-sharing Executive – and their apparent control over the local broadcasting agencies, the strikers lost the propaganda 'battle' in 1974. The rationale behind their resistance to the Sunningdale Agreement and the strength of their feelings, were, by and large, unappreciated by the media, which tended to report the strike as a 'revolt'.[166] However, unionists were, within a comparatively short period of time, to be reassured, at least in terms of the security situation, by a new Secretary of State. Roy Mason adopted a tougher approach to the terrorist threat and unionists applauded a number of his security policies, including the employment of the SAS on the border, increased troop provision and the extension of the 'Ulsterisation' policy started by his predecessor, Rees.

164 J. Callaghan, *A House Divided* (London 1977), p. 20. 165 K. Bloomfield, *Stormont in Crisis – A Memoir* (Belfast 1994), p. 219. 166 Indeed, in comparing the tactics of the UWC to the IRA the *Daily Mirror*, 24 May 1974, suggested that intimidation was the striker's main feature. Terence Lancaster wrote: 'Behind the strike has been the barricade, the bludgeon and the boot. And behind all of these has been the gun'. A detailed analysis of media coverage of the 1974 strike is given in my doctoral thesis.

Differences between Labour's front and back benches have been apparent since partition, but were especially noticeable during the the 1980s. The most consistent champion of Unionism's 'enemies', Sinn Fein, was Ken Livingstone, at the time leader of the GLC. Referring to the proposed extradition of two Maze escapees Gerard Kelly and Brendan McFarlane, Livingstone claimed they were 'political refugees' who 'should not be returned to their enemies'.[167] The lack of interest in, and knowledge of, this on the left in the unionist predicament was also reflected in debates at party conferences where rank and file members called for an end to strip-searching, the release of 'political' prisoners such as the Birmingham Six and the Guildford Four, the banning of plastic bullets and the repeal of the Prevention of Terrorism Act, and the issues of troop withdrawal and Irish unity.[168] Loyalists were perceived by many delegates to be the chief obstacles on Labour's preferred route of unification. One delegate at the 1983 Conference, supporting a motion demanding a break in the bipartisan policy and calling for troop withdrawal, pinpointed the loyalists as the main obstacle to progress in Northern Ireland:

> For too long now we have all been walking on eggs in fear of the Orangemen. It is time we asked the Protestant people straight – will you go into history as the quisling garrison of a foreign power or will you join with your fellow Christians, including southern Protestants, in building a united, socialist Ireland?[169]

It has been argued that Labour's attitude both to the unity issue and the unionist community has altered since the 1992 election defeat and Neil Kinnock's subsequent resignation. Indeed, since Tony Blair's appointment as party leader in 1994, there have been allegations of 'a shift of policy' on Northern Ireland, with a potential Labour government 'moving away from acting as a persuader for a united Ireland by consent'.[170] However, this 'shift' was not as pronounced as some imagined. Desmond McCartan, in a *Belfast Telegraph* report on Labour's 1994 Conference, observed that suggestions Blair was 'steering Labour towards a pro-unionist stance and a radically different view of the Province' were 'total nonsense'.[171] With the substance of policy remaining the same and grassroots sympathy for long-term Irish unity as firm as ever, it was only the tone of the message which had been altered to blend with 'new' Labour's 'clean' image. Thus, McCartan argued that, rather than shifting party policy to embrace unionists' interests, Blair 'has given a touch to the tiller on a course for the safety first route to the ultimate destination'.[172] Yet, following Labour's resounding election victory in May 1997, Tony Blair and his new Ulster Secretary, Mo Mowlam, were keen to 'woo' the Ulster Unionist leadership, whom they increasingly perceived to be the key participants in any talks process. In a 'no unity in my lifetime' speech to a Belfast audience, Blair endeavoured to ease the anxiety of the union-

167 *Today*, 17 May 1986. 168 These two were discussed at the 1979, 1980, 1981 and 1983 Conferences. 169 Michael Kenny, Boothferry CLP, seconding a motion at the 1983 Conference. 170 *Independent*, 3 October 1994. 171 *Belfast Telegraph*, 7 October 1994. 172 Ibid.

ist community. A *Times* editorial suggested that soothing words in the ears of David Trimble and his colleagues might well facilitate their willingness to countenance the prospect of political compromise (at least that of a non-constitutional nature).

> Mr Blair's rhetoric should provide a nervous Unionist majority with the reassurance it seeks ... By making clear that he is personally committed to the Union and has no plans to put Ulster on the slippery slope to a sell-out, Mr Blair can, with greater authority, persuade the Unionists that change is the price of making the current constitutional realities more acceptable to nationalists.[173]

Bipartisanship was an important element in the formulation and delivery of British policy in Northern Ireland. The first Secretary of State for Northern Ireland, William Whitelaw, acknowledged its importance maintaining that whilst he would 'frequently encounter emotional opposition from both extremes', he could rely in general on 'a broad consensus of support throughout Parliament' and consequently, if 'carefully handled', Westminster could be a 'potential source of strength to me at moments of extreme crisis'.[174] Whilst there were to be frequent cases of divergent views being held on the periphery of parties, they responded in unison to the various political initiatives proposed for Northern Ireland over the years and made their joint, ritualistic condemnations of terrorist violence. This is not to say that the front benches constantly agreed on their Irish policy. Despite the common approach taken on the majority of political initiatives, there were perennial differences over aspects of security policy and 'human rights' issues, although the extent of these depended on the degree of rift between the parties at a particular time.[175] Yet the bipartisanship which was forged early in the Troubles set a definite pattern for future responses. Thus Northern Irish issues were to be regarded as being so far above party politics that when Ulster Secretaries later found themselves ensnared in Irish traps of their own making, the parliamentary and media response was one of supporting the alleged miscreant and condemning the aggrieved. Such an instance was Peter Brooke's singing 'O My Darling Clementine' on RTE shortly after 10 Protestant workers had been killed by the IRA. Normally such an act of political folly would have led to condemnation from all sides of the House and pressure being placed on the Minister involved to resign. However, in this instance there was overwhelming parliamentary and press support for the offending minister and criticism of unionist politicians.[176] Only the *Sun*, in its 'Sack the Singing Minister' editorial, reflected the mood of anger in loyalist heartlands.

173 *Times*, 17 May 1997. 174 W. Whitelaw, *The Whitelaw Memoirs*, London 1989, p. 88. 175 Therefore, in the early 1980s when there was a great distance between left and right in Great Britain, pro-republican elements within the Labour left, such as Ken Livingstone, were to the fore, criticising government actions, particularly in the security field. 176 *The Daily Mail*, 21 January 1992 claimed that Brooke's mistake was 'nothing' compared to 'the stiff-necked obduracy of Ulster's community leaders', whilst the *Independent*, 25 January 1992,

> Ulster has known much grief and horror. It has never known such an irresponsible, witless, careless display of indifference from a government minister. We cannot begin to understand, let alone excuse, the behaviour of Ulster Secretary Peter Brooke ... Unionist MPs have demanded his resignation. We share their outrage. *If Mr Brooke has not the decency to resign the Prime Minister must sack him.*[177]

Unionists' sense of political isolation has therefore increased during the last 25 years. This has been especially apparent in the 'distancing' nature of the relationship between front-bench Conservatives and Unionists. Although the political 'separation' of Conservatism and Unionism has not resulted in a political 'divorce', this has been largely due to Tory pragmatism which has manifested itself in Government 'touting' of Ulster Unionist support in parliament, rather than a resurgence of widespread 'fraternal' feelings between Conservatives and Ulster Unionists.[178] Thus Tory administrations had adopted an increasingly 'neutral' stance towards the issue of the Union and the volume of backbench support which had characterised the much closer relationship between the respective groups during the Edwardian period, never materialised during the current conflict. Moreover, although loyalist fears of Labour intentions were also to be dissipated on account of the acceptance of a bipartisan approach to Northern Ireland which, by necessity, required the adoption of 'moderate' policies (not to mention Labour's long spell in the political 'wilderness'), unionists were not to feel any 'safer' in their countenance of a political future which would be controlled by an administration supporting the aim of long-term Irish unity. Unionists were, therefore, to experience even greater feelings of isolation than the largely Catholic Civil Rights movement during the late 1960s.

ENNISKILLEN – ITS EFFECT ON THE ENGLISH

> When I go to Westminster tomorrow my colleagues will be gracious and sympathetic. But when they go home to their constituencies next week they will have forgotten Ken Maginnis and the people of Fermanagh and Tyrone.[179]

The Enniskillen bombing in 1987, although it did not claim the greatest number

claimed that unionist reaction to the Brooke gaffe was 'unforgiving and unchristian enough to make them yet more deeply disliked'. 177 *Sun*, 20 January 1992. 178 Governments of differing political hues which lacked an overall Commons majority were not above negotiating 'alliances' with the UUP in their efforts to stay in power. This was the case both with the Callaghan government of the late 1970s and John Major's administration, especially between 1994 and 1997. David Trimble was regarded as being more likely to capitalise on such dependency than his predecessors, especially when Major's government lost its parliamentary majority late in 1996. The *Times*, 13 December 1996, warned the Ulster Unionist leader to 'avoid trying to be too clever by half' as there 'is nothing to be won from stating that Ulster is as British as Huntingdon or Sedgefield, and then behaving in a manner which suggests that it is not'. 179 *Guardian*, 9 November, 1987.

of fatalities in the Troubles, was undoubtedly the single incident of terrorism within the province which made, for a prolonged period, the greatest impression on British public and politicians alike.[180] I have chosen it as a case study for this reason and would like to pose a number of questions. Why did the Enniskillen bombing arouse so much interest in Britain, particularly when other attacks in Northern Ireland had not? What were the main features of the national media's coverage of the attack and how did these reflect existing views about the conflict in Northern Ireland in general and about the unionist position in particular? What changes, if any, were there in the mainland reaction to the unionist position in the wake of the bombing?

What lay behind the IRA's choice of Enniskillen for the 'Poppy Day' bombing? Obviously it's difficult to fathom the logic behind the justification of such an attack, particularly when the bombing divided the republican community itself. However, it can be argued that a number of factors influenced the decision to bomb the Remembrance Day ceremony in the Fermanagh town. Provisional strength and the existence of a 'maverick' fringe within the area's republican community, the need to revive morale in the period of a major arms interception, as well as Enniskillen's military connections, all made the town's Remembrance Day parade a potential target for an IRA attack.

Enniskillen, the county town of Fermanagh, with its 'mixed' population and its close proximity to the border, had experienced much suffering in the conflict before November 1987. However, this had, in the main, been restricted to attacks on security personnel, notably 'easier' targets, such as off-duty members of the RUC and the UDR.[181] Despite this previous emphasis on 'easy' targets, the IRA was well aware of Enniskillen's long history as a military base. Enniskillen had been a garrison town since the 17th century and its mainly Protestant regiments, such as the Royal Inniskillings, had a distinguished record in earlier overseas campaigns. Indeed, the military significance of the town was pinpointed by the BBC in their early coverage of the bombing.[182]

Clearly the IRA appreciated the symbolic significance of an attack on what they perceived to be a military target, a 'triumphalist' British commemoration of their dead in two previous military campaigns. What they seemingly failed to grasp was that the British, and more importantly from the republican perspective, Americans and European, differentiated between British soldiers carrying out their duties in Ulster and British forces remembering their fallen comrades

180 The explosions at the La Mon House Hotel in 1978 and the Droppin Well pub (1982) each claimed a greater number of fatalities than the Enniskillen attack. 181 Local MP Ken Maginnis pointed out in Parliament that there had been 169 IRA killings in his constituency and that there had only been 14 resulting convictions; quoted in the *Guardian*, 10 November 1987. 182 The town's military background was a theme which the media established early in its coverage of the bombing. A BBC1 bulletin of 9 November had an 'Old Soldiers' feature, showing the Duke of Gloucester inspecting old members of the regiment and zoomed in on a display of photos and medals of local military heroes. The report ended with a former Royal Inniskillings captain, Willie Park, declaring that he found it 'hard to fathom Irishmen doing this to each other'.

from previous campaigns. Indeed, in practical terms it had been rather more than an attack on British soldiers, as both the operationally successful Enniskillen bomb and the unsuccessful 150 lb landmine at Tullyhannon near the Irish border (which had been scheduled to go off at a time when a Boys Brigade band would have been playing at a Remembrance Day parade), were inevitably going to involve large numbers of civilian casualties.

Despite the clear risk to civilian life the IRA were obviously prepared to take a gamble with such a device. Whilst the British media were clearly unaware of the sectarian nuances implicit in attendance and participation in a Remembrance Day parade (and, indeed, the distinction between 'our' civilians and 'theirs'), the local brigade of the IRA were not. Therefore, while a small number of Catholics might have been involved in the parade, the vast majority of participants and observers who would have been remembering British forces killed in military conflict, clearly would have been expected to have been Protestants. The Provisionals had just suffered, a severe blow, both in military and propaganda terms, with the *Eksund* arms-interception. A republican counter-attack, or 'spectacular', was clearly need to raise republican morale and Enniskillen was perceived, at least by republicans in Fermanagh, as a likely response.

A 30–50 lb device (small by Ulster standards) had been left in St Michael's Catholic memorial hall which was only twenty yards from the war memorial. The blast occurred at 10.45 on Sunday 8 November, just fifteen minutes before the memorial service had been due to start. Indeed, Sir John Hermon, the RUC Chief Constable, said that a large number of young participants in the parade (an estimated 245) had been delayed three minutes behind the band and had been due to arrive at the memorial at the time of the blast. The hall itself had not been searched, a fact which was later to be of some controversy.[183]

Despite the comparatively small size of the device involved, the effects of falling masonry and collapsing buildings proved to be devastating. Many eyewitnesses reported that their first recollections after the loud blast had been those of the rising dust and the horrendous screams and moans of the injured. David Hearst wrote of the dreadful confusion;

> For a few seconds, it looked as if the town had suddenly been plunged into a thick fog. But the fog was dust settling on a scene of carnage. Children screamed for their parents and the injured screamed for help. those who were still on their feet began to pull frantically at the rubble to free bodies.[184]

Although the holocaust which would undoubtedly have occurred if the bomb had exploded when the full parade had assembled, had been avoided, the toll of civilian casualties was the worst to occur in the province since the Droppin Well bomb five years previously (in this attack, seventeen had died, including eleven civilians). Eleven people died and 63 were injured (19 seriously) in the Enniskillen blast. *Daily Mirror* photographer Michael Martin, an eye-witness, wrote about

183 This is referred to in greater detail later. 184 *Guardian*, 9 November 1987.

'desperate rescuers clawing at the rubble' and, like others who described the carnage, used a series of images, including fallen poppies, smashed wreaths, bloodied children's uniforms and 'a coat of dust'.

> Smashed wreaths were trampled under foot, old soldiers were helpling rescuers in the rubble and children were wandering in a daze looking for friends or parents. They'd all been spruced up in their smartest Scouts, Guides and Brownies uniforms. Now they were covered with dust and blood. The dust coated everything like shroud and through it all the cries of the wounded drifted like some terrible nightmare.[185]

Most national papers did not have their own journalists or photographers present at Enniskillen but many despatched their reporters as quickly as possible to describe post-explosion traumas and deveopments. Sue Carroll of the *Sun* did this in her report, 'Fear of a town bathed in tears'.

> In Enniskillen, the air is thick with fog and fear and the smell of death. Poppies scattered among the rubble are a tragic and pathetic reminder of the disaster. The carnage and devastation of the bomb have left the small Irish town shocked and stunned. Nobody, not even in war-torn Ireland can be prepared for the horror of murder on this scale. Amidst the mayhem relatives, some crying, some just staring into space, others praying, stood in the town centre last night surveying the debris. The enormity of the blast has shaken Enniskillen to its roots, but there are few signs of rage – only grief.[186]

A significant contribution to the volume of 'external' media interest in, and impact of, the Enniskillen incident was the ready availability of good quality video recording of the bombing. A local shopkeeper, Raymond McCartney, who had intended to take a film of the parade on his VHS video camera, hastily switched his camera on to the drama unfolding in front of him. His eleven minutes of videotape were used by the BBC, ITV and RTE, all of which, having no personnel in Enniskillen, took several hours reaching the border town, and were subsequently relayed by television companies all round the world. McCartney's video brought home the horrors of the bombing in a way that previous bomb aftermath coverage had failed to achieve. Although the BBC thought it prudent to cut the soundtrack from McCartney's video and ITV omitted some of the more harrowing images from its earlier bulletins, the edited use of a live recording of a catrastrophic event had a profound effect, particularly on external audiences whose experience of such an event would have been minimal.[187]

Enniskillen certainly made great impact on the national audience. The story not only dominated the news bulletins for most of the week leading up to the

185 *Daily Mirror*, 9 November 1987. 186 *Sun*, 9 November 1987. 187 In a *Sunday Times*' report (15 November 1987), Martha Wohrle argued that the video 'kindled dulled emotions with powerful images of confusion and chaos and a distressing soundtrack of stifled whimpers'.

victims' funerals, but it also encroached in to other news areas, including programmes such as 'Kilroy' and Question Time'.[188] Enniskillen was also 'different' in the sense that it was not allowed to 'evaporate' like other Ulster tragedies. Thus television used new angles on the 'old' story to rekindle interest in the event. In the early days after the attack, attention was focused on the forgiving, dignified figure of Gordon Wilson. After the funerals of the victims, the visit of the Prince and Princess of Wales on 17 November and the suffering and stoicism of some of Enniskillen injured dominated the headlines.[189] Indeed, the story appeared regularly in the national bulletins until the Remembrance Day service two weeks after the explosion and programmes relating to the event were transmitted nearly two years after the explosion.[190] The Enniskillen tragedy was featured in over fifty BBC TV national broadcasts, including studio audience discussions, religious broadcasts, interviews with victims and political and security experts, as well as news bulletins.

The 'longetivity' of the Enniskillen incident was unparalleled in covereage of Northern Irish events, and unquestionably so, since the mid 1970s. The story became a 'perennial', appearing regularly over the years. Therefore, the visit of a group of children injured in the blast to see the Changing of the Guard was featured on the BBC's late evening news in February 1988 and the start of a scheme for helping Enniskillen teenagers was featured on 'Breakfast Time' in May 1988.[191] Rapidly, Enniskillen became a subject of 'anniversaries', with follow-ups on the bombing. This included live coverage of the re-arranged Remembrance service in the town two weeks after the bomb, 'Enniskillen at Christmas', Gordon Wilson's 'Breakfast Time' interview just before Christmas, the Queen's Christmas Message, the News Review of the Year (where, as with other news reviews Enniskillen was reported as being one tragedy in a 'year of disasters'), 'Songs of Praise from Enniskillen' and 'Enniskillen One Year On'.[192]

The media's early assessment was that here was an Irish story which, although it had emanated from the same violent backdrop as so many other newstories from the Province, was 'different' in terms of the community's response to the violence which had provided new hopes for a peaceful future. Most of the early news bulletins featured not only extracts from the amateur video recording, but interviews with eye witnesses and political reaction. The bombing was considered, from the off, as a landmark, which required brief contextual analysis, and thus not only was the immediate background supplied (such as the *Eksund* arms haul of the previous week), but also the political events on the road to the Enniskillen bombing, including the signing of the Anglo-Irish Agreement. The late evening news bulletin of the day of blast devoted itself largely to the story of the bombing.[193] The story was considered to be of such magnitude that it was

188 BBC1 *Kilroy* 10 November 1987 and *Question Time*, 12 November 1987. 189 I return to this subject later. 190 This featured the opening of an integrated school in the town. 191 BBC1 *Nine O'clock News*, 28 February 1988 and BBC *Breakfast Time*, 16 May 1988. 192 The respective dates of these BBC1 broadcasts about Enniskillen were; 22 November, 21 November, 21 December, 15 December, 29 December (all 1987), 6 January and 8 November (both 1988). 193 BBC1 *Evening News*, 8 November 1987.

split up into five sections – the scene in the town as darkness fell, the amateur video coverage, the political response, an impromptu 'memorial' service in the town and the security background to the attack – which were each considered in turn. Apart from transmission of the video recording of the explosion, the early bulletins focused on the bulldozers removing rubble in the darkness, eye witness accounts from survivors relating their experiences from hospital beds and security chiefs deflecting criticism that the Catholic hall had not been searched before the military parade. The bulletins featured the eerie image that for many became the personification of Enniskillen - the juxtaposition of the War Memorial 'Tommy' and the bombed Catholic hall in the background.[194]

The initial political response

The response of British political and religious leaders to the events in County Fermanagh was unparalleled. They recognised that Enniskillen was different not just in terms of the scale of the bombing but also in its sacrilegious aspects and the fact that it appeared to break the 'ground rules' of the conflict.[195] The volume of rebuke was unprecedented, with the 'groundswell of outrage' quickly becoming 'an avalanche of damnation'.[196]

Nothing was, of course, different in the nature of the British response to Irish bombings. English politicians, devoid of any real answers, were united in their condemnation of the attack. Yet with Enniskillen, the tenor of the condemnation, its harshness, and the manner in which they vied with each other in their condemnation, was unique. The Prime Minister clearly moved by the attack, emphasised the sacrilegious nature of the bombing.

> Every nation should honour its dead – and we should all be able to stand and honour them in peace.[197]

In stressing that her government would actively pursue the terrorists, she maintained there would be 'no hiding place' for them and appealed directly to republican sympathisers in North America, trusting that anyone 'who ever had sympathies for the terrorists, will not have any more now'.[198]

There was cross-party condemnation of the attack. Labour leader Neil Kinnock described the bombing as 'an atrocity against ordinary people'.[199] The Liberals also condemned the IRA, with its Ulster spokesman David Alton calling for 'increased co-operation with the Irish Republic' and in an unusually harsh criticism of the minority community, urged Catholics to 'end their ambivalence and join the RUC'.[200] Despite their vehement condemnation of the IRA the government offered little immediate hope to the beleagured Protestant community liv-

194 Ibid. **195** Some argue that such 'ground rules' – the acceptance by both sides that only soldiers and policemen (and presumably not terrorists) were 'legitimate' targets – reflected one perspective (the republican) more than the other (unionist). **196** P. O'Malley, *Biting at the Grave – The Irish Hunger Strike and the Politics of Despair* (Belfast, 1990), p. 251. **197** BBC1, *Late Evening News*, 8 November 1987. **198** Ibid. **199** P. O'Malley, op. cit., p. 252. **200** *Guardian*, 10 November 1987.

ing close to the Irish border. Secretary of State Tom King admitted 'there isn't an easy solution' to such breaches in security and, far from reassuring the community he cautioned the Protestants, urging that 'anger mustn't take the form of retaliation and people taking the law into their own hands'.[201]

Opponents of the Prime Minister criticised her reluctance to alter her Ulster policy. Writing in the *Standard,* Enoch Powell condemned English politicans and public alike for their 'surprise' at what had happened in Enniskillen, implying that such a tragedy was 'the almost inevitable result of recent Government policy'.[202] Powell pinpointed the significance of the Anglo-Irish Agreement and maintained that 'there has to be an end to the differential treatment of Ulster and a reassessment of English political interpretation of the problem' which had culminated in an Anglo Irish Agreement as shameful to Britain as it was injurious to Northern Ireland'.[203]

Mrs Thatcher's party colleagues joined with her in condemning the IRA, but this condemnation did not lead to their calling for a reintroduction of internment or even supporting Ian Paisley's call for an emergency debate which was overwhelmingly rejected.[204] Unionist sympathisers, the Friends of the Union, didn't join Peter Robinson-led unionists demands for tougher action, but one of them, Ian Gow, did use the debate as an opportunity to endorse Unionist demands for an end to the Hillsborough Agreement, though at the same time warning disenchanted loyalists to refrain from adopting the tactics of the IRA.

Enniskillen presented the Labour Party with a problem. Neil Kinnock urged northern nationalists and southern politicians to reconsider their opposition to extradition. As the *Guardian* commented, 'Labour said and did all the right things which could have been expected of it in the circumstances'.[205] Its front-bench Northern Ireland spokesman Kevin McNamara joined his party leader in condemning the bombing. Like Tom King he rejected retaliation, recommending 'cold anger mixed with a determination to support the forces of law and order'.[206] The Shadow Secretary was on unsteady ground when he argued that Enniskillen had 'given the lie to the suggested that any democrat can flirt with those who support the policy of the bomb and the ballot box'.[207] This comment brought shouts of 'tell that to your own Labour MPs' from the Ulster Unionists'.[208]

The party was embarrassed not so much by the left's long-standing cordial relationship with Sinn Fein, but more specifically the involvement of National Executive member Ken Livingstone and front-bench spokesperson for employment affairs, Claire Short, with a Troops Out meeting just over a week after the bombing. Although Short was to pull out of the meeting, it clearly caused Labour some embarrassment. The Tories were not slow in extracting political capital from the issue. The chairman of the Tory back-bench committee on Northern Ireland, Sir John Biggs-Davison, argued:

201 Ibid. **202** *London Evening Standard*, 10 November 1987. **203** Ibid. **204** *Guardian*, 10 November 1987. **205** *Guardian*, 17 November 1987. **206** *Guardian*, 10 November 1987. **207** Ibid. **208** Ibid.

> ... it's hard to understand how much a meeting could take place in the light of last Sunday's massacre. It's astonishing and deplorable.[209]

Even those papers traditionally sympathetic to the left and their demands for Irish unity, criticised that 'minority of Labour activists' who masqueraded as 'the moral grotesqueries of the Gerry Adams Fan Club'.[210] The *Guardian* pointed out that this was a potentially 'damaging' liaison for Labour,

> Two hundred and twenty odd Labour MPs can react in a decent, humane fashion to Enniskillen. But a couple of opportunists or revolutionary romantics can destroy the whole thing, exposing Labour to the very damaging charges that it can't keep its house in order, is split down the middle or is soft on terrorism.[211]

The *Independent* criticised Livingstone's 'tactically inept' position, claiming that it would 'marginalise' Unionists who clearly would 'not be bombed into leaving' the province.[212] The *Independent's* cartoon, 'The Boy Stood on the Burning Deck' depicted Livingstone on the deck of his sinking 'Support for Sinn Fein ship'.[213]

British media coverage of the Enniskillen bombing

The national media were quick to exploit the image of one individual's extraordinary capacity to forgive as being symbolic of Ireland's growing mood of atonement. By concentrating of this aspect of Enniskillen, the media avoided the attack's underlying cause, particularly the government's apparent inability to protect its citizens. Although it seemed slightly incongruous for an increasingly secular society to be stressing the essentially Christian virtue of forgiveness, this was the predominant feature of British coverage of the bombing: a forgiving response of a provincial society, one which surmounted political and military barriers and which promised fruitful change emanating from below, rather than being devised and implemented by those from above.

The personification of this willingness to forgive and the torch-carrier for future peace hopes was Enniskillen draper Gordon Wilson, who had not only suffered injury in the explosion, but had also lost his daughter Marie, a trainee nurse at the Royal Victoria Hospital in Belfast. Gordon Wilson quickly became for the national media the 'voice' of Enniskillen. An honest, dignified man, he was perceived to be the antithesis of the perpetuators of the violence and the local politicians who appeared either unable or unwilling to break the deadlock. Television cameras focused on his remarkable capacity for forgiving those who had taken the lives of his daughter and fellow citizens. On 9 November he told the nation that he 'had prayed for the bombers last night'.[214] He gave an emotional description of Marie's last moments, ending with the words, 'Daddy, I love

209 *Sunday Times*, 15 November 1987. **210** *Guardian* 17 November 1987. **211** Ibid. **212** *Independent*, 17 November 1987. **213** Ibid. **214** BBC1 *Six O'Clock Evening News*, 9 November 1987.

you very much' and added that he and his wife had 'no ill feeling towards the IRA'.[215]

The *Daily Express* also highlighted Wilson's propensity towards forgiveness. The *Express*'s headline, 'Marie's father mourns with dignity and a remarkable lack of bitterness', concentrated on this apparently new Irish angle.[216] John Burns' centre page report highlighted the feelings of the Wilsons, but gave the impression that they represented the feelings of other grieving Enniskillen families. Burns wrote with passion about how the Wilsons 'prayed for the bomber' who 'would have to face his Maker' and wondered in amazement at the unselfishness of the local community.

> In other homes (apart from the Wilsons) in this backwater town there are tears for the victims. Yet no one talks of bloody vengeance against the killers and all strive to hide you from their tears. Time and again you are rocked by the unfailing niceness of the bereaved. Whenever their self control slips they quickly apologise for their tears, yet you want to weep with them.[217]

Other papers exploited the forgiveness theme. The *London Standard*'s headline the day after the bomb was 'I forgive Marie's Murderers'.[218] The *Daily Mirror,* which was to establish a Marie Wilson Fund, said that Gordon Wilson 'has shown ... how indomitable the human spirit is' and other papers, including the *Independent, Today* and the *Sunday Times*, also concentrated on this feature.[219] Indeed, it was this specific characteristic of the Enniskillen bombing which was later to feature in the Queen's Speech. Clearly the Queen's advisers acknowledged that a chord had been struck with the British public.

> From time to time we ... see some inspiring examples of tolerance. Mr Gordon Wilson ... impressed the whole world by the depth of his forgiveness. His strength, and that of his wife, and the courage of their daughter, came from their Christian conviction.[220]

Gordon Wilson was often cited by the national media as an example of how Christian charity and forgiveness could conquer those agents of sectarian division in the Province and hold out hopes of a better future. The *Sunday Times* noted that 'what local bitterness there has been has been limited and held in check' and praised the contribution of a 'remarkable' man, whose 'display of simple Christian faith' promised to 'cut the ground from beneath the extremists who prefer conflict to compromise'.[221] The same paper, like others, was quick to grab the opportunity of lashing out at unionist politicians. Although Ian Paisley had restricted his Enniskillen reactions to a renunciation of IRA violence and a re-

215 Ibid. 216 *Daily Express*, 10 November 1987. 217 Ibid. 218 *London Evening Standard*, 9 November 1987. 219 *Daily Mirror*, 10 November, *Independent*, 11 November, *Today*, 11 November, and *Sunday Times*, 15 November, 1987. 220 BBC1, *The Queen's Christmas Message*, 25 December 1987. 221 *Sunday Times,* 15 November 1987.

newed call for tighter security measures, some journalists afforded themselves of the opportunity of contrasting Paisley's belligerence with the tolerance of Wilson.

> If Mr Wilson can forgive what right have others to call for revenge? Not for the first time, it's the Rev Ian Paisley who is out of touch with the public yearn for peace, not Mr Wilson.[222]

A few days later it was Marie's funeral which was highlighted by the media, with *Today* devoting its front and double centre pages in a six photo coverage of the funeral, under the headline, 'Enniskillen says farewell to Saint Marie'.[223] The *Independent* described the great cross-community sympathy for the Wilson family, quoting the Methodist minister's description of the nurse who was 'like a whirlwind breathing life and vitality' into Enniskillen.[224]

Many papers concentrated on the clear contrast between the destruction of Marie's own life and her obvious care for the lives of others. To many, particularly the tabloids, it was this angelic quality which, along with the statue of the soldier bowing his head in front of the blast damage, were to become the potent symbols of Enniskillen. The *Daily Mirror* not only singled out Marie as the embodiment of the tragedy, but decided that her vocation, the caring of the sick, would make an appropriate vehicle for a fund appeal. In a page feature article, 'Front line angels', Mary Riddell spotlighted the Royal Victoria Hospital in west Belfast, where Marie had been a student nurse. Describing the scene in the maternity unit 'where smiling nurses masked their grief as they worked', the *Mirror* appealed to its readers for donations which would help alleviate the burden of an over-stretched hospital staff.[225]

Although he was to resist the temptation of forming a peace movement in the wake of the Enniskillen blast, Wilson did not slip back into anonymity. He continued to be closely involved in a plethora of fund-raising events associated with the bombing and was to lend his sympathy to the parents of the Warrington bomb victims in March 1993. Gordon Wilson was appointed to the Irish Senate in 1993 in recognition of his work to foster reconciliation and he was involved in an ill-fated meeting with the IRA in April 1994. Tragically Wilson was to gain further exposure in the national media following the death of his son Peter in a road accident. The *Daily Mirror* asked in December 1994, Gordon Wilson – how much grief can one man bear?'[226] When he died suddenly, eight years after the Enniskillen bombing, the national media mourned the passing of 'a great man of peace'.[227] Yet through all his personal suffering Gordon Wilson maintained his forgiving, dignified approach, the bedrock of which was, he argued, Christian love.

> That's (love) what helps to keep me going, to get through my days and to sleep at nights. Love God and your neighbour. In life and after death there's only one ultimate standard by which we are judged. Marie showed that to us

222 Ibid. 223 *Today*, 11 November 1987. 224 *Independent*, 11 November 1987. 225 *Daily Mirror*, 13 November 1987. 226 *Daily Mirror*, 9 December 1994. 227 ITN, *News at Ten*, 27 June 1995.

all as she lay under the rubble at the Cenotaph, holding my hand, with her life slipping away. The bottom line is love. There's nothing more I can say ...[228]

Although the national media was to maximise the forgiveness theme – this response, in stressing the need to avoid a backlash, obviously was in accordance with British policy in the province – the local press also investigated the degree of suffering of Enniskillen victims long after the explosion and queried the extent of forgiveness in the wider Protestant community. Jane Bell's *Belfast Telegraph* report – 'Head Ronnie Hill retired on Monday, but he didn't know. He's still in a coma' – graphically illustrated the extent of suffering of Enniskillen victims some time after the event.[229] Bell informed her readers that Ronnie Hill 'needs round the clock care as he lies and sits in his hospital room. Tubes feed him and help his breathing. The only independent movement he can make it to open and close his eyes'.[230] His wife Noreen felt that the Poppy Day bombing had 'sadly made no difference' and attacked the gunmen, arguing that 'if they were human, they could not do it. I don't know how anyone could support them'.[231]

The story's obvious 'human angle' appeal was a vital component of press and TV coverage of the attack. The high profile given to the story and the graphic detail, particularly in the context of pictorial coverage of the explosion and its aftermath, was quite unusual in the mainland presentation of the Irish troubles. Empathy, even with apparently innocent victims of violence in Northern Ireland, has not always been an easy matter for the external audience. This is in itself less the result of 'English insensitivity' and rather more their failure to comprehend the political and social complexities of the Ulster situation. However, due to Enniskillen's wider implications, the fact that the bombing had occurred in an old garrison town and at such a 'typically British' ceremony meant that the external audience were more prepared to pay attention as its background was one easily within their own experience and understanding. The location and the nature of the ceremony attacked by the IRA constituted an act of sacrilege as far as many of the tabloids were concerned. The *Sun* contained 3 large photos of the Enniskillen carnage, including one with the caption, 'Death in the Debris' and its headline the day after the bomb was 'Poppy Day massacre – 11 dead and 63 maimed by the IRA'.[232] The report noted the 'merciless savagery' of the IRA and concluded:

Eleven men and women, wearing their Remembrance Day poppies with pride. Red poppies that became bathed in the blood they symbolise. They were cut down at a service for heroes – with a bomb planted by the IRA cowards.[233]

The *Daily Mirror* also picked out the sacrilegious aspect of the Remembrance Day attack in its coverage. Leading with the headline, 'Poppy Day of Blood – a blot on mankind' the Mirror stressed the 'role-reversal' of 'bandsmen and march-

228 A McCreary, *Marie – A Story From Enniskillen* (London 1990), p. 112. 229 *Belfast Telegraph*, 3 November 1988. 230 Ibid. 231 Ibid. 232 *Sun*, 9 November 1987. 233. Ibid.

ers with World War medals' (who) ran from the parade in a desperate attempt to rescue victims'.[234]

Aligned to the forgiveness theme of media coverage was that of community cohesion in the explosion's aftermath. The idea that, since the community as a whole was so totally appalled by the attack they could look optimistically to the future, was featured in a number of television reports. Thus *Newsnight* and the main *BBC Evening News* bulletin spotlighted Enniskillen 'looking to the future' and another BBC report observed how teachers were trying to prevent their children from becoming more insular in their attitudes as a result of the bombing.[235] Another report looked at 'the after-effects of the Remembrance Day bomb on the community'.[236] Special emphasis was placed in several reports on the explosion's repercussions on local schoolchilren. Carmel McQuaid noted that despite local schools' attempts to ensure a speedy return to normality, there were many cases of pupils 'suffering delayed reaction', with several instances of 'insomnia, nightmares, depression, unsettled behaviour and outbursts of weeping' being reported.[237]

Enniskillen was portrayed by the national media as an attack on the wider community and not simply one aimed at the Protestant section of that community. The joint involvement of local Catholics and Protestants who had fought 'shoulder to shoulder' and 'with heroism' in previous conflicts was noted by Ted Oliver in the *Daily Mirror*.[238] The *Sun*, too, emphasised that, despite the exclusively Protestant fatality list, parades in the town were not perceived by many, including the RUC, to be solely Protestant occasions. The reactions of a police officer witness to the blast, who had noted that the march had 'not been just a Protestant parade' but that there had been 'Catholics there too, paying their respects to the dead', were recorded.[239]

Indeed, this perception that the bomb, rather than being a blatantly sectarian, 'anti-Protestant' act, was a crime against the wider community and indeed, humanity in general, was of crucial significance in ensuring that unionists were unable to turn the Enniskillen outrage to their political advantage. It could be argued that this perception was one largely constructed by the national media which did not desire the outrage to be given a 'political' dimension. In other words, by restricting coverage of Enniskillen to an attack on the wider community, the national media was not providing unionist politicians with sufficient leverage to turn the Enniskillen bombing into propaganda 'fodder' for their anti-Anglo-Irish Agreement campaign. Therefore, as has been noted, coverage of the explosion concentrated on the scale of human losses, the unusually large measure of Christian forgiveness to emerge from Enniskillen and the sacrilegious nature of the IRA's attack on the 'war dead'. It was these facets which made Enniskillen 'different' in the eyes of the British media, and not the belief that one section of the Northern Irish community was being specifically targetted by terrorists emanating from another section of that community.

234 *Daily Mirror*, 9 November 1987. 235 BBC2 *Newsnight* and BBC1 *Evening News*, 13 November 1987. 236 BBC1 *Breakfast Time*, 10 November 1987. 237 *Times Educational Supplement*, 11 March 1988. 238 *Daily Mirror*, 9 November 1987. 239 *Sun*, 9 November 1987.

Some academics, however noted that Enniskillen was 'different' because the vast majority of the Enniskillen victims were Protestant civilians rather than being, in the main, Protestant members of the security forces. Padraig O'Malley stressed this 'sectarian' nature of Enniskillen because it broke 'the generally accepted ground rules of the conflict' where attacks by republican terrorists would not be regarded as 'sectarian'.[240] This distinction, of course, ignores the deeper motivation of republican terrorists, merely taking at face value the IRA's intention of killing security personnel, regardless of their religion. The counter-argument that members of the security forces, living in Ulster, who are more likely to be Protestant and therefore likely to provoke – from the republican viewpoint – a politically-positive counter attack by loyalist terrorists, is less liable to be broached in the national media, which tends to restrict the term 'sectarian' to loyalist attacks. It is interesting to note in the context of the Enniskillen bombing, the different usage of the term 'sectarian' within the *same* report. Robert Rodwell's *Standard* report dealt with the victims of the violence without mentioning their religion, whilst in a short paragraph at the end, describing an attack on Catholics in north Belfast, he noted, '8 Roman Catholic youths were shot last night'.[241]

Thus the religious composition of the Enniskillen victims was rarely referred to. Where it was, reference was indirect, such as where the victims worshipped or were buried. Papers like *Today* reported the names of the churches in their descriptions of the funerals and the *Express* mentioned the Armstrong couple who 'sang together in the town's Darling Street Methodist Church Choir' and also noted that 'six devoted members of the same church' (Enniskillen Presbyterian) were victims of the blast.[242] However, few papers deemed it necessary to analyse why the suffering was exclusively Protestant nor was the issue of Protestants being directly targetted by the IRA dealt with at length in the press, (for instance in a leading article). Fleet Street rather chose to contextualise Enniskillen as a republican response to the *Eksund* arms find, thereby ignoring its place in the framework of an IRA 'genocide' policy in the border areas.

Ironically the external audience's only awareness that the bombing had a sectarian dimension emanated from the speeches and statements of others, principally from the Catholic community itself. The *Standard* was one of a number of papers to print John Hume's statement regarding the magnitude of Enniskillen which he described as 'the worst act of provocation against the Protestant community in the whole of 17 years of the conflict'.[243] In a similar vein, the *Times*, on its front page, reported a statement from the Irish Catholic bishops (without actually commenting on its implications), where they 'called on the Irish people to attend Sunday Mass in large numbers to show their collective solidarity or sympathy with the Protestant community'.[244]

'Suffering children' was another powerful media image of the Enniskillen bombing. Apart from focussing on the tragic fate of a young adult (Marie Wilson), the *Sunday Times* presented an in-depth, illustrated life story of the student nurse,

240 P. O'Malley, op. cit., p. 252. 241 *London Evening Standard*, 9 November 1987. 242 *Today*, 11 November 1987 and *Daily Express*, 10 November 1987. 243 *London Evening Standard*, 9 November 1987. 244 *Times*, 14 November 1987.

'Born into strife; the life and death of Marie Wilson' – the *Sunday Times* and much of the national media also highlighted the physical and psychological suffering of those injured in the blast like Stephen Ross and Lisa Cathcart, as well as the suffering of those young people who had lost parents and relatives in the bombing, most notably Julian Armstrong (who had been injured in the blast) and that of his older sisters.[245] The *Express* wrote about how 'orphaned Julian Armstrong was yesterday struggling to come to terms with loss of his parents'.[246]

Another example of Enniskillen youth personifying the resilience of the town was provided by six-year-old Lisa Cathcart, who had been the youngest casualty. A photograph of her playing with a typewriter presented by NIO minister Richard Needham, under the caption, 'Lisa's keys to recovery', was featured in the *Express*.[247] The media also concentrated on youngsters like Stephen Ross, who had been badly injured in the blast but who showed resilience in overcoming some of the problems caused by his serious injuries. The horrific facial injuries suffered by the apparently normal teenager were given special treatment by the media. The *Daily Mirror* combined its reporting of the horrible injuries suffered by Stephen, a 15-year-old Enniskillen schoolboy, with an appropriate condemnation of the IRA's account of the event. In a front page report dominated by a photo of Stephen clearly in pain under the title, 'The IRA regrets – the brutal truth behind the terrorists' lying claims', reporter Joe Gorrod told *Mirror* readers that Stephen was 'so badly injured in the blast that he needs a cage to keep the bones of his face together'.[248] He proceeded to castigate the hypocrisy of the IRA 'apology' for the attack by relating it directly to the suffering of Stephen, 'a boy in an iron mask' lying 'suffering in hospital ... shaming IRA claims that they 'regret' the Enniskillen massacre'.[249]

Stephen Ross was one of the many Enniskillen survivors to receive the interest and sympathy of the Royal Family, an interest which, coming as it did chiefly from the Prince and Princess of Wales, inevitably captured media attention. *Today's* front page coloured photograph of the grieving Wilsons at their daughter's funeral was under the headline, 'Courage that touched the heart of Prince Charles' and its double-page, five-photo account of her funeral, 'Marie did not die in vain', led on the Prince's phonecall message to another Enniskillen survivor, Austin Stinson, stressing his 'extreme sympathy' with the Wilsons and saying how 'very upset' he and his wife were by the whole incident.[250]

It was not only the tabloids who concentrated on the 'healing' effect of royal interest and how this managed to bring 'the smiles back to Enniskillen'. The *Times* led on a similar theme the day after the royal couple had visited the town. The front page report announced how the injured had been 'cheered up by the

245 *Sunday Times*, 15 November 1987. 246 *Daily Express*, 10 November 1987. *Today* (23 November 1987), also wrote about the loneliness and despair of the 'orphan Armstrongs'. 247 *Daily Express*, 10 November 1987. 248 *Daily Mirror*, 12 November, 1987. 249 Television bulletins also portrayed Stephen as being representative of the stoicism and cheerfulness of the Enniskillen community. In an interview with John Thorne – BBC *Six O'Clock News*, 12 November 1987 – the teenager recalled the explosion and explained the extent of his injuries. 250 *Today*, 11 November 1987.

royal visitors' and had three photos of the royal pair meeting some of the casualties.[251] One featured Princess Diana sympathising with an injured policeman by his hospital bed, another showed her signing an autograph for an injured teenager and the third photographed her with Gordon Wilson who later told the press, 'The visit has helped me. Princess Di is a lovely girl'.[252] Even the Queen who rarely visited the province or even made public statements on the situation there, was sufficiently moved both by the timing and nature of the Enniskillen bombing to issue a message shortly after the explosion.

> I was deeply shocked to hear of the atrocity which took place at Enniskillen today and of the innocent victims who were sharing in the nation's Remembrance. My heartfelt sympathy goes to the bereaved and injured in their distress.[253]

The importance of Gordon Wilson's forgiveness message and the royal sympathy for the victims of Enniskillen should not be underestimated. Apart from further damaging the militant republican cause, they undoubtedly influenced the swing of public opinion (albeit a temporary one) to the unionist case (see below), as well as managing to direct the British public's attention away from their government's inability to cope with the terrorist threat in Northern Ireland.

Enniskillen – apportioning the blame

As has been mentioned, much of the early coverage of the bombing concentrated on its 'human' angle – the extraordinary depths of forgiveness exhibited by Gordon Wilson and others, the sacrilegious nature of the blast, the 'Britishness' of the occasion and the stoicism of the townspeople. Early analysis tended to centre on the security aspect. However, it was not long before attention turned to apportioning blame for the incident. It is my contention that, despite the increase in the volume of sympathy for bomb victims and a definite, if short-lived, upward shift in support for the presence of British troops in the province, British analysis of the explosion concentrated more on the faults and weaknesses of Irish parties than delivering an in-depth investigation of British policy and attitudes in Ireland.

It is interesting to note that detailed television coverage of 'grassroots' loyalist feelings, as distinct from those 'forgiving' elements within the local community, were restricted to a *Newsnight* analysis of unionist reactions to the blast.[254] Even more intriguing is the degree of attention paid to analysing the effects of the incident on the Catholic hierarchy, the response of Sinn Fein and of politicians and public in the Irish Republic. The reactions of the Catholic bishops to the

251 *Times*, 18 November 1987. **252** Ibid. **253** The Queen, reported in the *Guardian*, 9 November 1987. **254** BBC2 *Newsnight*, 9 November 1987.

bomb were featured on 'Breakfast Time' and the response of Catholic congregations to their bishops' denunciation of the IRA observed on news bulletins.[255] *Newsnight* gave a more analytical treatment of the theme on 13 November in their feature, 'Roman Catholic Church's toughest message on terrorism'.[256]

A lot of coverage was given to the muted reaction of the political representatives of the IRA. Paul Kerrigan, leader of Enniskillen Council, was followed by a large group of journalists, waiting for his reaction to the bombing and allegations of disagreement within the republican movement were raised in a BBC evening news bulletin.[257] Although some observers reminded their audiences that the IRA had not strictly adhered to their own 'code' in the past, there was a general feeling that the republican organisation had broken their own ground rules and in making 'no attempt to phone a warning' and that it was 'impossible to see how such an operation could have been planned without envisaging civilian casualties and Protestant ones at that'.[258]

Patrick Bishop questioned the true morality of republican thinking. Although conceding that the Enniskillen bombing was bound to produce 'an almighty row inside the Republican movement', Bishop concluded that the rationale behind the Provisionals' 'regret' would have more to do with propaganda damage to the movement rather than genuine moral outrage from within the republican movement, at the deed itself. Writing about how the IRA would deal with the local volunteers responsible for planting the Enniskillen bomb, Bishop concluded sardonically:

> Nor should we expect the miscreants' punishment to be too harsh. Killing civilians is not a kneecapping offence in the IRA list of crimes.[259]

'Breakfast Time News', the day after the bomb, argued that the 'no warning' nature of the Enniskillen attack 'breaks the current IRA pattern'.[260] Academics and journalists alike accepted that the 'no warning' nature of Enniskillen was one factor which made it 'different' to other blasts. Padraig O'Malley distinguished between the killing of local security force members and what had occurred at Enniskillen, arguing that the former 'at least fit into the established ground rules of the conflict'.[261] O'Malley maintained that Enniskillen 'broke' these established ground rules and had resulted in the 'degeneration' of 'acceptable' into 'unacceptable' violence.[262] David McKittrick was another experienced writer who wrote about how the IRA had broken their 'self-imposed rules'.[263] Yet this takes republican claims and dogma at face value and ignores earlier breaches of those very ground rules. Perhaps the most infamous case was the Darkley 'massacre' of November 1983, which had a religious backdrop, though it wasn't to gain the headlines which the events of Enniskillen managed to achieve.

Criticism was averted from the British government for the clear breaches in

255 BBC1 *Breakfast Time*, 9 November 1987. 256BBC2 *Newsnight*, 13 November 1987. 257 BBC1 *Nine O'Clock News*, 10 November 1987. 258 *Spectator*, 14 November 1987. 259 Ibid. 260 BBC1 *Breakfast Time News*, 9 November 1987. 261 P. O'Malley, op. cit., p. 252. 262 Ibid. 263 *Independent*, 9 November 1987.

security preceding the Cenotaph blast and foisted on to the government of the Irish Republic. This was particularly true of the Tory tabloids. In its front page 'exclusive' report by John Burns, the *Express* led on 'RUC name bomber – Haughey faces extradition test'. In locating the whereabouts of the bomber, Burns wrote of the way the IRA used the apparent sanctuary or border areas within the Irish Republic; 'at present the bomber is lying low in his Donegal bolthole, just 30 minutes drive from Enniskillen'.[264] Burns' concluding indictment of the Irish government was a damning one:

> Now Irish premier Charles Haughey will have to show whether he has the political will to show IRA killers that there is no hiding place for them in the Republic and that they will be extradited to face British justice.[265]

The *Standard* was another English paper to attack the government of the Irish Republic, particularly in relation to the extradition issue. Noting that extradition had been 'a keystone of the Anglo Irish Agreement', the *Standard* went on to claim that the Republic's degree of willingness to implement the extradition provisions would be an indicator of 'how committed Mr Haughey is to keeping good relationships with Mrs Thatcher and improving cross-border security'.[266] The *Times* differentiated between Haughey's sympathies with the republican cause and that of Garret Fitzgerald, the Irish premier and leader of Fine Gael, who had been a signatory to the Hillsborough Ageement. The *Times* maintained that '... the government of the Republic wriggles uneasily to rid itself of its predecessor's commitment to tighter extradition laws'.[267] Only whenever it fitted into the existing British media agenda did press and television select other 'Irish' dimensions, notably the visit of the Mayor of Dublin to the town and the holding of a minute's silence for the victims of Enniskillen.[268]

Unlike the British press's open condemnation of the behaviour of the IRA and the apparent inactivity of the government of the Irish Republic, their criticism of their own government's security weaknesses, was veiled. The *Standard* argued that the Enniskillen bombing had highlighted the need for Northern Ireland to be placed higher on the political agenda and urged the Prime Minister to exert more influence on Irish policy.

> For too long Anglo-Irish affairs have been dealt with in a low-level at the London end. This is an opportunity for Mrs Thatcher, who was largely responsible for getting the Agreement through and weathering the antagonisms in Ulster and in her own party, to take the reins back into her own hands.[269]

Although other Conservative papers resisted from directly attacking the government ministers involved, the scale of the Enniskillen disaster was justification

264 *Daily Express*, 12 November 1987. 265 Ibid. 266 *London Standard*, 9 November 1987. 267 *Times*, 9 November 1987. 268 The cordial relations between Dublin and Enniskillen were featured on a number of TV news bulletins in November 1987 (and indeed, afterwards). 269 *London Evening Standard*, 9 November 1987.

enough for their devoting considerable space to unionist unrest. For example, the *Express*, in a double page article, 'War on the IRA!' noted the virulence of the unionist protest in Parliament. Their political editor Robert Gibson noted how 'angry' unionists were united in demanding 'martial law and a return of internment'.[270] He went on to describe their attack on the Ulster Secretary:

> In heated and emotional scenes unionists savaged Northern Ireland Secretary Tom King for his low-key, soft response to the Poppy Day massacre.[271]

Predictably, the *Daily Mirror's* criticism of King was more virulent in its tone, accompanied with the demand that the 'ineffectual' Secretary of State 'should go'.[272] Some of the Tory papers in particular proceeded to criticise security arrangements, even going to the extent of questioning army and police statements. The *Express* reported Ian Paisley's claim on television that police had told him the Catholic hall opposite the town's war memorial had not been searched because there could have been 'a serious reaction' from the Catholic community.[273] Other papers featuring this story included the *Standard* which reported Hermon's statement that the rooms had been considered 'safe'.[274] The *Standard* went on to report Paisley's 'amazement' that a search hadn't been made and noted his quest for a full scale debate on the security situation 'which had seriously deteriorated'.[275]

The political representatives of the Protestant community were not to enjoy a sympathetic national 'press' after the bombing. Many serious commentators agreed with British politicians in their consideration that, by refusing to accept the Anglo-Irish Agreement gracefully, unionists were guilty of stalling the political process and were, as a result, guilty by default of prolonging the bombing campaign. The *Sunday Times* was perhaps the most specific in its criticism. In its leader, 'Out of tragedy – hope', it maintained that 'the British and Irish governments must continue to shoulder their responsibility', and that an essential task was 'to strive to make the Anglo Irish Agreement more productive'.[276]

Not only was the Hillsborough Accord a way out of the Irish morass but it was the Unionists who were blocking progress (something which would only occur if the 'locals' were prepared to compromise).

> Ulster's Protestant leaders must (also) drop their dog-in-the manger attitude to the reality around them. Co-operation with the SDLP makes sense in every count, nothing will be achieved without it. Unionists must push at the British government's open door and seek talks on a new way towards power-sharing. In the final analysis, it is only Northern Ireland's people who can resolve their problems.[277]

The *Guardian* saw the Anglo Irish Agreement as the way out in even more emphatic terms, but approached it rather differently. In their leader, 'A time to

270 *Daily Express*, 10 November 1987. **271** Ibid. **272** *Daily Mirror*, 9 November 1987. **273** *Daily Express*, 10 November 1987. **274** *London Standard*, 9 November 1987. **275** Ibid. **276** *Sunday Times*, 15 November 1987. **277** Ibid.

mourn, but also to listen', the paper used a combination of sympathy – albeit low-level – for Protestants, with a touch of paternalistic advice for the unionist community whilst at the same time maintaining their espousal of the Hillsborough 'route'.[278] Quoting John Hume's comment that Enniskillen had been a 'provocative' act against Protestants, the *Guardian* praised the SDLP leader's 'statesman-like' qualities before stressing the need for both communities to see that the hope for the future lay in the Hillsborough Agreement.

> The only threat at present to the existence of the IRA and other violent forms of republicanism would be the sense among Nationalists that they have benefitted from the agreement and among Unionists that they have lost nothing of importance.[279]

Apart from its noticeable restraint in sympathy for the Enniskillen victims, the *Guardian* made little reference in its leader to the frustration, anger and difficulties faced by the unionist community in trying to cope not only with its direct loss but also with the threat posed by its own paramilitaries. The *Guardian*'s advice was, as they admitted themselves, 'sanctimonious'. By offering a psychological explanation of terrorists' motives, by offering a theoretical rather than a practical analysis of the province's problems, the paper agreed with Conor Cruise O'Brien's condemnation of 'politics against the last atrocity'.[280] By stressing the 'only hope' formula of defeating the IRA by 'pulling the rug from under their feet by co-operation between peoples and governments', the *Guardian* too argued that, in effect, the British were powerless in political and military terms in the province, with the locals holding the key to a permanent solution.[281]

In their reporting of the understandably emotive response of unionist representatives, the British press sympathised more with British political leaders 'who have beaten their heads against Ulster's brick wall of hate', than they did with the leaders of the Protestant community whose 'megaphonic, incandescent incoherence outshadowed the stifled, small voice' of moderation in Northern Ireland (as represented by John Hume). Criticising unionist parliamentary condemnation of the attack, Andrew Rawnsley noted their 'frightening determination to build more funeral pyres in Ulster from the bodies of their own dead'.[282]

On the rare occasion where a British paper did sympathise with the unionist position, it could usually be attributed to the recognition of the special place held on the British or Irish right by the writers. Thus voices such as Conor Cruise O'Brien and particularly Enoch Powell were outshouted by those in the British media which saw unionists as incorrigible bigots. This latter, pessimistic interpretation, of what appeared to be a hopeless and illogical situation, where 'hardly anything that has happened in the past 19 years makes any sense at all' dominated a report in the *Express* by a veteran reporter of the Ulster conflict, Jon Akass. Lamenting the demise of the notion of Ulster as an independent republic, Akass

278 *Guardian*, 9 November 1987. 279 Ibid. 280 Ibid. 281 Ibid. 282 *Guardian*, 10 November 1987.

bemoaned that 'it was not to be' and added that we are stuck for ever with the gleeful gunmen and roaring bigots like the Reverend Ian Paisley'.[283]

Subsequent media coverage looked more fully at unionist reaction to the bombing. Peter Taylor's *Newsnight* report observed the attitudes of many unionists at local level.[284] Although it was clearly important to gauge the local Protestant response, it was inevitable that this response would, in the heat of the moment, be more emotional than logical, and that a broader, more rational, response from the unionist community province-wide, would have been more pertinent in the circumstances. A former Ulster Unionist councillor in Fermanagh, Bertie Kerr, filmed driving his tractor, maintained that because of the bomb there could be 'no possibility of Catholics in government, whilst voting for the IRA', and other local unionist figures, including local MP Ken Maginnis and Raymond Ferguson both dismissed any possibility of power-sharing.[285] Another local Unionist Party councillor Samuel Foster, who had witnessed the blast, denounced the terrorists whilst Martin Smyth pointed out that there had been no improvement in security since the Anglo-Irish Agreement. This argument formed the substance of Unionist Party leader Jim Molyneaux's meeting with Mrs Thatcher at which he called for a complete review of security in the wake of the Enniskillen attack.

The bombing also coincided with the second anniversary of the signing of the Anglo-Irish Agreement. Indeed, unionists were to use the emotional backdrop of Enniskillen to highlight their ongoing opposition to the Hillsborough Accord. The BBC featured a unionist demonstration in London protesting against the Agreement on one of its bulletins. The short news item contained film of a group of loyalists marching behind a pipeband on their way to Downing Street, where they delivered a message to Mrs Thatcher. Ian Paisley was to claim that the Enniskillen tragedy had 'brought home to the (English) people what is happening in Northern Ireland'.[286] Unionists' responses to the Enniskillen bombing and their continued resistance to the 1985 agreement, therefore,appeared to the British public to remain uncompromising and diehard in their nature and might well have resulted in loyalists conceding some of the 'moral high ground' which they had briefly gained as a result of the Enniskillen blast.

Public opinion in Britain has never been highly sympathetic to the unionist case.[287] However, for a brief period after the Enniskillen bombing, mainland opinion became noticeably more sensitive to the need for maintaining a military presence in the province. In a Marplan poll, conducted for Channel 4's *A Week in Politics*, there was a sharp reduction both in the number of Britons who wanted the troops withdrawn from the province and also in the proportion of those who wanted Northern Ireland to become part of a united Ireland.[288] The issue of the withdrawal of troops illustrates a softening in British resistance to unionist protestation. Of 1185 people interviewed between 20–24 November 1987, 46% wanted troops to stay in the Province as long as violence continued (this compared with

283 *Daily Express*, 10 November 1987. 284 BBC2 *Newsnight*, 9 November 1987. 285 Ibid. 286 BBC1 *Six O'Clock News*, 12 November 1987. 287 Public opinion and the Northern Irish question will be considered in more detail later. 288 Channel Four, *A Week in Politics*, November 1987.

34% in a Marplan poll conducted in January).[289] The bombing also persuaded some individuals who had previously supported the recent political developments in Northern Ireland to reconsider. Brian Walden wrote in the *Sunday Times*:

> The Anglo-Irish Agreement was a benign fudge which I supported believing it would have anything other than a marginal impact ... The accord between them (Ireland and Britain) must never be seen as a solution to the problem.[290]

In conclusion, it would be foolish to underestimate the unique effect which the coverage of the Enniskillen bomb had on the British public. For perhaps the first and only time they were able to fully empathise with the civilian population of Northern Ireland. The event was seen as so catastrophic by the media in Britain as well as many politicians, that it was believed it would prove to be a watershed in the history of the Troubles, with the acknowledged 'decency' of the ordinary people somehow overcoming the evil forces of terrorism. Not all observers were tricked into formulating such hasty conclusions. David McKittrick reminded his *Independent* readers that there had been 'a great many false dawns' in Ireland over the past twenty years. He added:

> The IRA could yet salvage something from the wreckage. A retaliatory loyalist outrage or even a recklessly fired plastic bullet could begin to dull the impact of Enniskillen in the nationalist ghettos.[291]

Despite the unprecendented degree of empathy in Britain with the predicament of ordinary people in Northern Ireland, and some evidence of a short-term increase in support for both troop involvement in the province and the constitutional guarantee, the 'Poppy Day' bombing was not to lead to a closer awareness of, or identification with, the unionist predicament. What was more apparent in the national media's coverage of Enniskillen was its condemnation of the IRA, and indeed, its apportioning the blame to the various groups in Ireland. By interpreting the 'story' in this manner – that is, within the traditional framework of Britain having to act as peacemaker between two 'unreasonable' and 'irrational' forces in Ireland – the story became depoliticised and was confined to an, albeit very moving, emotional 'human interest' angle. As a result, unionists were unable to capitalise on tragic events of that November morning and their ostensibly just claims for resisting the Hillsborough Agreement continued to be ignored in Britain and further afield.

289 Ibid. 290 *Sunday Times*, 15 November 1987. 291 *Independent*, 17 November 1987.

CHAPTER THREE

Why don't they like us? Loyalists and the British media

> We as Ulster loyalists protest against the gross irresponsibility of the BBC and ITV in the reporting of day to day troubles in Northern Ireland ... We question the right of the mass media to continually distort the news in favour of the terrorists and the politicians whose loyalties are to subversion and not to the constitution of the country. No time or expense is spared in the interviewing the gunman, or travelling to the refugee camps for on-the-spot stories. Yet hundreds of Protestant families are without homes, having been evicted at the point of the gun, loyalist women and their children are living in fear, business premises have been burned and looted, and little of this side of the story is told.[1]

COVERING THE SAME OLD STORY

The start of the modern Irish conflict in 1968 presented the British media with a sizeable dilemma. Clearly this was a major news story which demanded immediate and detailed media attention. However, the media found themselves ill-prepared for the latest Irish Troubles. Only a handful of programmes had focused their attention on the region and most of these had protrayed its inhabitants in a prototypical 'stage-Irish' manner.[2]

The early street demonstrations and the public disintegration of the Ulster Unionist Party received disproportionately high media treatment (particularly when compared to more serious security incidents from the mid 1970s). National (and indeed, international) journalists, photographers and TV cameramen saturated the province, their numbers increasing dramatically as the potential for violence increased from march to march. Although the tone of media coverage was to radically alter with the emergence of the IRA towards the end of 1970, media treatment of the conflict, whilst periodically attaining high levels, was to decline somewhat from the mid 1970s. This was due to the monotonous nature of Ulster news stories and the lack of progress in both political and security fields.

1 A group of loyalists writing in the 'News Letter', 12 August 1971, quoted in R Cathcart, *The Most Contrary Region – The BBC in Northern Ireland 1924–84* (Belfast, 1984), p. 221. 2 These included a number of reports by Alan Whicker for the *Tonight* programme in the 1950s and early 1960s which depicted the eccentric nature of its inhabitants, and Richard Dimbleby's renowned interview with Northern Ireland premier Basil Brooke, in which the *Tonight* presenter asked of the Prime Minister, 'What exactly is this I-R-A?' (see Cathcart op. cit., p. 190–1).

With the decline in violence levels and the introduction of an 'Ulsterisation' policy around this time, there was a growing recognition by the media of the unofficial political line of an 'acceptable level of violence'.[3] Consequently the media duly reported incidents involving serious injury or loss of life (although the degree of space allotted to the killings of soldiers inevitably declined to a brief mention on a news bulletin or a short paragraph in a national paper), only concentrating in greater detail on large-scale security incidents or on signs of political development. As the conflict endured, television in particular used the occasion of anniversaries to remind their audience of the origins of the conflict.[4]

Apart from fluctuations in the level of reporting, there were distinct modifications in the media's perception of what was happening in Northern Ireland. The first phase of the conflict produced an over-simplistic account of what was going on in the province. English journalists, with little background information, had initial problems coping with the complexities of the unfolding situation, and as indicated below, the situation tended to be contextualised in terms of stereotypes. These 'visiting firemen' tended to exhibit more sympathy to the Catholics, whom they portrayed as the 'underdogs', reserving their venom for dissident unionists (most notably Ian Paisley).[5] These attitudes were to change when the IRA campaign started and the loyalists' role as 'baddies' was taken on by the Provisionals, with loyalists taking on a 'supporting' role as 'Uglies'. This attitude shift was not an overnight phenomenon and Paul Wilkinson, an expert on terrorism, suggested that it was only on account of the media filming incidents such as Belfast's Bloody Friday in 1972 that fully convinced the British public of the dangers posed by republican terrorists.[6]

> TV crews were soon at the scenes of the crimes and the reports that sped down the wires to the news capitals of the world seemed to convince many TV editors, and certainly those in Britain, that they could no longer remain neutral toward such events. They therefore decided to show the horrific consequences to a public halfway persuaded to thinking of bomb attacks as romantic, Robin Hood-style adventures.[7]

3 The conflict's most bloody year was 1972 when 467 people were killed. Casualties declined from the mid 1970s, although there were occasional exceptions to this pattern, such as in the post H Block period in 1981, the post Hillsborough Agreement period and during the early 1990s, when there was a resurgence in loyalist terrorism. 4 The 25th anniversary of the sending-in of the troops produced two major TV documentary series. These were BBC2's *25 Bloody Years* and Channel Four's *The Long War*. 5 See below for Max Hastings' 'conversion' from being pro-Catholic to his adoption of a strong anti-terrorist position. Also, Northern Ireland proved to be a useful 'training-ground' for young journalists, many of whom forged their reputation there (they included Jeremy Paxman, Martin Bell, Henry Kelly, Bob Fisk, Simon Winchester, Simon Hoggart and Mary Holland). Making a similar point, Richard Clutterbuck, in *The Media and Political Violence* (London 1981), suggested that the Irish situation, in providing such journalists with 'a chance to make their names', also handed them 'an incentive to make their stories as lively as possible' (p. 88). 6 26 bombs exploded in central Belfast on 21 July 1972, killing 11 and injuring 130. 7 P. Wilkinson, *Terrorism and the Liberal State* (London 1977), p. 31.

Initially, therefore, the media's reporting of events in Northern Ireland left a lot to be desired. A combination of greater experience of on-the-ground conditions and instructions from broadcasting chiefs and editors, requesting their staff to take a calm, dispassionate look at incidents, led to a greater sophistication in reportage.[8] Although this was not to fundamentally alter the grassroots loyalist conviction that the media were 'against' them (as expressed in the introductory quote), sections of the media were eventually to become more aware of shifts in the unionist perspective.

A number of writers have pointed out that as most people in Great Britain have little direct experience of the Irish conflict and are 'almost entirely dependent on the mass media for news and interpretation of events' in the province, it is imperative that the quality of such coverage is of the highest standard, as it 'influences the extent to which British people can participate in an informed discussion about their government's Irish policy'.[9] The production and maintenance of 'quality' media coverage of the Northern Irish situation has not been assisted by the early decision to place such coverage within the usual, factual 'bulletin' framework. This has meant that the normal news 'package' – factual on-the-spot reports and interviews with leading political personalities (more often or not, British Ministers) – has generally failed to provide a background context apart that is, from a reminder of the last atrocity) to unfolding events. This lack of a relevant context mitigates against a proper understanding of the complexities of the Irish problem and the resulting confusion of a mainland audience which has not fully grasped the relevant background frequently manifests itself in rapid dismissal of the problem on account of the 'irrationality' of the communities involved, as well as fostering the development of widespread apathy.[10]

The more complex the political case, the deeper is the confusion of the receiving audience, as unionists have found to their cost. Occasionally this bemusement has prompted journalists in Great Britain, unable to disguise their guilty consciences over persistent ignorance and apathy towards Ulster, into requesting more open and intensive debate of the issues involved. Peter McKay expressed such sentiments in the *Evening Standard* in 1990.[11] Demanding that television should mount an 'Ulsterthon', McKay admitted:

8 Alasdair Milne, in *DG – The Memoirs of a British Broadcaster* (London 1988) stressed the need for broadcasting caution 'in such a highly charged and emotional situation' as existed in Northern Ireland. An ex-Director General of the BBC, Milne recalled 'at all events we took our own decisions to be cautious and pick our way a-top-toe through this minefield' (p. 110).
9 L. Curtis, *The Propaganda War* (op. cit.), p. 2. The *Sunday Times* Insight team also stressed the importance of delving into the headlines, maintaining it was 'impossible to judge what is happening in Ulster day to day if one omitted a study of the origins of community conflict' (quoted in *Sunday Times* Insight team, *Ulster* (London 1972), p. 8. 10 My experiences teaching several courses on the Northern Ireland conflict (mainly in adult education centres in the London area during the 1980s) reinforced this feeling that people in England were blatantly unaware of what was going on in Northern Ireland, and certainly the enrolments on a number of the courses reflected the apathy! See my article on one of these courses in Irish Studies in Britain *Yer Man About the Bush – Northern Irish Studies in Britain*, 11/1982. 11 *Evening Standard*, 18 January 1990.

> Isn't it time we decided to talk openly and honestly about Northern Ireland and not just pretend it is a God-forsaken place fit only for contemptuous saloon-bar dismissal – 'I'd pull out and let them get on with it' – each time its citizens are blown to bits or shot dead? I suggest a week-long TV debate about the province and its troubles, presented by Mr Terry Wogan and Miss Gloria Hunniford.[12]

The one-dimensional nature of the reporting of the Ulster situation – what's been called 'a shopping-list in death and destruction' – has been criticised for presenting the British public with 'a series of decontextualised reports of violence' which 'failed to analyse and re-analyse the historical roots of the Irish problem'.[13] It was also unpopular with many Irish people who believed that the 'fix' of violence in daily news bulletins gave an unrepresentative and unhelpful impression of life 'across the water'. Recalling a period when he was living in Canterbury, distinguished Irish historian F.S.L. Lyons regretted the impact of such 'cycle of violence' reporting on mainland viewers.

> English public opinion had little option but to take a view of Northern Ireland as a place where bloodthirsty bigots of various obscure sects murdered each other incessantly for reasons no sane man could fathom. I longed them to say what I still say – show us the place as it really is, show it to us in all its human ordinarinesss, its quirky humour, it stubborn contraryness, its integrity. Show it to us, above all, as a place inhabited not only by evil men ... but also by decent human beings.[14]

It was this emphasis on security and broader issues, such as questions over the integrity of the English judicial system and political censorship, which tended to dominate media interest in Northern Ireland.[15] This limited presentation of the Irish conflict is mirrored in the comparatively small number and restricted range of investigative programmes. Only two series explaining the historical background to the discord in Ireland were transmitted in a period of over 15 years and these were transmitted at approximately the same time.[16] Most documentaries concentrated on a 'non-unionist' agenda, featuring several cases of alleged miscarriages of justice and other 'humanitarian' cases, censorship issues and political developments which were increasingly in the hands of London and Dublin

12 Ibid. 13 This was a central theme in Rod Stoneman's 1983 film for Channel 4, *Ireland – Silent Voices.* The quote is from P. Schlesinger's *Putting Reality Together – BBC News* (London 1978), p. 243. 14 F.S.L. Lyons, *The Burden of Our History* (Queen's University pamphlet, 1978), p. 26. 15 Political, and indeed internal, broadcasting pressure led to the banning, postponing or editing of at least 48 programmes before 1980. (L. Curtis, op cit). A number of controversial programmes including BBC1's *A Question of Ulster* (January 1972), 'Tonight's' report of an operational IRA unit in Carrickmore during July 1979, *At the Edge of the Union* (September 1985) and Thames Television's *Death on the Rock* (April 1988), reflected the ferocious ongoing debate between journalists and politicians over the role of broadcasting in a divided society. 16 The two series concerned, R. Kee's BBC1 *Ireland – A History* and Thames' *The Troubles* were both screened in 1980/81 (I refer to the latter series in the Thames section).

rather than Belfast and the likelihood of a cessation of violence. The fact that loyalists were regarded as being fundamentally reactive in both political and military fields explains their peripheral role in such analytical programmes.

Whilst a growing number of enlightening documentaries about the unionist predicament were transmitted, particularly in the late 1980s and 1990s, these were the exception, rather than the rule (this is developed later in the chapter). For instance, opportunities to highlight the particular plight of border Protestants were either ignored or partially covered.[17] An exception was Ronald Eyre's 1990 programme in the *Frontiers* series which looked sympathetically at such an often ignored community.[18] Mark Steyn's review of the programme in the *Independent* referred to the cameras panning round the tombstones in a Protestant graveyard, before accentuating the dearth of sympathy for unionists in Great Britain.

> It was filled with the bodies of young Protestant sons, their headstones inscribed, 'Murdered by the IRA'. It ought to make you weep, except that the English save their Irish tears for bandsmen in Deal and Australian tourists. No one in these islands is as unloved as the Ulster Unionists.[19]

My main intention in this chapter is to consider how loyalists have been depicted by the British media and also to assess the effects of this portrayal on national public opinion. I'm therefore less concerned about the central area for research on this subject of media coverage in Northern Ireland – namely the wider question of political censorship of broadcasting related to the Irish conflict – and focus instead on how the largely one-dimensional, selective nature of the broadcasting agencies in particular, have mediated against an adequate analysis of the unionist predicament. In this introductory section I look at the way in which the media's agenda has been dominated by republican and 'human rights' issues, with loyalist concerns such as political isolation, deteriorating security and border 'genocide', being largely confined to the periphery of national media coverage. I also focus on the tendency of the media to scapegoat loyalists for political failure in Northern Ireland (this is illustrated below with specific reference to the 1991 Brooke talks). My television and press sections provide more detailed illustrations of how the unionist case was portrayed, both negatively and positively, in the media. The TV section's focal point is an analysis of the quality of in-depth coverage of programmes relating to unionism. I attempt this by concentrating on a number of leading investigative programmes and TV channels, tracing both the extent and nature of their coverage of 'loyalist' topics. In the press section I conclude that having mutual 'friends' and 'enemies' (army and IRA respectively) did not mean that the British press and Ulster Unionists were

17 This was the case in C. Gebler's BBC2 series, *Plain Tales from Northern Ireland*. Set entirely on the border, the fears of the loyalist community only appeared indirectly in two of the six films (*One Family in Rosslea*, 2 September 1993 and *Business as Usual*, 16 September 1993). 18 BBC2 *Frontiers*, 'Long Division – A Border', 18 July 1990. 19 *Independent*, 19 July 1990.

necessarily staunch bedfellows and I stress the support given in the press for government initiatives on Northern Ireland and their condemnation of a variety of unionist misdemeanours. However, I also observe evidence of a growing awareness of what was behind these negative characteristics. In my final section I shall discuss the findings of a small survey on loyalism which I conducted in various parts of Great Britain. I based many of the questions in this survey around central images of loyalism, several of which are developed in the case studies and elsewhere in this thesis. I turn first to the domination of the media agenda by nationalists and republicans.

A republican agenda

Some writers have assumed that the undermining of the republican case in the British media has automatically resulted in a more sympathetic presentation of the loyalist case. As I hope to illustrate later, there is no real correlation between the two. It is correct to state, however, that the British press in particular, has been extremely critical of both political and military republicanism (this is explored in greater detail in the press section). Indeed, by their condemnation of republican paramilitarism, albeit in an increasingly ritualistic manner in Northern Ireland, the national media were uniquely united, even if those on its liberal fringe periodically qualified their abhorrence of terrorism by criticising govermental security policy. However, by affording such attention to Sinn Fein/IRA, the British media was considered to be providing them with the 'oxygen of publicity' and the consequence of this was the Thatcher Government's decision to deny them appropriate channels of communications (in the form of the 1988 Broadcasting Act).

The assertion that republicans gained the upper hand in the propaganda battle without winning the publicity 'war' outright, is a reasonable one. Although mainstream American political opinion gradually shifted from covert espousal of the Sinn Fein cause to overt backing for the joint approach of British and Irish governments, the party succeeded, over a period of many years, in damaging Britain's reputation as a liberal, democratic state, both in Europe and America, less on account of their own 'freedom-fighting' campaign but rather as a result of the British response, which, particularly in the 1980s, appeared to outsiders to be intransigent and inflexible.[20] Thus the Sinn Fein message was listened to with interest outside the United Kingdom in spite of the violence associated with it and its comparatively limited political backing, due to an unimaginative British response and the general unawareness of a third dimension in the conflict, namely that of the loyalists. By choosing the appropriate agenda and language, Sinn Fein were able to consistently score propaganda successes. Their listing of British military 'excesses' (such as a 'shoot-to-kill' policy, the risk of civilian injury due to the use of plastic bullets and allegations of brutality in interrogation centres),

20 The H Block prison dispute is a good illustration of this. The *Sunday Times* (31 May 1981), in a major article, 'Is Britain losing the propaganda war?'sought the opinions of 64 editors in 24 countries to Britain's handling of the hunger strike. Their chief finding was that 'editor after editor said that the death of the hunger strikers had improved the image of the IRA'.

the adroit tactic of the hunger strike which breathed new life into what many considered to be a dying movement in 1981, and their decision to call a ceasefire in 1994 before the British had initiated a meaningful all-party conference, thus enabling them to pose as 'peace-makers', all succeeded in putting British authorities on the defensive.[21] Although most of the British press failed to see the 'logic' behind IRA attacks (the term 'senseless' was frequently and invariably inaccurately applied to describe their tactics), some writers were astute enough to pinpoint the true motivation behind republican propaganda. Paul Wilkinson, argued:

> The purpose of Provisional propaganda directed at British and at most uncommitted audiences, was less to convert them but to confuse and embarrass. By creating doubts, minds that were determined might be changed. If the man on the Clapham omnibus began to wonder whether his troops were indeed misbehaving, and whether the law was being abused, and whether government policy was sectarian and unjust, then he should worry ...[22]

It was on account of their perceived control of events in Ulster that Sinn Fein/IRA were allowed to dominate media coverage. Apart from focusing periodically on the government's political options and the army's role in the province, the bulk of coverage was dominated by the republican perspective.[23] This domination of the media agenda ignored Sinn Fein's 'minority' party status in both Northern Ireland and the Irish Republic, but resulted in its party conferences ensuring substantial treatment in the British broadsheets.[24] The *Independent* devoted nearly a page to the 1990 conference, whilst the *Guardian* described Gerry Adams as 'the apostle of the bullet and the ballot box' following his 1991 conference speech.[25] Great attention was paid to Sinn Fein leaders' speeches and actions. Indeed, Gerry Adams was, for many years, the most profiled, non-elected politician in Europe. Profiles of him appeared in several television programmes and papers. These included the *Independent*'s description of the Sinn Fein President as 'the Castro of the Emerald Isle', the *Sunday Times* feature 'In the Shadow of the Gun' and John Ware's 1995 *Panorama* reassessment of the Sinn Fein leader.[26]

21 Even the language of the conflict was dictated by Sinn Fein. Examples lie both in the origins and one-dimensional application of terms such as 'demilitarisation', 'shoot-to-kill' policies, 'miscarriage of justice', and 'sectarian' attacks. 22 P. Wilkinson, ed., *British Perspectives on Terrorism* (London 1981), p. 267. 23 This was also reflected in a plethora of TV dramas with a Northern Irish backdrop, the majority of which relied heavily on IRA characters. 24 Gerry Adams was defeated by the SDLP's Joe Hendron in the 1992 Westminster election. Sinn Fein was polling just over 10% of the vote (a similar figure to the virtually unheard Alliance voice) and their 'power' tended to lie in council chambers. 25 *Independent*, 5 February 1990 and the *Guardian*, 4 February 1991. 26 *Independent*, 1 November 1986, *Sunday Times*, 8 May 1983 and *Panorama*, 30 January 1995. (the later programme is discussed in greater detail in the Panorama section). These, features, whilst not exactly eulogising the Sinn Fein leader, sought to 'humanize' Gerry Adams and his colleagues. A good instance of this was a *Guardian* article (4 August 1997), entitled ' The man from the Falls', which examined 'behind the chilling facade' of Adams and found 'a man of surprising warmth and vision'.

British coverage of his trips to America in 1994 and 1995 were copious in detail, if vitriolic in their tone. *The Daily Mirror* in its leader, 'Death of an old friend', maintained that 'the moment when Adams flew into New York, the special relationship that existed between Britain and America was finally killed off'.[27] Another leading Sinn Fein member, Martin McGuinness, also received a considerable amount of media attention. He was featured in the controversial BBC programme *At the Edge of the Union*, where he was portrayed as a family-loving, church-going republican activist, whilst ITV's *Cook Report* exposed his background as the IRA's military commander in the north.[28]

The chief result of Sinn Fein's dominance of the media agenda on Northern Ireland has been the marginalisation of the unionist community. Unable as an intrinsically reactive force to dictate 'military' events, they are politically fragmented and bereft of friends. Despite the acceptance that their position has to be considered, their numerical majority in the province is increasingly irrelevant, both in terms of Westminster's political response and the media's presentation of the confict. Whilst media perception of the unionist case has been modified during this decade, the unionist position is still not taken as seriously as the nationalist, or republican, one.

Miscarriages of justice

A significant ingredient of British media interest in Northern Ireland was their coverage of several miscarriage of justice cases which, with the notable exception of the UDR Four (see below), exclusively involved Catholics. In a sense, this was inevitable. Due to the very nature of the conflict, loyalists were clearly less likely to have been involved in contesting legal decisions related to terrorist cases, particularly in Great Britain. What perhaps is of greater importance was the decision of news agencies to select specific types of 'human rights' stories (such as those alleging that individuals, or small groups, had failed to get justice) at the expense of other potential stories, including the rights of farmers to live without the threat of physical violence, simply on the grounds of their religion.[29]

The knee-jerk response of the British judiciary in the mid-1970s to the demands of the British public for quick, punitive action against IRA terrorism, was to result in the shame-faced reaction of the judicial establishment several years later when the reviews of several cases, including those of the Guildford Four, the Birmingham Six, the Maguire Seven and Judith Ward, reinforced the impression that such an establishment possessed a blatant anti-Irish bias. Respected journalists and writers such as Ludovic Kennedy and Robert Kee, church leaders both in Ireland and Britain and sections of the British left (Labour MP Chris Mullin was prominent in the campaign for the release of the Birmingham Six)

27 *Daily Mirror*, 2 February 1994. 28 BBC1, Edge of the Union, quoted in *Radio Times*, 3 September 1985 and ITV, *The Cook Report*, 28 April 1993. 29 The ocasional feature on the IRA's 'genocide' policy of Ulster border Protestants was transmitted on television, but although such killings greatly outnumbered those involved in 'miscarriage' cases, media coverage very much favoured those in the latter category.

united in their demands for the original convictions against those involved in the Guildford and Birmingham pub bombings to be reviewed.[30]

During the run-up to the appeal cases, sections of the press and a number of TV programmes focused on the inadequacies of the prosecution's argument in the original trials and presented what they claimed to be 'new' evidence. Yorkshire TV concentrated on the Maguire Seven and the Guildford Four cases.[31] They argued that their documentary, 'Aunt Annie's Bomb Factory', which proclaimed the innocence of Ann Maguire and her family 'reveals how the legal process can be swayed, resulting in dubious justice'.[32] The same commerical company assembled two powerful 'drama-doc' programmes on the Guildford Four case, putting pressure on the government as well as the legal authorities to reopen the case.[33] ITV were later to produce a similar investigative programme, 'Who Bombed Birmingham?', which was also to have a profound effect on influential opinion in Britain and Ireland.[34]

The release of those convicted for the Guildford and Birmingham bombings earned substantial headlines in the British press and the experiences of the cleared men and woman resulted in a number of them (notably Paul Hill and Gerard Conlon) becoming minor 'celebrities'.[35] The broadsheets, in particular, rendered special treatment to the early days of freedom for the Birmingham Six. Gerry Hunter's 'return to the free world' was featured in the *Observer*, whilst the *Independent* featured both Hugh Callaghan's story of events and John Walker's 'rapturous' return to Derry, noting how local people 'thronged around a man who has become for them a living icon of British injustice'.[36] Even those tabloids which had reservations about the verdicts, covered the release of the Birmingham Six in depth. The *Daily Star* devoted several pages to the story, speculating that the compensation for each of the released 'might top the million mark' and argued that 'as Sinn Fein are so interested in justice, they might now like to finally identify the guilty men'.[37] Both press and TV concentrated on the feelings of those imprisoned and their families. The *Daily Mirror* ran a two page story on 'the women who wait in hope – crying out for freedom', whilst Melanie McFadyean's

30 R. Kee, *Trial and Error – The Maguires, The Guildford Pub Bombs and British Justice* (London 1986) and C. Mullin, *Error of Judgement – The Truth about the Birmingham Bombings* (London 1986). 31 Between March 1984 and January 1990, Yorkshire TV, in their documentary series *First Tuesday*, presented eight programmes with a Northern Irish theme, five of which were concerned with 'human rights' cases (in a letter from Yorkshire TV, 2 July 1990). 32 Yorkshire TV, *Aunt Annie's Bomb Factory*, 6 March 1984. 33 Yorkshire TV, *The Guildford Time Bomb*, 1 July 1986 and *A Case That Won't Go Away*, 3 March 1987. 34 Thames/Granada, World in Action, *Who Bombed Birmingham?* 28 March 1990. Other programmes featuring miscarriages of justice involving Catholics included RTE/ITV's *Dear Sarah*, 2 July 1990 (based on Maguire seven member Guiseppe Conlon's letters to his wife), Panorama, *The Guildford 4 – The Untold Story*, 13 December 1990 and BBC1 *Rough Justice*, 1 April 1993 (based on the 'wrongful' conviction of Patrick Kane for his involvement in the murder of two soldiers in west Belfast in 1988). 35 Hill, who was later to marry into the renowned Irish-American Kennedy family, had his book on his prison experiences serialised in the *Observer* (3 June 1990), whilst the section in Conlon's book pertaining to his father's death in prison formed the basis for the Oscar-winning film, *In the Name of the Father* (1994). 36 *Observer*, 17 March 1991 and *Independent*, 15 March 1991. 37 *Daily Star*, 15 March 1991.

New Statesman and Society's feature praised the 'courage' of the relatives of the Birmingham Six', 'women who weren't prepared to sit back and do nothing'.[38] Television also featured the long, frustrating and worrying wait of the Birmingham women both in a 1985 *World in Action* programme and an *Everyman* version of the same 'angle' five years on.[39]

A rare occasion when Protestants found themselves featured as victims of miscarriages of justices was the case of the UDR, or Armagh, Four. This case was so intriguing because it involved four members of the security forces who had been convicted of murdering a Catholic and the ensuing campaign for their release involved loyalists in an unprecendented contesting of decisions taken in Ulster's courts. The UDR Four had expressed their innocence at the time of their trial in 1986.[40] A campaign to reverse the initial legal decision was to result in Northern Ireland Secretary Peter Brooke granting an appeal which ultimately led to the acquittal in 1992 of three of the group.[41]

The uniqueness of the case was its essential feature and one highlighted in the *Guardian*, which remarked it was the first time that 'widespread allegations of a miscarriage of justice have been voiced by unionists'.[42] The irony of Protestant Ulstermen serving in a regiment of the British Army contesting the legal decisions of British courts, was another conspicuous characteristic of this case. The extreme dilemma facing the UDR Four was vividly described by a leading campaigner for their release. Ian Paisley Junior wrote of the Armagh Four:

> These men have been caught between the devil and the deep blue sea. On the one hand they are Protestant, British and ex-soldiers who were part of the British way of life in Ulster. They detested the ideas of those who challenged the Northern Ireland system accepting that the police, army and courts were doing a job that had to be done. On the other hand, they are now precariously placed out on a limb, claiming that they were wrongly convicted by the system they supported.[43]

The same author, whilst questioning the correctness of this particular decision, proceeded to argue that the very fact Protestant soldiers had been prosecuted and jailed for terrorist offences was valedictory proof of the basic equity of Northern Ireland's legal system.[44]

Whilst recognising fundamental differences between this and other 'miscarriage' cases involving Catholics, the media also observed some similarities. One was that the bulk of evidence against the UDR soldiers, had been extracted from them in custody under alleged duress and that their confessions were subse-

38 *Daily Mirror*, 2 February 1990 and *New Statesman/Society*, 23 February 1990. 39 ITV, *World in Action* (exact date unavailable) and BBC1 *Everyman – The Birmingham Wives*, 8 December 1990. 40 The UDR four – James Hegan, Neil Latimer, Winston Allen and Noel Bell – had been convicted of the murder of Adrian Carroll in Armagh in 1983. 41 Neil Latimer remains in prison. 42 *Guardian*, 13 February 1991. 43 I. Paisley, Jnr, *Reasonable Doubt – The Case for the UDR 4* (Cork 1991), p. 13. 44 In a letter (11 June 1990), Ian Paisley Jnr argued that the initial verdict 'proved the professionalism of the RUC at the expense of the UDR'.

quently withdrawn. Another was that, like the IRA bombings in England in 1974, the killing had been the work of a paramilitary group (in this case, the Protestant Action Force). In a report, 'New doubts over Armagh Four guilt', the *Independent on Sunday* suggested that there was 'new' evidence in the case which 'supports the theory that a loyalist paramilitary organisation carried out the killing' and that this would 'add to growing pressure for the case to be reopened'.[45] Television coverage of the incident, restricted as it was to three 'non prime-time' programmes, pursued the same investigative approach adopted in other 'miscarriage' cases. Miriam O'Callaghan's *Newsnight* report mentioned the 'profound effect' of the case on 'a community unaccustomed to questioning the workings of the Northern Ireland legal sysem'.[46] Using scientific 'experts', the report questioned the reliability of police statements. Andrew Morton, an expert in cases of disputed authorship, maintained that 'the men's alleged confessions to the killing of Adrian Carroll, a Catholic, in Armagh in 1983, were unreliable'.[47] Channel Four allotted two programmes to the case, one before and the other after the acquittal, both of which stressed the case's unique quality and fallibility of the legal system which had produced such convictions.[48]

Although the Armagh Four did, therefore, eventually gain national media exposure and their campaign team were adroit enough in marshalling substantial support (much of it emanating from sources not normally sympathetic to the unionist cause), this was nowhere near the scale of the other cases involving Irish Catholics.[49] In particular, the case received little publicity in the tabloid press. Why, therefore, did this whole incident fail to generate the media attention which other miscarriage of justice cases had warranted, paticularly since it was generally acknowledged to be 'different'? Robert Kee suggested it was the location of the trials which was the significant factor in explaining the comparative dearth of publicity. Writing in the *Sunday Times* about 'the curious case of the Armagh Four', Kee argued that 'the lack of attention was due to the appeal court being held in Northern Ireland and not Great Britain'.[50] The scale and location of the attack – a street killing in an Ulster town was unlikely to seriously compete for equal media space with incidents involving large numbers of people in English towns and cities – were other factors which might explain this differential in media treatment. Another explanation lay in the response of the Protestant community. Whilst the UDR Four case did lead to many unionists asking questions of the judicial system, it's also true to say that the greater fragmentation of the unionist community (particularly along class lines) and its reticence in challenging their province's legal structure, mitigated against their campaign group harnessing widespread support, even within Northern Ireland.

Unionists, therefore, have lost out in a number of ways in the propaganda

45 *Independent on Sunday*, 27 May 1990. 46 BBC2 *Newsnight*, 12 February 1991. 47 Ibid. 48 Channel Four, *Armagh Four – Free For All*, 6 March 1991, and *Critical Eye – Loyalty on the Line*, 5 November 1992. 49 An estimated 200 MPs, academics and writers lent their support to demands for a retrial and one of the parents of the imprisoned UDR soldiers even joined Birmingham Six campaigners on a Dublin platform (quoted in *Independent on Sunday*, 27 May 1990). 50 *Sunday Times*, 28 June 1992.

'war'. Part of the explanation is due to their own poor presentational skills and distrust of the media. Also, they have not been aided by the media's contextualisation of the conflict which, as I've already indicated, presents Britain trying to separate two warring factions. Consequently loyalists have, on the whole, been unable to make long-term capital from the horrific results of PIRA's bombing campaign, with sections of the British media suggesting that such terrorism was directly attributable to unionism's own negative legacy. A proper understanding of the loyalist position has hardly been helped by the republican domination of the media agenda mentioned earlier and the media's selectivity of stories which has, with a few notable exceptions, mitigated against unionists. Thus, emphasis has been given to British and Irish governments' political initiatives, incidents of mainland violence, the calling of the IRA ceasefires, in 1994 and 1997 and Sinn Fein 'tours' of America, all of which have underlined unionists' growing sense of alienation, ignored their pleas for self-determination and provided scant coverage of their sense of suffering at the hands of terrorists for over a quarter of a century. As a result, the central images associated with unionism (which are examined in detail elsewhere) – unionist intransigence, bigotry and their reputation as 'blockers' or 'wreckers' – tend to be, in the main, negative ones. David Butler has argued that even analytical accounts of loyalism in the British media are over-simplistic, and amount to little more than cementing earlier, easily recognisable representations of loyalism.

> British documentary dispatches have been inclined to condense the socio-political complexities of protestant politics (landed aristocrats, small farmers, industrial labourers ... immobilists, devolutionists, integrationists, religious rednecks) into Paisley's demagogic form ...[51]

Butler has also asserted that those attempts to counter loyalism's 'ugly' image have generally been 'defensive and apologetic rather than (being) robust arguments in favour of their interests'.[52] This is, I believe, a fair assessment of media accounts of loyalism, though as I point out, there has been an increase in the number of genuine attempts to explain, if not actually sympathise with the loyalist predicament.

The 1991 Brooke talks

Several instances of the negative portrayal of loyalism are outlined in other parts of this chapter and in the Enniskillen case study. I have tried to bring them together in a 'mini' case study, based on media coverage of a set period, centred round the 1991 Brooke talks and I turn to this next. I decided to carry out an in-depth study of media coverage of Northern Ireland during a two month period in 1991. The main event which occurred during this period was the first Brooke talks about Northern Ireland's political future.[53] I was fascinated by the manner

51 D. Butler, *The Trouble with Reporting Northern Ireland* (Aldershot 1995), p. 129. 52 Ibid.
53 Subsequent talks (sometimes referred to as the 'Brooke-Mayhew talks') occurred in 1992.

in which the media reported such a major initiative, and particularly by the way in which the unionists were portrayed as the 'wreckers' of these talks. I chose a specific period – 29 April to 28 June 1991 – and recorded all references made to Northern Ireland during that period emanating from *BBC1 News*, BBC2's *Newsnight*, ITN's *News at Ten*, the *Times*, the *Guardian*, the *Daily Mail* and the *Daily Mirror*. As TV bulletins provide most Britons with their 'daily news intake', I decided to check the leading bulletins as well as the more analytical *Newsnight* programme.[54] Two of my chosen papers were tabloids and represented different strands of British politics, as did the designated broadsheets. Although these news agencies provided my central focus, I also took note of other papers and programmes with a Northern Irish dimension.[55]

The findings on the degree of coverage were, on the whole, rather predictable. The tabloid press frequently failed to mention Northern Ireland and covered the talks process in considerably less detail than the 'qualities'. Out of an estimated 55 editions covered in the survey the *Daily Mirror* failed to mention Northern Irish issues in nearly half of them (27 editions), with the *Daily Mail* also failing to do so in 24 editions. *The Mirror* only gave 'detailed' coverage to Ulster on seven occasions (these included 'non-talks' issues such as the cases of the Maguire Seven and Guildford Four), whilst the *Daily Mail* only provided 'detailed' coverage on 5 occasions. On the other hand, the broadsheets dealt more generously with the situation in Northern Ireland, with *the Guardian* giving 'detailed' treatment to Northern Ireland 27 times, and the *Times* on 21 occasions (the *Times* only failed to cover Northern Ireland on three occasions, with the *Guardian* omitting it twice). Obviously it was not easy extricating purely 'loyalist' stories from those dealing with the wider talks process, but I estimated that unionists were portrayed in a negative light on at least 30 occasions, compared with 9 news items proving to be sympathetic either to the unionist position directly, or by placing criticism on their opponents.

Undoubtedly the main impression the British public gleaned from the media coverage of the talks was one of petty squabbling and bickering, mainly fermented by the unionists, who inevitably became readily associated with its failure.[56] There were at least 25 'strong' criticisms of the unionist tactics during the talks, with only 1 'mild' criticism of the SDLP's decision to withdraw from the talks until

54 They also offered, in terms of news presentation, a variety in style which, to some degree, reflected the differences between taboids and broadsheets. 55 It's also important to point out that, although the Brooke talks were the main Northern Irish new item of the period, they did not monopolise media coverage, even of Ulster issues. Therefore, the usual coverage of terrorist and counter-terrorist attacks continued, with a contrast in the depth of coverage afforded to the deaths of 3 IRA members on Coagh on 3 June and a similar fatality count in an IRA attack on UDR members in County Armagh on 3 May. The latter story only appeared on page 6 of the *Mail on Sunday* (31 May) and was featured in a similar manner on television bulletins, whereas the Coagh killings got prominent coverage in most news agencies. Of the four TV documentaries relating to Northern Ireland which were transmitted in this period three were critical of the security forces and legal system (these included programmes on the Maguire Seven case and the Stalker enquiry). 56 This was evident in John Ware's *Panorama* report on the talks (21 October 1992).

unionist misgivings about procedural arrangements had been assuaged.[57] A mood of pessimism was prevalent in sections of the British press from the start. One report even suggested that the lone protests at Stormont of a DUP councillor might well represent 'the lack of common ground for Mr Brooke's talks'.[58]

Impressions of continuing loyalist intransigence and stalling tactics abounded in media reports. The *Times* considered the unionists to be deliberately behaving awkwardly. In the leader 'Up and Down in Ulster', they argued that both unionist parties 'have decided to make a mountain out of a molehill, until their counterparts run out of time or patience'.[59] The belief that unionists were again failing to concede ground resurfaced, particularly when negotiations invariably ended in an impasse. Thus, a *News at Ten* headline announced that 'Unionist leaders refused to make any concessions' regarding the locations of the talks.[60] This impression was also echoed on BBC1's *Question Time* where a Labour MP with republican sympathies, Clare Short, expounded on unionist failings over the years and audience members criticised unionists 'for not making concessions'.[61] Ironically, it was left to one of the architects of the Anglo-Irish Agreement, Garret Fitzgerald, to 'defend' loyalist fears and to expain why they felt threatened![62]

The media considered that loyalist concern over the appointment of the Conference Chairperson constituted a deliberate attempt to wreck the talks. Therefore, their rejection of Lord Carrington for such a role (he had condemned unionist 'bigotry' in his autobiography) was castigated for producing what *News at Ten* considered to be 'a political fiasco' and *Newsnight* deemed to be unionists' 'latest obstacle'.[63] Mary Holland avowed that they had deliberately chosen this 'stalling' tactic where they could do damage to the overall negotiation process rather than simply boycott the talks and run the risk of being overtaken by political events. Holland wrote in the *Observer*:

> There is widespread suspicion that the Unionist leadership is now involved in an elaborate exercise designed to scupper the talks while avoiding the blame that will fall on whoever is seen to destroy an initiative offering hopes of bringing the violence to an end.[64]

Perhaps the strongest criticism of unionist behaviour came from Joe Haines. Writing in the *Daily Mirror*, Harold Wilson's ex-advisor berated the 'patience' of British Governments in endeavouring to 'talk round' Ulster Unionists, because that was 'the last thing the Unionists want'.[65] Haines even proceeded to liken the Unionists to the IRA, arguing that they had similar 'wrecking' motives.

> If you don't like the game, object to the rules. That's what the Ulster Union-

57 The media tended to report the SDLP's quitting the talks as a response to unionist bickering, rather than providing an opportunity to investigate the party's increasing hostility to the likely outcome of such discussions, (namely power-sharing). 58 *Guardian*, 1 May 1991. 59 *Times*, 3 June 1991. 60 ITN, *News at Ten*, 7 May 1991. 61 BBC1 *Question Time*, 16 May 1991. 62 Ibid. 63 ITN, *News at Ten*, 30 May 1991 and BBC2 *Newsnight*, 30 May 1991. 64 *Observer*, 19 May 1991. 65 *Daily Mirror*, 3 June 1991.

> ists are up to in the talks about Ireland's future. The Unionists and the IRA are playing a different game from all the others. Talks which succeeded would diminish the role of both.[66]

Other negative characteristics of unionism highlighted by the media during this period included its 'illogical' nature, division in the unionist ranks and the seemingly irrelevant belligerence of their leaders, past and present. Tim Jones' *Times* report on the eve of the talks, assessed the 'achievements' of that loyalist icon, Edward Carson, derisively suggesting that these included 'raising a volunteer army to fight the British for the right to remain British and being involved in talks with the Kaiser that led to suggestions that the province could become part of the German empire in preference to being swallowed up by 'papists'.[67] Further traits of media coverage were journalists' inability to treat seriously unionists' argument and a stressing of their isolationism. Thus, Jeremy Paxman described the contrast between the unionist leaders' stern appearance on entering 10 Downing Street with their 'all smiles' exit as a further example of loyalists 'huffing and puffing', which had not affected the initiative and 'which remains to fight another day'.[68] The isolation of unionism's leaders was personified in a Steve Bell cartoon in the *Guardian*.[69] Bell's cartoon strip portrayed Molyneaux and Paisley arriving for talks on a desert island (they were the sole 'delegates' for the 'conference' there). The cartoon went on:

> Paisley: We could set up our independent Protestant state right here on Rockall.
> Molyneaux: But there are no people here, Ian!
> Paisley: People? People? Who needs people?[70]

On the eve of the talks there was an anticipatory air of change in the unionist perspective. Owen Bowcott optimistically proclaimed that 'both unionist parties are facing up to the prospect of an accommodation with the Republic and power-sharing with a Catholic minority', while Richard Ford suggested that in their acknowledgment of the talks framework, unionists had 'accepted their opponents' analysis of the problem'.[71] *News at Ten*'s innovative device of highlighting change in attitudes across three generations of the Brownes, a north Belfast Protestant family, accentuated hopes for compromise 'after 6 years of impotent protest by the Protestant community against the Anglo-Irish Agreement'.[72] Miriam O'Callaghan's *Newsnight* report, in covering a wide range of Protestant opinion (including Ballylumford power workers and the players of Ballynahinch Rugby Club) arrived at similar conclusions. She argued that 'apathy rules in the Protestant community' and that 'receding power has ground Protestant resistance to sharing power'.[73] Although she admitted that unionists were still 'haunted by the

66 Ibid. 67 *Times*, 1 May 1991. The 'Times Diary' that day also referred to ill-feeling between Peter Robinson and John Taylor. 68 BBC2 *Newsnight*, 15 May 1991. 69 *Guardian*, 21 May 1991. 70 Ibid. 71 *Guardian*, 29 April 1991 and the *Times*, 29 April 1991. 72 ITN, *News at Ten*, 30 April 1991. 73 BBC2 *Newsnight*, 30 April 1991.

ghosts of Terence O'Neill and Brian Faulkner, Unionists who were destroyed as they dared to compromise', O'Callaghan maintained that their increasing political isolation had forced many of them into reassessing their political future, which had resulted in many accepting their dilemma that 'they have to talk about the Anglo-Irish Agreement to get it reversed'.[74]

Other journalists were less optimistic about the chances of a successful outcome to the talks. David Selborne, in a perceptive *Sunday Times* article, 'Among the Accused', described a recent visit to Belfast where he had found attitudes, particularly among Protestants, 'beyond the reach of negotiation'.[75] In his conclusion he dismissed 'triumphalist' feelings in the Protestant community, arguing that the predominant impression was of 'a worried, alienated people' who, Selborne believed, formed 'a majority with a minority complex'.[76] He continued:

> Left behind, politically and economically by most of the rest of Europe, under direct rule from Westminster, and lacking a normal democratic process, Ulster cries out for redemption.[77]

Compared with the media's response to later events (most notably the IRA ceasefire), there was little sympathy for unionism at this time beyond the occasional explanation of their alienation or the sporadic rebuke of the Dublin government. Therefore, the *Times,* whilst criticising unionists 'for not having much interest in forcing the talks to succeed', proceeded to argue that concessions 'could not be expected to come solely from the unionist direction'.[78] The *Times* leader, 'When all else fails', went on to argue that Articles 2 and 3 of the Irish constitution should be amended:

> The Unionists had agreed in principle to talk with the Irish government while these clauses remain – a substantial concession – but they demanded in return either that the Irish government express an intention to have the constitution amended, or that more of the talks should take place in the Irish capital ... What price would he (Charles Haughey) pay in order to take part in talks with Unionists.[79]

The 'on-off' nature of the talks was a constant feature of their coverage in May and early June. A *News at Ten* report argued that Peter Brooke 'had been doing his best' to produce a compromise with the parties but that 'each side blames the other about where to meet'.[80]

This image of petty squabbing and failure of negotiations to proceed beyond the 'talks about talks' stage did, of course, fit the prevalent conception that Britain held the line between two unreasonable factions. Papers on the right praised

74 Ibid. 75 *Sunday Times*, 5 May 1991. 76 Ibid. 77 Ibid. 78 *Times*, 16 May 1991. 79 Ibid. The *Daily Mail* (8 May) also maintained it was a matter of 'take but no give from Dublin'. 80 ITN, *News at Ten*, 10 May 1991. Indeed, when the parties did agree to meet face-to-face the 'News at Ten' bulletins (on 5 June) led with the headline, 'They agree for once – the Northern Ireland talks are on'.

Ulster Secretary Peter Brooke and premier John Major for 'rescuing' the talks.[81] It was the Conservative Government's sense of duty rather than open support for the unionist cause which was the *Mail's* main message in their leader, 'Brooke's burden'.[82] In stating that unionists' procedural bickerings possessed 'all the characteristics of a childish spat', the *Mail* suggested that the government was following the only sensible line.

> Unless we are prepared to abandon part of the United Kingdom to the rule of gunmen, there is no choice but to overcome such frustrations and persevere with the kind of patient diplomacy undertaken by the Northern Ireland Secretary.[83]

ULSTER UNIONISM – ITS PORTRAYAL IN THE BRITISH PRESS

> The interests of this minute minority of the population (Ulster's Protestants) are thus determining policy for the entire nation. Our leaders courageously say that they will not be budged by terrorist outrages because they will not submit to an extremist minority, but the uncomfortable truth is that British policy has been hijacked by an extremist minority, the loyalist majority in Ulster, which may not command the sympathy of the whole electorate.[84]

Background

At the start of the Troubles, the British media had saturated the province with journalists, photographers and cameramen, most of whom were ignorant of what was unfolding in front of them.[85] The next phase of press reporting occurred in the post-Ulsterisation period when the main events were still duly recorded, but in significantly less detail. Some of these characteristics were still evident in the press's coverage of Northern Ireland in the 1990s, but there was also apparent a growing sophistication amongst journalists, of changing trends (notably amongst the loyalist paramilitaries), as well as an abundance of 'Irish anniversaries' (such as Bloody Sunday, the early marches of the Civil Rights movement and the sending-in of the army in 1969), which served to remind the national audience, every so often, of the origins of the conflict.

Apart from changes in the manner in which the national press, as a whole, covered events in Northern Ireland, there have inevitably been differences between individual papers' coverage of these incidents, on account of their differing political perspectives. As I argue later, the fact that most of the national press pursued a right-of-centre perspective did not mean they were especially sympathetic to the unionist position, though they might have shared an antipathy to-

81 *Daily Mail*, 16 May 1991. 82 *Daily Mail*, 1 June 1991. 83 Ibid. 84 Neil Lyndon in the *Independent*, 4 March 1992 (the article first appeared in the *Spectator*). 85 Eamonn McCann whimsically recalled in *War and an Irish Town* (London 1974) that the *Daily Mirror* had 12 reporters in Derry in October 1968, several of whom were looking for 'a local Danny the Red' and any locals who had been 'discriminated against'!

wards the IRA and, to a lesser extent, the government of the Irish Republic. Whilst Northern Ireland was deemed to be a 'non party-political' issue which produced an unofficial bipartisan approach for a considerable period of the Troubles, sections of Fleet Street were not above exploiting any difficulties which governments, of a different political hue to their own, were confronted with. Therefore, the *Sun*, referring to an increase in sectarian violence in mid 1970s Belfast, put the blame squarely on the shoulders of the Labour Government.[86] The paper's leading article, 'Wake up Rip Van Wilson', argued:

> The men of violence are only too eager to fill the vacuum left by dithering politicians. The Government must stop fiddling while Belfast burns and soldiers and civilians die.[87]

The central problem which the British press had to cope with was one of mainland apathy. This reflected itself in the press in a number of ways. Obviously the main one was a reduction in the degree of coverage of events, particularly in Northern Ireland itself, although incidents which had a significant number of casualties, or which were 'different', such as 'human' bombs, 'rogue' policemen or the killing of a nun by the IRA, were covered in detail.[88] Many papers, in some cases a little self-righteously, acknowledged their duty not just to reflect opinion on Northern Ireland but also to help mould public attitudes towards accepting their responsibility and duty to the province. Consequently they continued to report what was happening there as honestly as they could. To sustain the level of interest of its public, the British tabloid press, in particular, utilised a variety of 'human interest' stories to revive the flagging interest of their readers in events across the Irish Sea.[89] 'New' angles on the conflict were explored, mainly by the broadsheets, again with the intention of renewing mainland interest in a seemingly never-changing news story. These included variations on the usual 'cycle of violence' theme, such as joyriding, and representations of economic depression in Ulster.[90] However, there were also more optimistic news from the province, including the opening of integrated schools, economic regeneration, a boom in tourism, the popularity of opera at Castleward in Co. Down and a series of stories on 'peacemakers' and 'healers'.[91] Occasionally an article apeared in the British press which would completely contradict the one-dimensional impression held

86 *Sun*, 2 November 1974. On the other side of the political spectrum, the *Daily Mirror's* response to the IRA's killing of a judge and his wife was to demand the resignation of the Conservative Secretary of State for Northern Ireland (the *Mirror's* headline, on 27 April 1987, was, 'Time to go, Mr King'). 87 *Sun*, op. cit. 88 Each of these is referred to later in this section. 89 Several of these are referred to elsewhere, particularly in the case study on the Enniskillen bombing. 90 The *Guardian's* feature on joy-riding (2 May 1992) was 'Streetwise in Belfast – children of the Troubles', whilst the *New Stateman's* main feature (29 January 1982) concentrated on 'the future that doesn't work – Strabane, the unemployment capital of Europe'. 91 *The Daily Express* (7 May 1982) described the integrated Lagan College in Belfast as providing 'a new lesson in unity for the Children of the Troubles'; the *Independent on Sunday* (25 June 1995) announced Sainsbury's intentions to open several branches in Northern Ireland as being indicative of the 'peace dividend on its way' (to Ulster); the *Guardian* (3 Janu-

by those on the mainland with little personal experience of Northern Ireland. Walter Ellis wrote in the *Sunday Times* about 'the good war' enjoyed by Ulster's middle class and outlined some of the advantages of their lifestyle.

> The native bourgeoisie is extensive, growing and doing better than ever in its history. In Belfast, where a 4 bedroom house in a good area, with 2 bathrooms and a garden like a park can cost under £100,000, and where a typical mortgage is less than £30,000, professionals can afford to enjoy themselves, just as they can in Manchester or Leeds. And so long as Whitehall continues to bump in the subsidies – now in excess of £3 billion annually – the rich of the province will continue their affable feuding all the way to be bank.[92]

I intend, in this section, to discern how Northern Ireland's Protestant community has been portrayed in the British press. In my evaluation of the degree of press sympathy for unionism, I will be considering other inter-related factors. This assessment involved an analysis of the experiences of mutual 'friends' and 'enemies' of loyalism, such as the army, RUC and IRA and the government of the Irish Republic. I contend that, as with television coverage, press analysis of the loyalist position (with the exception of the Ian Paisley stereotype and the increased awareness of changes in the structure and political philosophy of loyalist paramilitariasm particularly during the 1990s) tended to be more low-key than corresponding treatment of nationalists. I conclude that because Tory tabloids, in particular, castigated Sinn Fein/IRA and were sympathetic to the army's plight, this did not mean they were automatically pro-unionist. Indeed, despite the right of centre bias in the British press, this was not reflected in widespread Fleet Street backing for the unionist position. Therefore, even papers like the *Times*, *Daily Telegraph*, *Express* and *Mail*, backed political initiatives ranging from direct rule and the Anglo-Irish Agreement to the Downing Street Declaration and the Framework Document, as well as vehemently opposing grassroots loyalist activity (such as the UWC strike and Ian Paisley's 'hill marches') and loyalist terrorism. Such papers were more vociferous in their condemnation of IRA attacks (particularly those occurring in Great Britain) and the perceived ambivalence of Irish Governments, than they were in supporting, or even explaining, the unionist responses to such groups.

There were, of course, exceptions to this restricted, understated treatment of the unionist case from the right wing press and I have included some of these in the final part of this section (also see the case study on the Enniskillen bombing and references to the ceasefire and the Shankill bomb). Apart from this failure to

ary 1991) described Belfast as 'a Hibernian Rio', whilst the *Independent's* travel section (18 August 1990) announced that 'despite 21 years of sectarian warfare, Northern Ireland's main city is bustling with building work, visitors and Porsches'; the *Times* (2 July 1994) wrote that the opera at Castleward 'drowns out the undertone of the Troubles' and there were numerous features on peacemakers such as Gordon Wilson (see Enniskillen case study), Mairead Corrigan and Betty Williams (see elsewhere) and 'healers' such as eminent Ulster surgeon, William Rutherford, whom the *Guardian* (1 October 1986) described as 'the man who heals Ulster's wounds'. 92 *Sunday Times*, 19 August 1990.

gain 'political' sympathy from substantial sections of the Tory press, unionists had to face constant criticism from papers on the left, including the *Daily Mirror*, *Guardian* and the *Observer*. Clearly I have had to be selective in choosing illustrations from a wide number of reports over the years but I have tried to reflect prevalent trends and emphasis within British press reporting of Northern Ireland.

MUTUAL FRIENDS AND ENEMIES

With the media agenda on Northern Ireland being dominated by security matters and political initiatives concocted by others (often, indeed, ignoring loyalist interests), unionists tended to pick up national media 'scraps'. In this section I shall be looking at a range of 'enemies' (most notably the IRA, but also at governments of the Irish Republic and Americans sympathetic to the republican cause) and also at 'friends', particularly those in the security forces.[93]

Some commonly-shared experiences, such as the effect of bombings on respective communities in Great Britain and Ulster, will be referred to later in this chapter. The categories are not, of course, quite as neat as I've made them out to be. Therefore, the degree of criticism levied at these groups varied not only within certain groups but also from paper to paper.[94]

Loyalists' main enemy has been the IRA and its political representatives.[95] They have also been perceived – on account of their periodic mainland bombing campaigns – to form the chief terrorist threat to national security interests. Hence there was a clear commonality of interest between unionists and the British public in this security sphere. It goes without saying that the IRA's military campaign was a 'headline-winner' for many years in Fleet Street, but it is beyond my remit to delve into such media treatment in depth. What I intend to concentrate on is how press denunciation of IRA excesses might have assisted unionists' political case and amplified loyalist grievances to a wider audience.

Although security incidents earned most publicity, the volume devoted to specific incidents declined over the years and coverage tended to be decided on factors such as the location of the incident and the size or nature of any resulting casualties. Therefore, single killings of army personnel which had warranted substantial coverage in the early 1970s were barely guaranteed a single paragraph by the end of the decade. Only when there were several army fatalities in an Ulster incident was it deemed 'worthy' of Page One treatment. Greater space was afforded to reporting attacks on British soldiers as distinct from locally-recruited security forces and particularly for IRA attacks on the British mainland.[96] The

93 Press coverage of loyalists' relationships with their political 'friends' is dealt with in detail in the first chapter. 94 The Press's harsher treatment of the local security forces (namely the RUC and the UDR/RIR) is referred to later in this section. 95 I mainly focus on the IRA here, though Sinn Fein and the influence of Gerry Adams, is observed elsewhere. 96 Although the UDR was technically a regiment of the British army (its largest, in fact), many regarded it as being 'different' to other regiments.

Provisionals were aware as early as 1972 that 'a bomb in London is worth twenty in Belfast' and they intermittently mounted campaigns in London and other mainland cities, which were to prove damaging to British society, both in human and economic terms. The tabloids were especially vitriolic in their censure of IRA violence. Following the Harrods bombing in London, where six people were killed and over ninety injured, the *Star* promised that 'God will be their Judge', whilst the *People* led with the succinct headline, 'Bloody IRA bastards!'.[97] The *Mail's* plea for Britain's large Irish community to assist police in detecting those responsible, would have struck a chord with loyalists in Northern Ireland. Referring to republican sympathisers, the *Mail* leader argued:

> Let them recognise this bombing for what it was – a deliberate and obscene desecration of the Christian festival of peace and goodwill ... Nothing could do more for the standing and esteem of the Irish community in Britain that one of their number should come forward and let the authorities know where these monsters are to be found.[98]

The Hyde Park attack the previous year had prompted sections of the 'quality' press in particular, to adopt a political tactic long requested by loyalists.[99] In a leader, 'Murders most foul', the *Times* called for the Irish government to renounce their claims over Northern Ireland'. It went on:

> It is crude fantasy to invoke the 'self-determination of a people', as the IRA does, as a pretext for suppressing the self-determination of a province which strongly affirms its desire for no changes in allegiances as often as it is asked.[100]

Another press demand, this time following a series of blasts at railway stations in London in 1991, reflected hard-line loyalist concerns.[101] The *Sun*, leading with the words of an eyewitness to the Victoria blast, 'I saw roses covered in blood – nightmare on platform 3', demanded immediate action to restrict the movement of terrorists.

> We should SEAL the border between the Republic and Ulster, except for checkpoints and insist that all Irish carry passports.[102]

Many of the mainland attacks did not reserve their criticism for the IRA or Sinn Fein. In the wake of the Birmingham pub bombings in 1974, the *Sun*, after spelling out the urgent need to 'smash the IRA', demanded ' a combination of tough, short-term measures at homes and positive long term ones in Ulster'.[103]

97 *Daily Star*, 20 December 1983 and the *People*, 18 December 1983. 98 *Daily Mail*, 19 December 1983. 99 Eight soldiers were killed and over forty were injured by IRA bombs in Hyde Park and Regents Park. Seven army horses were also killed in the Hyde Park blast and it was the image of a severely injured horse, Sefton (which was to survive the blast), which lingered in the memory. The *Daily Mirror* (21 July 1982) alleged 'these (bombers) are not real men, they're bastards!'. 100 *Times*, 21 July 1982. 101 One person was killed and over forty injured in the blast at Victoria station. 102 *Sun*, 18 February 1991. 103 *Sun*, 25 November 1974.

They argued that without such action 'the likely mayhem (against the Irish in Great Britain) will be too terrible to contemplate'.[104] The consequence of such press clamour for increased surveillance of Irish people travelling between the two islands was the Prevention of Terrorism Act.[105] However, such legislation and the presence of British troops in the province for another twenty years, did not result, as the *Sun* had forecast, in a 'smashing' of the IRA, and attacks were to continue on the mainland. Critical comments were directed at a plethora of public officials for a litany of security blunders. One such case was the Deal bombing in 1989.[106] The *Independent* noted 'concern over Ministry of Defence placing security with private companies', whilst *Today* simply demanded, 'Sack the bunglers!'[107] The *People* also castigated the authorities for allowing further carnage at Bishopgate in 1993.[108] It fumed:

> IRA bastards use a 10 ton tipper truck to bring death to the City of London again yesterday. But why did something so obvious not cause suspicion? If we are to wage effective war against the IRA, there must now be an urgent review of security at their more likely targets.[109]

The *Daily Express* sought another scapegoat for failed security and consequently started to question its support for an earlier Tory initiative on Northern Ireland (the Hillsborough Agreement). The *Express*, reporting an IRA attack on a military base in Kent, blamed the Irish government.

> The Eltham outrage is as good a time as any to remind Mr Haughey that the first priority of the Anglo-Irish Agreement is to halt terror attack in both our nations. If his government cannot provide effective legislation then the conclusion can only be that the agreement is a useless and outdated document.[110]

These calls for tighter security both within and outside the national terrority were a constant feature of press reporting of bombings in Great Britain, and their rigour contrasted with the basic, 'dry' content of reports based on the more frequent instances of violence in Northern Ireland. Only when such attacks were on a large scale, for example, the Enniskillen and Shankill blasts, did the press seriously challenge, what were for most of the conflict, administrations favoured

104 Ibid. **105** This act, a draconian piece of legislation, ironically passed by a Labour administration, was to prove both unpopular and unsuccessful (at least in terms of resulting convictions). The fiery public mood at the time demanded swift apprehension of those responsible: this was a factor in the speedy arrests and convictions of six Northern Irish Catholics for the Birmingham bombings. **106** The IRA bombed the barracks of the Royal Marines School of Music in Deal, Kent in September 1989. Ten bandsmen were killed and 22 injured. **107** *Independent*, 23 September 1989 and *Today*, 23 September 1989. **108** The IRA explosion at the Nat West Tower in the City of London killed one person, injured over 30 and caused over £1 billion damage. The ease with which they were able to transport a ton of explosives to the centre of London without causing suspicion promoted the *Sunday Times* (2 May 1993) to bewail that this represented 'the failed fight against terrorism'. **109** *People*, 25 April 1993. **110** *Daily Express*, 15 May 1990.

by the majority of the national press. Unionist demands for governmental resignations following security lapses were routinely reported in press reports but rarely won backing.

Predictably it was some of the more extreme tabloids which were to respond in a hasty, knee-jerk manner to such attacks. The *Star's* ultra-militaristic response to the ongoing 'tit for tat' killings in the province, coincided with the feelings of many loyalists, although their motivation was purely pragmatic and their sympathy confined to troops serving in the region. In its 'Kill or Cure?' leader the *Star* asked:

> Just what is going on in Ulster? We're pouring in millions to keep our soldiers there and fund a massive security operation. But tit-for-tat tribal murders are now as regular as daybreak. The Government plan to throw yet more of our boys into that black hole of despair. Yet, surely, these will be as useful as a fridge in Hell unless all our forces get one simple order from the top – Gloves off – go get the killers![111]

Some papers maintained their condemnation of terrorist violence even after the ceasefire. Referring to the term 'decommissioning', the *Mail* labelled it ' a weasel word' and demanded:

> ... the gangsters give up the assassin's rifle and the coward's bomb. And if this demand is not met soon, they should seriously question whether the peace process can possibly continue.[112]

The government of the Irish Republic was a regular quarry for denigration from the conservative British press, particularly as they offered a diversionary, more easily identifiable target from the press's normal 'enemy', Sinn Fein/IRA.[113] The main reasons for this press resentment towards Irish politicians included their apparent reluctance to ease extradition arrangements involving suspect terrorists wanted either in Northern Ireland or Great Britain, their failure to apprehend suspect paramilitaries in their own terroritory, which had proven to be the origin of many terrorist attacks and the perceived political immobility of an Irish government reluctant to make its state a more attractive proposition to unionists, either in terms of dropping its constitutional claims over the north or over 'moral' issues (including divorce and abortion). As was mentioned above, the Irish government were criticised for appearing unwilling to fulfil their obligations in the security field, as laid out in the Hillsborough Agreement.[114] After an IRA 'human bomb' had killed six soldiers and a civilian in 1990, the *Mail* asserted:

111 *Daily Star*, 16 November 1991. 112 *Daily Mail*, 19 May 1995. 113 Some papers from the other side of the political spectrum deliberately played down the Irish dimension, questioning the degree of feeling in Ireland for unification. The *Guardian*, 2 September 1987, referring to an Irish opinion poll, sugested that citizens of the Irish Republic were 'losing their desire for unity', with over 60% believing that it would never happen, or at least would not occur within a century. 114 See the earlier reference to the Eltham bomb in 1990.

> We have surely now arrived at a turning point in relations between Britain and Eire. Following a series of failures by the Irish government and courts to go through with the process of catching, prosecuting and punishing IRA criminals, this must surely be the last chance to show that the south really means to make the Anglo-Irish Agreement work. If this vile outrage cannot stir it into action, what can?[115]

Another terrorist incident resulted in an equally forthright attack by *Today* on Irish premier Charles Haughey, which reflected a widespread view that Irish politicians were ambiguous on the security issue.[116] *Today* maintained that Haughey had given 'precious little sign of matching his words with actions' and outlined what was urgently needed from the Irish leader.

> What Mr Haughey must do now is give a bold and unmistakable sign to the terrorists. He could move troops northwards to harry the IRA's cross-border raiders. He could make it easier for suspect terrorists to be extradited to Britain ... Mr Haughey owes it to his Government, his country, the people of Northern Ireland and Britain to act with spirit and imagination. And to act now.[117]

A long-standing source of unionist discontent had been with Articles 2 and 3 in the state's constitution which claimed jurisdiction over the whole of the Irish island. Several papers challenged the Republic's government on this 'annexation' goal, arguing that it wasn't only the unionists who needed to modernise their political thinking. The *Sunday Times* pondered;

> Is the Irish government serious about contributing to a lasting solution of Northern Ireland's continuing crisis or not? If so, will it recognise that the abandonment of the old Unionist ascendancy must be accompanied by the withdrawal of constitutional claims which the Irish supreme court says have legal force?[118]

The British press placed a lot of attention on the American response to events in Northern Ireland. This was on account of America's leading superpower status and the 'special relationship' enjoyed between the two countries for a consid-

115 *Daily Mail*, 26 October 1990. 116 The incident which had prompted the paper's attack on Haughey was the coach killing of eight soldiers in County Tyrone. 117 *Today*, 23 August 1988. Other tabloids chose less familiar Irish political targets upon whom to unleash their venom. The *Daily Star*, 31 August 1988, exposed a weapon-selling scandal involving Irish soldiers and identified the 'culprit' as Irish Defence Minister, Michael Noonan, 'a gentleman farmer', who, the *Star* suggested, 'should be sacked today and put out to grass with his cows'. 118 *Sunday Times*, 8 July 1990. Its 'sister' paper, the *Times* (22 June 1994) was to criticise 'constitutional horse-trading' between British and Irish governments, maintaining that what was required from Dublin were 'imaginative security resources and swift devolutionary reform' which would 'contribute far more than the spent rhetoric of the Downing Street Declaration'.

erable period (which was cemented during the Thatcher-Reagan years), as well as the potentially detrimental influence of a strong pro-Irish lobby on US policy relating to Northern Ireland.[119] The main focus of British press interest was, indeed, in this area of American susceptibility to republican propaganda, and it was most apparent during the hunger strike in 1981 when the British government opened up a publicity department in Washington and during Gerry Adams' visits to America in 1994 and 1995, when the warm reception and high profile afforded to the Sinn Fein President dominated press headlines in Britain.[120] In decrying the volume of support and particularly dollars, emanating from America's 50 million-strong 'Irish' community, the British press castigated a number of leading American political figures, including Congress Speaker 'Tip' O'Neill and Robert Kennedy, but reserved its most bitter rancour for a republican fund-raising group, Noraid.[121] The *Express* exposed Noraid involvement in supposedly cultural, non-political events, like St Patrick's Day celebrations, describing one American event as 'this parade of deadly lies' and accused the IRA of 'milking St Patrick's Day for sympathy and dollars'.[122]

On the whole, American Presidents did not become too deeply involved in the Irish question, but Bill Clinton expressed an early interest, offering to send an American peace envoy to Northern Ireland. This angered many editors in London, who, despite their support for the 'special' relationship, were wary of American intervention in British affairs.[123] The *Daily Express* was emphatically opposed to Clinton's offer of help. In a blunt editorial, 'Keep Out Clinton', the *Express* asserted

> Unless we've missed something, Ulster has not become America's 52th state ...Why on earth should we indulge their whim to dabble in the complexities of Northern Ireland ... Of course we want good relationships with President Clinton. But not so greatly that we must give him Ulster to play with.[124]

119 There is an interesting ambiguity about American media coverage of Northern Ireland. Jack Holland, in *The American Connection: US Guns, Money and Influence in Northern Ireland* (Dublin 1989, p. 234), has argued 'the remarkable thing about the American press is that, in general, it has stayed closer to the British government than has its British counterpart'. However, if this is so and American media responses to the Adams' visits in the mid 1990s suggest otherwise, it fails to explain British obsession in endeavouring to offset the perceived public relations damage caused by the presentation of the republican case in the American media. 120 The *Dail Mail* (3 July 1981) devoted its centre pages to a story about the daughter of an IRA hunger striker, who had enjoyed substantial television coverage. Labelling her 'the Propaganda Child', the paper described the ten year old as 'turning a nation against Britain'. Reference to Gerry Adams's American visits is made elsewhere in this section. Suffice to say here is that clear evidence of Sinn Fein's dictating the propaganda 'war' is provided by the visits of Tory back-bencher and ex-Northern Ireland Minister, Michael Mates and Unionist MP, Ken Maginnis, to America, in endeavours to counteract republican propaganda. 121 There was a significant shift away from the sympathy for the republican cause in 'respectable' American political circles from the mid-1980s onwards. This owed less to the effects of British counter-propaganda and rather more to the efforts of John Hume in persuading such politicians to give their backing to ongoing British-Irish initiatives. 122 *Daily Express*, 17 March 1984. 123 The feeling amongst many editors was that Clinton's trip was arranged to bolster his showing in domestic opinion polls. 124 *Daily Express*, 18 February 1993.

Despite critical leaders such as the above and anger over the 'megastar' reception provided for Gerry Adams during his trips to America, there proved to be a re-evaluation of British press thinking towards the Clinton administration, following his visit to the province at the end of 1995.[125] Although the *Times* had warned on 25 November that 'Ulster must look beyond Clinton's visit', maintaining that 'the prospects of the peace process should not be confused with the success or failure of a presidential visit', its response to the presidential trip a week later was noticeably upbeat.[126] Recognising the universally popular nature of Clinton's reception in Belfast and Derry, the *Times* admitted:

> Mr Clinton's trip was more than an exercise in political pageantry. It has pushed the process forward in the broad sense that it made clear how high the stakes have become and how great the cost of failure would be.[127]

Due to a combination of the prolonged nature of the Irish conflict and a gradual reduction in the number of army casualties from the mid 1970s onwards, press coverage of such attacks were inevitably less frequent and detailed.[128] This was in sharp contrast with the immense press interest in the army's intervention in Ulster, when the troops were portrayed as rather heroic figures, or what they were frequently referred to, 'our boys over there'.[129] Rhona Churchill's *Daily Mail* report of the army's initial experiences caught the prevalent mood of British press and public alike.

> Over and over again they said patiently and politely, 'Would you mind very much moving on please?' And people have moved on. This was the British Tommy in action here. You felt proud of him.[130]

Even when the level of violence sharply increased after 1970, (with the additional factor of IRA involvement) and it became apparent to many that the army's task was becoming an increasingly difficult, dangerous and thankless one, they managed to retain press support, despite foreign media criticism of British military 'excesses' (such as Bloody Sunday).[131] Although papers like the *Guardian*,

125 Most press coverage of Clinton's visit was ecstatic in its tone. The *Express*, which had been so critical of Clinton two years previously, led on how 'Cathy's plea had won the heart of a President' (the child concerned, Catherine Hamill, had lost her father in the violence and had made an emotional rendition of her peace poem during Clinton's visit to Mackie's factory in west Belfast; quoted in *Daily Express*, 1 December 1995), whilst the *Independent* (2 December 1995) suggested that the American President had unearthed 'a formula for reviving Irish spirits'. 126 *Times*, 25 November 1995. 127 *Times*, 2 December 1995. 128 In addition, the 'Ulsterisation' policy – that of giving increased responsibility for security to the locally-recruited forces – made it less likely for British soldiers to be the target for IRA attack. The increased involvement of the RUC and UDR from the mid 1970s was not popular with loyalists. As the *New Statesman* (28 May 1976) keenly observed, 'the death of a single policeman at the hands of the IRA always angers the Protestants more than any number of casualties among British soldiers'. 129 See the TV section for a more detailed account of the army's early involvement in Northern Ireland. 130 *Daily Mail*, 16 August 1969. 131 The *Daily Tel-*

Observer and, to a lesser extent, the *Independent,* were to question specific military operations and tactics (most notably, the allegations that they were pursuing a 'shoot to kill' policy against suspect terrorists), this tended to be less damning than their criticism of RUC or UDR 'misdeeds'.[132] When the army were under pressure from nationalist accusations of using 'excessive' force, they could always rely on the support of the conservative press. One of the clearest illustrations of this was the *Daily Mail*'s fund-raising on behalf of a soldier, Private Lee Clegg, imprisoned for the killing of a Catholic.[133]

The press, like television, was fond of its army 'heroes'. Frequently tabloids delved into the personal backgrounds of soldiers killed or severely injured in the violence. This 'human interest' aspect was an essential tool which tabloids felt obliged to implement in combating growing public apathy with Northern Ireland. Frequently they exploited the 'peace-keeper's' role of the army, characterising troops as the protectors and friends of local people. Such a case was the *Daily Star's* front page photo and report of a Royal Green Jackets soldier befriending a little girl in a Belfast street which informed readers that 'to this little girl he was a friend, to the IRA he was the enemy. So they killed him'.[134]

It was evidently difficult for the press to present a picture of military 'heroes' fighting a 'glorious' war in Northern Ireland.[135] Nevertheless, papers like the *Daily Telegraph* endeavoured to ensure that soldiers serving in Northern Ireland would not be 'forgotten' by the British public. Hence the *Telegraph* featured a poem written by a soldier, Stephen Cummins, killed by terrorists in March 1989, which they speculated might be converted into a pop song.[136] A number of papers also reported on the 'ruined' lives of those soldiers horrifically maimed in Ulster's violence, frequently attacking the poor levels of compensation for the injured.[137] The *Mail,* in a feature, 'Building a new life – the forgotten soldiers' – portrayed the suffering involved in the rebuilding of the lives of five injured soldiers, describing in detail 'the incredible courage of the men shattered by the IRA's weapons of hate'.[138]

Most press comment was supportive of John Stalker, Deputy Chief Constable of Manchester, in his attempts to conduct an enquiry into the killings by the RUC of six Catholics in 1982. Some papers, like the *Guardian*, were fully in support of the enquiry and criticised RUC reluctance in assisting Stalker with

egraph, 31 January 1972, blamed the IRA for the deaths of 13 civilians in Derry, claiming that 'their blood is on its hands'. 132 It is interesting to compare the defensive approach adopted by several Tory tabloids regarding the killings of three unarmed IRA members in Gibraltar in 1988 with the lack of support given to the UDR during a three-year period of prolonged criticism which led to the regiment's demise in 1992. 133 *The Times* (5 July 1995) maintained that Clegg's release was a 'private matter' and was 'irrelevant to the peace process'. 134 *Daily Star*, 27 March 1982. 135 Indeed, several reports contrasted the 'messy' character of the Ulster conflict with the 'glorious' nature of the Falklands War. A *Times* feature (4 March 1983) noted how soldiers had been heroes at Goose Green but villains on the Shankill Road'. 136 The *Daily Telegraph's* headline (25 November 1995) read 'Dead soldier's poem moves a nation'. 137 The *Daily Express* (18 August 1989) lamented that 'a soldier's life is valued at £1700'. 138 *Daily Mail*, 27 August 1981.

his quest.[139] One of the few editorials which had reservations about Stalker's task was the *Evening Standard* which had pointed out that RUC reticence in assisting Stalker was not surprising, given the circumstances. The *Standard* maintained:

> There is no doubt that he (Stalker) was hated by some officers of the RUC. But what did he expect? Few policemen investigating another force are toasted in champagne by those whose careers they threaten.[140]

Few features articles were written on the bravery of RUC officers. Instead, they concentrated on reporting the force's problems and weaknesses. The Stalker case was one instance of this trend. Another example was when an unstable off-duty officer, Allen Moore, shot dead three people at a Sinn Fein office in west Belfast. Most of the tabloids led on the 'terminator' theme (Moore's target was believed to have been Gerry Adams). The *Express* told its readers the attack was the 'Revenge of the Terminator', whilst the *Star's* headline read, 'Rogue Cop in Gun Frenzy'.[141] The *Sunday Times*, in a special feature on the officer involved, 'All my Troubles', analysed the problems and tensions facing a police force living and working in a divided community. Referring to PC Moore, the *Sunday Times* asked:

> ... was it pressure of work that drove him over the edge? Loss of his friends? Or was he just another victim of the psychosis that has gripped Ulster since he was born?[142]

Most press coverage of the RUC was factual and what detailed analysis there was tended to be critical in its tone. Therefore the increasing professionalism of the force was slowly recognised and its expertise in the anti-terrorist sphere was underplayed in the national media. Chris Ryder, however, neatly summarised the force's achievements in his book on the RUC.

> In the process of pacifying Ulster and heading off the effect of the IRA campaign, the RUC became the most skilled anti-terrorist and innovative police force in the world and their techniques and expertise, which have been studied and copied by police forces internationally, made them the model for the rapidly changing style of tougher conflict policing throughout the rest of the United Kingdom.[143]

Despite considerable media reticence, it must be acknowledged that there was, particularly in the Hillsborough protest period, a growing acceptance of the RUC's even-handedness and professionalism. Casualties suffered by the local

139 The *Guardian* devoted substantial space to the story and at least three leading articles were written on the case ('Mr Stalker's odd ordeal', 10 June 1986; 'The veil drops over Stalker', 26 January 1988; and 'Stalker's Irish Jungle', 2 February 1988). 140 *Evening Standard*, 22 January 1990. 141 *Daily Express*, 5 February 1992 and *Daily Star*, 5 February 1992. 142 *Sunday Times*, 9 February 1992. 143 C. Ryder, *The RUC – A Force Under Fire* (London, 1989), p. 12.

security forces, unless their numbers were significantly larger than usual, tended to earn less headlines as the conflict deepened and attracted less interest than similar attacks on the army.[144] Following the RUC's greatest loss of life in a terrorist incident – an attack by the IRA on Newry police station, the *Times* decided that here was an opportunity to remind its readers that there was no distinction between 'terrorism' and 'crime'. In its leader, 'Murder is Murder', the *Times* argued:

> Solzhenitzyn has reminded us that violence is used to support a system of lies and that lies are used to justify relationships based on violence. Only lies can justify murder in the pursuit of political ends. Only lies can find any comfort or exculpation, for the massacre at Newry.[145]

The UDR received an even more hostile reaction from the British media and it was arguably a television documentary which provided its *coup de grace*.[146] However, there were occasional reports which exhibited more meritorious behaviour on the part of its members, as well as illustrating the dangers they had to live with on a daily basis. The *Daily Express* was one of a number of papers to include a photograph of a shotgun-wielding UDR man's wife, guarding him as he worked on his farm, whilst the *Daily Mail*, in a feature on the UDR's 'Greenfinches', told its readers about 'the girls who fight the IRA – their faces are pretty but their names remain secret'.[147]

Just as in the Moore case, UDR members who were guilty of breaking the law tended to receive significantly greater interest from the press than those who had died trying to ensure its maintenance. The killing of Penny McAllister, whose officer husband had been having an affair with UDR soldier Susan Christie, received substantial press and TV coverage. This interest was due more to the case's lurid sexual details rather than a regard for the story's Northern Irish background.[148] The main accusation of sleaze directed against the UDR was, however, centred around allegations that information relating to republican suspects had been passed on by UDR soldiers to loyalist terrorists.[149] As early as 1988, the *Observer* suggested that 'terror links dent UDR's credibility', whilst Liam Clarke was later to argue in the *Sunday Times* that 'the disappearance of documents naming the IRA suspects has called into question the performance of the UDR'.[150]

144 For instance, a 1,000-pound IRA bomb which killed four UDR soldiers in County Down only warranted a photo and short report on p. 5 of *Today*, 10 April, 1990. 145 *Times*, 2 March 1985. Paul Johnson's pertinent *Guardian* report on the same day, noted that 'as the police count their dead there are few other damp eyes – children jeer near the scene of devastation'. 146 The programme concerned, Panorama's *'Ulster's Regiment – A Question of Loyalty'*, is considered in more detail in the Panorama section. 147 *Daily Express*, 13 November 1981 and the *Daily Mail*, 14 May 1987. 148 The *Daily Mirror's* headline was 'A Fatal Attraction' (2 July 1992). 149 Although a tiny proportion of the regiment faced such charges (and indeed, some of those found guilty of attacks on Catholics, including three of the Armagh Four, were later to have the legal judgements reversed) the whole regiment, perhaps uniquely, was unable to counteract what transpired to be irreparable damage to its reputation. 150 *Observer*, 29 May 1988 and the *Sunday Times*, 24 September 1989.

Following the 1991 decision to merge the UDR with the Royal Irish Rangers, thereby creating a new Royal Irish Regiment, Edward Gorman, in his *Times* report, described the UDR as 'the regiment of the Troubles' which had the misfortune of 'suffering from an image problem almost from the day it was formed in 1970'.[151] The *Guardian* felt that the *Panorama* programme had confirmed all the suspicions that it and other left-of-centre papers had harboured on the regiment for a considerable period. Referring to the high number of terrorist-related charges brought against men who had served in the UDR, and touching on the Stevens enquiry which had been etablished to look into allegations of collusion between the security forces and loyalist paramilitaries, the *Guardian's* leader argued:

> The record of UDR men detected in illegal activities on behalf of 'loyalist' groups and the evidence of ... collusion which led to the setting-up of the Stevens inquiry, has sapped the regiment's credibility to a point when its right to continuance was under challenge even before the Panorama analysis.[152]

LOYALISTS AND THE PRESS – AN UNSYMPATHETIC EAR?

Although the majority of the national Press is supposedly right of centre, this did not manifest itself in many papers expressing open support for political loyalism. Indeed, whilst most on the political right wearied of events in Ireland, focusing any support towards the army or for government policy, those papers on the left were more open in espousing the political goals, if not the methods, of Irish republicanism. The *Guardian*, arguably more than any other daily paper, pursued a consistently pro-nationalist line.[153] Its revered owner and editor C.P. Scott had been an ardent supporter of Irish unity and had given great assistance to both Asquith and Lloyd George during the Home Rule campaign.[154] In 1949 the *Guardian*, referring to Dublin street graffiti, 'Arm now to take the North!', restated its broadly 'constitutional-nationalist' line.

> We would like to see them (Ulster) joining with other Irishmen within a national unit, but we hold that it is for their Parliament, not ours, to decide.[155]

More recently, the paper has, whilst devoting considerable space to several aspects of loyalism not generally covered in the British media, kept to a broadly nationalist agenda, concentrating on issues such as the politicisation in the early 1980s of the republican movement, and the 'diminuition of human rights' incurred in the policing of the conflict. Thus whilst opposing the IRA's military

151 *Times*, 19 July 1991. 152 *Guardian*, 23 February 1990. 153 The *Manchester Guardian* was founded in 1821 and was for many years closely associated with the Liberal Party. The *Guardian* readership in September 1997 was 428,010. 154 C.P. ('Great') Scott was the editor of the *'Manchester Guardian'* from 1872 to 1929 and its owner between 1905 and 1929. 155 *Guardian*, 18 May 1949.

campaign, it retained its favoured option of Irish unity. Indeed, as Geoffrey Taylor observed in his historical account of the paper, the *Guardian* 'reflected the ideas which led to the New Ireland Forum and then to the Hillsborough Agreement'.[156] The difference between the thinking of the paper and the Conservative government was that the *Guardian* frequently left little room for doubting its commitment to withdrawal and unification. In a short 'Troops Out' series, the paper's Irish correspondent, Anne McHardy, postulated that perhaps it was now the time – in the middle of the hunger strike – for Britain to indicate its intentions to quit Northern Ireland:

> The Unionist refusal to even consider a future outside the United Kingdom may perhaps be the strongest argument for Britain to at least indicate that it wants to leave. At present the guarantee can be paraphrased as 'We would not object to going if the majority wanted us to'. Perhaps after 12 years of stalemate, it's time to say 'we really would like to get out. How can we help you to survive without us'? If Britain did make such a declaration it would then throw the ball into the Irish court.[157]

Another leading 'quality' paper which supported the cause of unity was the *Observer*, which followed a similar line in its Ulster coverage to that of the *Guardian*.[158] The distinguished journalist Mary Holland penned many reports and features on the conflict. In an article (co-written with Anthony Bevans) her assessment of the Framework Document, whilst basically accurate in its forthrightness, also possessed a celebratory tone. They described the document as 'a victory without the guns', arguing that the Prime Minister 'gave the green light to a united Ireland with his plea for cross-border bodies ... Britain has a moral commitment, but will not stay a moment longer than necessary'.[159] Although the *New Statesman* was the only other leading journal to consistently press for withdrawal and unity (it first did so in 1971), many papers were far from consistent in supporting the union and 'siding' with loyalists in Northern Ireland (the *Daily Mail* and *Sunday Telegraph*, and to a lesser extent, the *Times*, were the chief exceptions).[160] Even the *Spectator*, on the right of the British political spectrum, and a journal which later provided expression for unionist grievances (particularly over the Anglo-Irish Agreement), expressed early disillusionment with Ulster and its unionists. Commenting on Harold Wilson's 1971 scheme of troop withdrawal and unity, the *Spectator* appeared to disassociate itself with the unionist cause;

> There is no disposition in England to hang on to any part of Ireland and what

156 G. Taylor, *Changing Faces – A History of the Guardian 1956–88* (London 1993), p. 156. **157** *Guardian*, 6/8 July 1981, quoted in G. Taylor, op. cit. **158** The *Observer*, one of Britain's oldest papers, was founded in 1791. Taken over by the Lonrho Group in 1981, its circulation dropped by over 200,000 inside six years and in September 1997 was estimated at 498,086. **159** *Observer*, 26 February 1995. **160** This is dealt with later in greater detail.

would best suit the British government and British opinion would be for a change of mind to take place whereby the majority in Northern Ireland became prepared seriously to consider the conditions under which the unification of Ireland could be made acceptable.[161]

Other papers adopted a more pragmatic approach to troop withdrawal and Irish unity. The *Daily Mirror* uniquely combined a vehement denunciation of IRA terrorism with an equally vociferous demand for that organisation's two fundamental objectives, troop withdrawal and unification.[162] The *Mirror* became increasingly frustrated with the immobile nature of the Irish conflict and their positive assessment of the 1984 Forum Report was indicative of their growing belief in Irish unity. The *Mirror* proclaimed that British authorities had to 'show courage' in dealing with the political problems of Ireland. In an editorial 'The Way Out', the *Mirror* argued:

> It is time to right the wrong and to reunite Ireland. It is the only solution which makes sense ... If the British Government offered generous resettlement grants to Northern Irish who preferred to come to Britain, then the long march to peace could begin. That *is* the way forward. It is time to take it.[163]

The *Mirror's* belief that Unionists' objections and fears over the Irish dimension – that they could be 'bought' by the offers of 'resettlement' grants – not only displayed their antipathy to the unionist population, but also their tendency to respond in a 'knee-jerk' fashion to acts of terrorism. Thus, the *Mirror's* response to the savage killing of two soldiers in west Belfast in 1988, contained a strange blend of 'logic' and moral righteousness.[164] Again noting that withdrawal was 'the only option', the *Mirror* maintained that this 'wouldn't leave Ireland in the clutches of the IRA' but rather that the latter 'only survived because of the British presence'.[165] The *Mirror* believed that withdrawal would, in itself, sweep aside old divisions and 'solve' the Irish problem.

> When we leave the Irish can decide to live together or die together. We believe they will make the sensible choice.[166]

161 *Spectator*, 18 December 1971. 162 The *Daily Mirror* started publishing in 1903. It was taken over by Robert Maxwell in 1984 and is currently Britain's second most widely-read daily newspaper, with a daily circulation of 2,442,078 in September 1997 (many Irish people living in Britain are believed to 'take' the *Mirror*). Incidentally Maxwell took the unusual step of making a personal call for troop withdrawal on the 20th anniversary of the sending-in of the troops, when he maintained, 'Britain cannot solve the Irish problem, because we caused it with partition in 1921, and we're still part of it' (*Daily Mirror*, 10 August 1989). 163 *Daily Mirror*, 15 August 1984. 164 Another instance of the Mirror advocating withdrawal – 'which wouldn't be defeat, but the road to lasting victory' – was its response to the IRA's mortar attack on Downing Street (*Daily Mirror*, 8 February 1991). 165 *Daily Mirror*, 21 March 1988. 166 Ibid.

The *Economist* was another left of centre publication which saw the political advantages afforded by Irish unification. Indeed, it had been, from the start of the Troubles, wary of substantial British involvement in Northern Ireland. In 1970, they pointed out that 'the British Government does not want to take Northern Ireland over' and two years later they were suggesting that an all-Ireland solution would be a popular one with British politicians.

> Ministers have made little secret of their belief that the most satisfying solution in the end would be if a political solution were created over the years in which the Protestant majority in the north could come to recognise a future for itself in a united Ireland.[167]

In the *Economist*'s case, the road to Irish unity was based on the notion that it would prove to be, particularly in the financial context, an attractive long-term prospect. In lambasting Ulster Unionists whom they maintained 'should be told ... that they cannot set their conditions for remaining in the United Kingdom', the *Economist* pleaded for the region's middle class to 'start to give the lead'.[168] It suggested that 'a better hope for Protestants is that, slowly, both North and South will come to see that together they would be clever, stronger and richer than they have been while apart'.[169]

In the first phase of the Troubles, unionists appeared to be regarded contemptuously by most sections of national and political public opinion. Though this was to level out as the conflict developed, and the terror campaign provided the media with more obvious 'hate' figures, the early images of the public disintegration of the Unionist Party manifesting itself in the ugly street clashes between Paisleyites and Civil Rights demonstrators and taciturn provincial politicians constantly filing into shabby buildings to backstab their leaders, were to linger in the media's subconscious. Though the press's initial over-simplification of the Catholics as the 'goodies' and the Protestants as the 'baddies' was to be altered as British involvement increased, it would be a shifting of roles, rather than a transformation of national opinion in favour of unionism, which would occur. Therefore, the British (despite the occasional misdemeanour) took on the mantle of the 'Good', the IRA and Sinn Fein became the 'Bad' and the increasingly less significant Protestants became the 'Ugly' group. Even the conservative press were categorical in distancing themselves from the loyalists and castigated the unionist establishment for failing to reform their system of government, particularly at local level.[170] A *Daily Mail* editorial insisted:

> It is nearly 25 years since the rest of Britain decided that everyone over 21, not just householders and businessmen, should be entitled to vote for his local

167 *Economist*, 16 May 1970 and 12 January 1972. 168 *Economist*, 23 May 1981. 168 Ibid. 170 Although all sections of the press appeared to advocate reform, some were supportive of the Unionist Government. Referring to a political 'enemy', Harold Wilson, the *Daily Telegaph* admitted 'he so far has wisely left Captain O'Neill to get on with the job ... he should continue to do so' (8 October 1968). The *Telegraph* has the higher circulation of any daily broadsheet (1,129,177 in September 1997).

council ... It is intolerable that council houses should be alloted for reasons of religion and not of poverty. It is intolerable that Catholics should be denied an equal chance of a job.[171]

A young journalist who would later become editor of the *Daily Telegraph*, wrote about how Unionism's negative traits cancelled out his natural conservative instincts and made him – like many other journalists at the time – side with the Catholics. Max Hastings wrote:

> As the weeks went by and personal experiences broadened a detectable feeling for the Catholics crept more and more into everything I wrote, coupled with a dislike for the Protestants, the Unionists, and much of what they stood for.[172]

Many journalists at this time focused on the antediluvian nature of Ulster politics which so distanced the region from the rest of the country. In doing so, they tended to restrict this notion of politics being conducted in a time-warp, to one side, the unionists. Alexander Cocksburn's description of loyalist behaviour, as he witnessed a number of unionist meetings around the province (mainly involving Paisley), personifies the negative feelings of the press towards unionism at this time. In his *New Statesman* article, 'Ulster – History's Blind Alley', Cocksburn catalogued a list of unionist warts.

> Old women rush at you in the streets of Armagh, screeching for Paisley and waving clubs. Captain O'Neill, Captain Long, the obsession with mean military titles. Dream-like too was the mad loyalist fervour of the unionist meeting in the Ulster Hall with its covenanteers and Union Jacks...The old slogans 'no Surrender', 'Not an Inch'. Not Rhodesia or South Africa, but Ulster ... For the loyalist citizens, the recent upsurge has been horrifying, but in a way hideously satisfying. In practice, no society in western Europe can the myth of salvation and the emotion of fear be so sharply etched on the Protestant as in Ulster ... here was a column of bigots, having soundly beaten a reporter, marching off home, singing hymns.[173]

Although it was the street violence which caught press attention, substantial coverage was also given to the friction within unionism at this time. Some journalists noted how the Protestant working class felt increasingly vulnerable – 'the poorer among the privileged are increasingly afraid' – and Jeremy Bugler, in his 'The House of Orange' feature for *New Society*, noted the challenges facing the Unionist Party.

171 *Daily Mail*, 24 April 1969. The *Mail*, founded in 1896, has a readership of 2,344,183 (September 1997). Max Hastings is currently editor of the *Standard*. 172 M. Hastings, *Ulster* (London 1969), p. 197. 173 *New Statesman*, 3 January 1969.

> Even if O'Neill does get a new brand of non-Orange Unionist, even if he does ride out the next political crisis and attack on his leadership, his hardest struggle lies ahead of him. This is to ensure the survival of the Unionist Party in an age when the Protestant working man's vote won't be cast according to his faith. This is the Orange nightmare.[174]

Of course, the early castigation of loyalists was to become less pronounced, even before the commencement of the Provisionals' campaign. For a considerable period the republican element within the Civil Rights movement and People's Democracy was underestimated and the excesses of the demonstrators were explained as the actions of 'hooligans looking for a punch-up or anarchists with a grudge against society'.[175] However, even the *Sunday Times*, which had swiftly forged a reputation for its critical analysis of the Stormont regime, conceded that within six months of the first civil rights marches, the constitutional issue was firmly at the centre of the conflict. It maintained:

> The master of sectarian violence is well out of its cage. The issue now is no longer civil rights or even houses and jobs. The issue is now whether the state should exist and who should have the power and how it should be defended and this is an issue on which the wild men on both sides have sworn for over 40 years, frequently in blood, that they will never back down.[176]

Like television, the British press has, both in its news reports and features, devoted considerable attention to what they discern to be the numerous negative characteristics of loyalism. These include bigotry, unionists' intransigence and unwillingness to compromise, their internal divisions and poor leadership, and their siege mentality (several of these features are illustrated in greater detail elsewhere). The *Independent*, which was not unsympathetic to the unionist plight, despaired of its eternally depressing nature and, referring to the Framework Document, implored Ulster to say 'yes'. The *Independent* suggested that it was in unionist interests to participate in discussions about the Province's future, but questioned their right to establish a veto over all political change. It argued:

> ... if unionist politicians fail to co-operate, they might find that cross-border institutions are developed without them ... The Protestant community effectively retains a veto over Northern Ireland's constitutional status, but not over all political change.[177]

The *Sunday Times*, too, were critical of unionists' inflexibility. In a leading article, 'Politics of the last atrocity', written in the aftermath of the Anderstown killings of two soldiers, the *Sunday Times* maintained that 'Unionists' intransi-

174 *New Society*, 12 December 1968 and 19 December 1968. 175 *Daily Express*, 7 January 1969. The *Express*'s circulation in September 1997 was 1,241,336. 176 *Sunday Times*, 27 April 1969. The *Sunday Times* had a circulation of 1,449,113 in September 1997. 177 *Independent*, 23 February 1995. The *Independent*'s circulation in September 1997 was 288,182.

gence, above all, has done much to fuel a 'troops out' mood in mainland Britain, where 50% tell pollsters they favour withdrawal'.[178] In denouncing such a strategy, the *Sunday Times* voiced their support for power-sharing. The article went on:

> Such an initiative would put the decent majority in Ulster on the spot. The British government is right to be steadfast in its refusal to allow the terrorists to win. But the rest of Britain is entitled to demand more help from those in Ulster, with most to lose if they ever did.[179]

A movement plagued by internal tension and disputes was another theme of the coverage. Even on those rare occasions when unionism was temporarily united (such as in the early phase of the anti-Hillsborough campaign), critics were pointing to signs of division. Although unionism was not again to experience the degree of dissension it had suffered between 1968 and 1972, there was ongoing disagreement between the DUP and UUP and even inside these parties, particularly the latter. David McKittrick wrote in 1992 of 'clear signs of poor organisation, inept negotiation and internal factions fighting' within unionism, maintaining that there was 'little sign of co-ordination between the Unionist parties, while within both there have been signs of internal disagreement'.[180]

Blatant bigotry and a discernible reluctance to forgive were other nullifying idiosyncrasies associated with loyalism. Bigoted motivation and attitudes were assumed to pervade all areas of life in Northern Ireland. Therefore, the *Times* reported that 'loyalists are angry that a Belfast boxer won a silver medal for the Republic of Ireland' and noted his 'snubbing' by Belfast councillors on his return to Belfast.[181] Loyalists also seemed impervious to what appeared to be a universal desire for peace. Describing the circumstances behind the killing in prison of a loyalist paramilitary by the IRA, the *Observer* asked tersely of his widow, 'does she want peace in Ireland?'[182] The feature in the *Observer* magazine proceeded to describe her unforgiving views which reinforced existing notions of loyalist bitterness and animosity. The loyalist terrorist's widow maintained that not only did she 'hate the people' who had killed her husband, but also claimed she had been 'brought up to have nothing to do with them' (Catholics) and avowed that her daughter 'will be the same'.[183]

Even loyalist claims to possess a genuine cultural identity of their own were challenged. Ronan Bennett, a writer with a republican background, underlined the narrowness of loyalist culture in a *Guardian* article:

> As long as the political outlook of loyalism is defined by sectarianism it is likely that Lambeg drums will continue to preside over its (Protestant) culture, as Seamus Heaney put it 'like giant tumours'.[184]

178 *Sunday Times*, 27 March 1988. 179 Ibid. 180 *Independent*, 15 September 1992. 181 *Times*, 15 August, 1992. Incidentally, Shankill Road man Wayne McCullough went on to win a world championship as a professional. Britain's oldest paper the *Times*, had, in September 1997, a circulation of 821,000. 182 *Observer*, 13 March 1994. 183 Ibid. 184 *Guardian*, 16

Occasionally journalists have delved more deeply into the reasons behind unionist reticence, suggesting that their apparent intransigence is not only damaging hopes for a political settlement which will ensure permanent peace, but also their own aspirations. Referring to the need for unionists 'to keep the peace process on the rails', Andrew Neil, in a not unsympathetic *Sunday Times* article, pleaded with unionists to refrain from adopting a nihilistic attitude to the Framework Document.[185]

> It is self-destructive for loyalists to let their distrust boil up into hatred now. They must compromise with a new reality ... The Unionists will wrongfoot themselves, to the detriment of their own interests, if they opt for a rejectionist position in which 1 million people are seen to thwart what the other 59 million regard as reasonable. Sinn Fein/IRA would love that.[186]

Although some positive comments have been attributed to unionist leaders, (alas, normally in obituary columns, as was the case with Harold McCusker and James Kilfedder, though James Molyneaux also received some praise, particularly for his response to the Downing Street Declaration), the inflexibility of unionist leadership was a basic component of national press coverage.[187] In the wake of the Brighton bombing, the *Times* suggested that the unionist population 'are owed a political leadership that is capable of distinguishing between conciliatory moves which do and conciliatory moves which do not put the union at risk'.[188] Nearly a decade on, following the Unionists' castigation of Ulster Secretary Peter Brooke's RTE gaffe, the *Independent* bemoaned the dearth of fresh talent in unionism's ranks, and suggested that this was partly a result of the absence of devolved government in the province. The substance of the *Independent*'s argument was as follows:

> In Britain, the rigidity of the Unionists' veteran political leaders is seen as a substantial contributory factor in prolonging Ulster's agony ... It is regrettable that because there is no devolved government in Northern Ireland promising and moderate young Unionists who might have replaced or diluted the old guard have had no political jobs in which to cut their teeth. In the late 1980s they gave up and moved into other professions. The older generation lives in the past, rarely venturing into the republic, and unaware of the extent to which its citizens have been Europeanised.[189]

Unionist leaders, therefore, have either been marginalised or stereotyped in the national media. Thus it is hardly surprising that those few 'heroes' to emerge from the Troubles have had their roots firmly in the Catholic community. With the exception of Gordon Wilson, who was applauded because of his perceived tolerance and willingness to compromise, there have been few Protestants who

July 1994. 185 *Sunday Times*, 5 February 1995. 186 Ibid. 187 An assessment of Molyneaux's leadership is given in the political chapter. 188 *Times*, 29 October 1984. 189 *Independent*, 25 January 1992.

have been fêted, over a prolonged period in the press. On the other hand, Catholic priests, members of the Peace Movement and politicians have enjoyed detailed and broadly favourable press attention.[190] For instance, there is no unionist equivalent of Gerry Fitt or John Hume. The former was a jocular, popular figure at Westminster and following his departure from Irish politics and subsequent elevation to the Lords, he was the subject of much media interest. The *Daily Express* serialised Fitt's fascinating life story, asserting that 'no politician has worked harder than Gerry Fitt to build bridges across Ulster's yawning sectarian divide', whilst the *Observer*'s profile, 'Gerry Fitt – Ireland's gift to the Lords' was also essentially complimentary in its tone.[191] John Hume has also received a broadly favourable press over the years, though he hasn't been eulogised in the British media as has been the case in America. One sceptical report displayed irritation with Hume's non-stop media appearances and his reputation as a 'peace-broker'. Criticising Hume's involvement in talks with Gerry Adams and Sinn Fein, the *Sunday Express* expostulated:

> In Ulster Mr Hume is seen for what he is: an embattled, grasping politician with a certain constituency. But in Europe and America he comes second only to Mother Theresa in the global sainthood stakes.[192]

Virtually all sections of the national press backed the various political initiatives in the course of the Troubles. This was particularly the case with the press's initial response to the Anglo-Irish Agreement and to both the Downing Street Declaration and the Framework Document. Even conservative papers such as the *Standard*, were critical of the predictability of the unionist response to the Framework Document, arguing:

190 Therefore, the Catholic leaders of the Peace Movement, Mairead Corrigan and Betty Williams, received enormous media attention. Photographed shopping in London, they were described by the *Daily Mirror* (16 September 1976) as 'the peacemakers ... Ulster's pioneers of hope'. It must be said that, although Catholic priests tended to receive more publicity than their Protestant counterparts, this was not always complimentary in its tone. Although the broadsheets in particular, covered the appointments of Irish Cardinals (and also their funerals) in depth, they alluded to the nationalist background of Tomás Ó Fiaich – the *Observer*, in a profile, commented that 'the purple mixes with the green' (22 January 1984) – and several papers were to be, in the years ahead, highly critical of his vehement denunciation of Britsh military 'excesses' and what they regarded as his ambiguous statements regarding republican terrorism. On the other hand, the press highlighted the courage and Christian charity afforded by other priests, including Revd (later Bishop) Daly in Derry during Bloody Sunday and the Revd Alec Reid who had tried to aid two dying soldiers in west Belfast (the front cover story in the *Sunday Times* magazine, 30 October 1988, described him as 'the broadest back in Belfast'). Protestant ministers, on the other hand, tended to be regarded in Great Britain as more overtly 'political' (largely on account of the prominence of certain unionist MPs) and one consequence was that the statements of Irish Anglican Archbishop Dr Robin Eames, received signficantly less press attention than those of his Catholic counterparts. **191** *Daily Express*, 20 July 1983 and the *Observer*, 10 July 1983. **192** *Sunday Express*, 13 March 1994. The *Sunday Express*' circulation in September 1997 was 1,261,690.

> The anger of the Unionists over the Ulster peace plan was not long in coming. And when it came it did so in traditional fashion – a walkout.[193]

Other papers on the right did, however, maintain their caution, even in giving their conditional support to such initiatives. The *Sunday Express* expressed such sentiments towards the Downing Street Declaration, following Sinn Fein's prevarication over the declaration.[194] The paper advised the government that 'a bent backward posture held for too long becomes humiliating, especially when it is clear that Sinn Fein is merely stringing the British Government along'.[195] The *Daily Telegraph*, especially in the early 1980s, was in favour of Northern Ireland's integration within the United Kingdom and was therefore sceptical of James Prior's 1982 devolution scheme, which they believed unionists had 'rightly' rejected.[196] At the heart of the *Telegraph's* resistance to devolution was their emphasis on maintaining the union of the national territory, rather than the specific interests of Ulster Unionists. Their editorial went on:

> ... the Government's fanatical devotion to devolution is inevitably seen by Ulster as a device for distancing Britain as far as possible from the Province, in the hope that she will one day be able to clear out altogether...It is more than likely that the Prime Minister has not thought this out, but it is high time that she did.[197]

In contrast with their opposition to Prior's 'rolling' devolution scheme, the *Telegraph* agreed with mainstream interpretation of the Framework Document. On the eve of the publication of the Document, they warned unionists:

> The Unionists should beware of destroying the best opportunity for peace that Northern Ireland has seen in a generation, when they still hold so many cards in their hand.[198]

Apart from Ian Paisley, loyalists were the subject of significantly fewer cartoons in the British press than republicans. This reflects the latter's proactive role in the conflict, rather than indicating press sympathy for unionists.[199] Indeed, utilising the Irish racial stereotype to paradoxically cover both communities in Ulster, many cartoons reiterated English feelings that one side was 'as bad as the other'. An early Cummins cartoon in the *Daily Express* clearly depicted both Catholics and Protestants as irrational, violent creatures, only being pre-

193 *Standard*, 22 February 1995. The Standard's circulation in September 1997 was 494,195. 194 *Sunday Express*, 22 May 1994. 195 Ibid. 196 *Daily Telegraph*, 8 March 1982. 197 Ibid. 198 *Daily Telegraph*, 2 February 1995. 199 Utilising stereotypes which can be traced back to 'Punch' in the mid 19th century, the Irish were portrayed as violent aliens from early in the conflict. Despite initial caution depicting terrorist violence, the press portrayed paramilitaries as scheming, unfeeling and thoughtless. See the *Daily Mail*'s Harrods bombing cartoon (19 December 1983) and the *Independent*'s cartoon relating to an IRA bomb which killed 3 police officers and a nun, (26 July 1990).

vented from killing one another by the duty-bound British 'Tommy'.[200] Jak's infamous cartoon, 'The Irish', castigated all terror groups, refusing to distinguish between them.[201] Therefore, loyalist paramilitaries were frequently represented in a similar fashion to the IRA, usually as barbaric, blood-thirsty killers, or perhaps as dim-witted Irishmen blundering their way through a clandestine meeting with shady-looking arms agents.[202] This lack of regard for the view of loyalist paramilitaries is quite at odds with the interpretation of Liz Curtis, who implies that the British media's tendency to understate the political nature of the activities of loyalist paramilitaries (instead labelling their deeds as 'criminal') indicates that they are 'siding' with Protestant terrorists.[203] There is no doubt that the British media were initially confused by several 'mystery' killings during the early Troubles and inevitably they distinguished between the various paramilitary groupings, whose political motivations and theatres of war were very different. However, it's important not to confuse differing interpretations of such behaviour with a pronounced 'favouring' of one group or side. Even in 1972, right wing papers were castigating loyalist paramilitaries. Denouncing the reluctance of the UDA to dismantle their 'no go' areas in Belfast, a *Sun* leader urged William Whitelaw, the Ulster Secretary of State, to 'prick the UDA balloon and send the movement's known leaders to confinement, beside the leaders of the IRA'.[204]

Therefore, media images of loyalist paramilitarism, and especially cartoon depictions, were far from flattering. These exposed the criminal and bigoted essence of loyalist violence and derided their organisations' ill-discipline, internecine bickering and general lack of political direction.[205] Indeed, by adopting a mainly one-dimensional usage of the terms 'criminal' and 'sectarian', the British media were reinforcing impressions that loyalist paramilitaries had less political creditibility then their republican counterparts.[206] However some journalists reappraised their interpretations of loyalist paramilitarism, particularly on account of its increased level of activity and marginally more systematic approach in the early 1990s, and they noted the ironical situation where the political representatives of loyalist paramilitarism appeared more 'moderate' than the leaders of mainstream unionism.[207]

John Darby has described Ian Paisley as a 'godsend' for political cartoonists in that he 'served as a convenient metaphor for loyalist bigotry and intransigence'.[208]

200 *Daily Express*, 12 August, 1980 (see appendix). **201** *Evening Standard*, 29 October 1982 (see appendix). **202** *Daily Telegraph*, 7 February 1992, and *Evening Standard*, 25 April 1989. **203** See Liz Curtis, op. cit. **204** *Sun*, 11 July 1972. **205** These underlying characteristics of criminality and bigotry were personified by the media coverage of the 'Tombstone Assassin' (Michael Stone) and the infamous Shankill 'Butchers'. **206** Greater detailed discussion of this theme, and other media representations of loyalist paramilitarism, can be found in my doctoral thesis, 'Loyal Rebels without a Cause?', op. cit. **207** Liam Clarke noted this in a *Sunday Times* article (16 October, 1994). Clarke wrote: 'The post-Shankill man admits to 50 years of Unionist misrule, apologies for the mistakes of the past and has set his sights on the working class loyalist votes traditionally garnered by Ian Paisley and his DUP. The further irony is that they (loyalist terrorists) are now, in their philosophy and sense of political pragmatism, far more moderate then the old hardliners they are set to replace.' **208** J. Darby, *Dressed to Kill – Cartoonists and the Northern Ireland Conflict* (Belfast 1983), p. 45–6.

Other unionist leaders were less frequently the subjects of cartoons, though James Molyneaux was sketched as the other half of a Laurel and Hardy act with Paisley during their anti-Agreement campaigning.[209] Even the *Daily Telegraph* portrayed the two veteran unionists as being cast adrift in their opposition to the Framework Document.[210] Molyneaux's successor, David Trimble, undoubtedly on account of the reputation as an Orange hard-liner which he had recently gained at Drumcree, was depicted by Steve Bell, in his cartoon strips, as a bigot in a bowler hat, whilst other *Guardian* drawings portrayed Trimble as being only marginally less uncompromising in his approach than Ian Paisley.[211] Darby argues that such cartoons illustrate the media's despairing image of Northern Ireland, displaying the province as 'the cuckoo in the United Kingdom nest', and pointed out that Ulster politicians (with the possible exception of Brian Faulkner) were shown as 'petty, fractious and irrelevant': in other words, complementing the more general image of 'the isolated, psychotic Irish'.[212] Darby also proposed that press cartoons did not distinguish, in their wrath and condemnation, between the two communities.

> Undoubtedly the PIRA were the universally agreed enemy, but few cartoonists in Great Britain found anything in the province with which to sympathise – there was a discernible ripple effect of general antipathy towards the Ulster people, and indeed the Irish.[213]

PRESS SUPPORT FOR THE LOYALIST PREDICAMENT

Although even papers on the right were to back 'initiatives' on Northern Ireland opposed by unionists, there were occasions when sympathy for their political plight was expressed. Peregrine Worsthorne, commenting on the 1986 by-elections in the province (caused by the resignation of Unionist MPs in protest at the signing of the Anglo-Irish Agreement) suggested that, in ignoring unionists' political will, Westminster was encouraging more extreme elements within loyalism to adopt 'unconstitutional' methods. In an article, 'The threat from threatened Ulster', Worsthorne asserted:

> No wonder Ulstermen feel threatened. They *are* threatened and the almost total indifference shown to last week's election results ... will not encourage them one little bit to go on putting their faith in the protection of the ballot box.[214]

Other journalists maintained that Westminster's dismissive treatment of unionist politicians had sustained those opposed to the union. In demanding that Ulster should be 'treated like any other province of the United Kingdom', Andrew

209 This was examined earlier. **210** *Daily Telegraph*, 23 February 1995. **211** *Guardian*, 24 October 1995 and 12 September 1995. **212** J. Darby, op.cit., p. 64. **213** Ibid. **214** *Sunday Telegraph*, 26 January 1986. The *Sunday Telegraph*'s circulation in September 1997 was 938,253.

Alexander, writing in the *Daily Mail*, maintained that the 'contemptuous' treatment of unionists by successive governments had been 'a stimulus to those who wanted to overthrow majority rule'.[215] The political haemorraging which might befall complacent governments as a result of their dismissal of unionism was spelled out by the *Sunday Telegraph*. Commenting on increasing unionist concern over the content of the Framework Document, the paper warned that Unionist MPs 'menaced the Tory majority in Westminster' and that growing loyalist dissent could be 'a shot across the Government's bows in the final stages of the negotiations'.[216]

A number of papers on the right noted the political marginalisation of unionists, identifying potential repercussions of their being constantly bypassed in political debate and negotiation. Even in 1976 the *Daily Telegraph* was pointing out that unionists had not only been passed over politically but were also being denied the necessary security protection. In a strongly-worded attack on Labour's Secretary of State, Merlyn Rees, whose 'dull hopelessness' in apparently accepting a 'no win' military scenario it deplored, the *Telegraph* contended:

> Well may the people of Ulster, Roman Catholic and Protestant alike, be filled with fear, anger and despair as they listen to the maudlin platitudes of Mr Rees. They have been deprived of their own Government and also of power and responsibility to maintain order within their borders. Where authority should reside there sits a man whose every word proclaims him an absolute stranger to the very idea of government.[217]

This notion of 'losing out' to the other side had been a long-standing loyalist grievance that was increasingly highlighted in the press during the 1990s (I expand on this below).[218] Certain conservative papers even encouraged unionists not to allow themselves to be fooled by the government and to be wary in affording them their trust. In maintaining that it was 'time for Ulster's constitutional parties to reclaim the initiative from the men of violence and their supporters', the *Times* leader, 'Ulster's true agenda', advised the Unionist Party leadership to 'review their strategy'.[219] The *Times* went on;

> James Molyneaux has stood by Mr Major, deducing correctly that Unionists could not be seen as wreckers of the peace process. But he must not confuse discretion with passivity. He must make clear to the Prime Minister that the declaration alone is not enough; that the Protestant community expects a strong commitment to devolutionary reform and that he can no longer take for granted the support of unionist MPs.[220]

215 *Daily Mail*, 25 October 1982. 216 *Sunday Telegraph*, 15 January 1995. 217 *Daily Telegraph*, 7 January 1976. 218 Norman Tebbit warned in the *Evening Standard* (30 November 1993) of the dangers of conceding too much to nationalists and at the same time provoking unionists into violence. 219 *Times*, 28 February 1994. 220 Ibid.

The *Mail's* veteran writer on Irish affairs, Andrew Alexander, even went as far as advising Ulster Unionists not to trust the Conservative Prime Minister. Writing in 1995, again during the tense atmosphere which prevailed prior to the publication of the Framework Document, Alexander noted the irony of a situation where the victims of duplicity were regarded by many as wrong-doers. In his article, 'Why should Major be trusted by Northern Ireland?' Alexander noted:

> He (John Major) once said it would turn his stomach to negotiate with terrorists. Yet his officials were conducting talks. Mayhew recently told Ulster Unionist leader James Molyneaux that he would be consulted on a framework document and said that no such document existed. Yet the leaked one dates from November. However, to read much of the Press one would think it was the Ulster Unionists and their allies who were up to no good.[221]

The *Times*, which warmed to the unionist position in the 1990s, complained that there was still miscomprehension at Westminster about what unionism entailed.[222] Following John Major's Guildhall speech, in which he made tentative gestures to Sinn Fein, the *Times* bemoaned the side-lining of the majority of Ulster's political representatives.

> The inability of the British political class to comprehend the extent to which unionists have been militarised and disenchanted since the Anglo-Irish Agreement in 1985, remains a serious obstacle to discussion of the province.[223]

The *Times* differed from the *Telegraph*, in its support for devolutionary reform in Northern Ireland. In calling for a 'rethink' of government policy and the establishment of an administrative assembly, the *Times* alleged that 'wooing Sinn Fein has done nothing but raise the party's profile and alarm the Protestant comunity in Ulster' and proceeded to warn the premier to 'think again' if his desire 'to be remembered as a peace broker in Ireland is sincere'.[224] The *Daily Telegraph*, on the other hand, pursued an integrationist policy.[225] Although this was out of step both with government policy and grassroots unionist opinion, the paper was unequivocal in its support for the union, realising that the secession of Northern Ireland from the Union would also have ramifications for Scotland and Wales. Max Hastings, writing in the wake of the horrific killings of two soldiers in west Belfast in March 1988, argued that there could be 'no retreat' from Northern Ireland, maintaining that no matter how fatigued the British people might be with the province, their duty and responsbility was to remain. Hastings argued:

> The first signal the Westminster Government must repeat for the hundredth time is that, for all the misery the IRA is still inflicting, the British will and

221 *Daily Mail*, 3 February 1995. 222 This shift can be partly attributed to the presence of 'pro-Union' journalists (such as Matthew d'Ancona) in the *Times*' team of leader-writers. 223 *Times*, 17 November 1993. 224 *Times*, 20 May 1994. 225 This was strongly influenced by the distinguished pro-Union *Telegraph* journalist, T.E. Utley.

> ability to maintain Northern Ireland as a part of the United Kingdom are not in doubt. We may be weary of the struggle but that does not mean for a moment that Britain is as such nearer to the abandonment of the province.[226]

This idea that every outrage, particularly those committed in Great Britain, meant a strengthening of British political and public resistance to conceding the terrorists' aim of Irish unity, was a favourite theme, particularly of right of centre papers and Conservative Governments. Following a 1991 IRA attack in St Albans, the *Sunday Express* used strident language to express their determination to resist terrorist pressure.

> Britain will never be terrorised into abandoning its citizens in the Province. Every outrage serves to strengthen the nation's resolve never to give in to the men of violence.[227]

A constant theme of right wing press coverage was the need to improve security both in the province and on the British mainland. Perhaps more than any other paper, the *Daily Telegraph* was vociferous in its condemnation of terrorism and its criticism of perceived governmental inefficiency in coping with such an onslaught. Indeed, the paper placed greater emphasis on the short-term primacy of winning the security 'war', at the expense of immediate political progress. After the killing of 10 Protestants by the IRA in 1976, the *Telegraph* argued 'no purely political action will suffice' and what was required was 'a firm and consistent security campaign, visibly, impartially and relentlessly directed towards suppressing terrorism from all quarters'.[228] In another, earlier, leading article, the *Daily Telegraph* had criticised those suggesting military withdrawal, arguing that 'if we wash our hands of Ulster we are in fact washing our hands of responsibility for our own security and survival', and castigated the failure of the authorities to protect its fellow citizens in Northern Ireland.[229] The *Telegraph* neatly pinpointed the predicament of Ulster's majority community:

> They have had to live in a society in which the forces of evil, malice, madness and violence which are everywhere present, so far from being properly repressed by public authorities, have been most improperly and outrageously rewarded. We are accustomed to saying that crime does not pay. It has paid handsomely in Ulster. Who can wonder now that a minority of Protestants, learning the evil lesson, now deal in the same coinage.[230]

226 *Daily Telegraph*, 21 March 1988. 227 *Sunday Express*, 17 January 1991. This resolution to combat terrorism to the end was never totally accepted by unionists who believed that political concessions were being made to nationalists, at their expense, which nullified the effect of such condemnations. 228 *Daily Telegraph*, 6 January 1976. 229 *Daily Telegraph*, 24 December 1975. Indeed, another leading article in the *Telegraph* (18 May 1976) described loyalist paramilitary attacks as 'an inevitable reaction to the horrifying truth... that, after all these years, the Government's security policy has not been able to protect innocent people'. 230 Ibid.

The reduced coverage of IRA attacks in Northern Ireland resulted in only the larger scale, most horrific incidents involving the loyalist community being covered in comparable detail to victims of IRA violence in Great Britain.[231] Indeed, loyalists for many years had been aggrieved at the differentiation in response to terror attacks committed in Northern Ireland and those executed in the rest of the United Kingdom. Unionist disquiet was particularly to the fore in the wake of the response to the Warrington bombing in 1993.[232] Papers led for days on the story and television unearthed in Colin Parry, father of young victim Tim, a mainland counterpart, in terms of his capacity to forgive, of Gordon Wilson.[233] Apart from the obligatory virulent reaction to such an attack – the *Sunday Mirror*, which devoted its first three pages to the story, led on 'Bastards – the IRA's gift for Mother's Day' – the press concentrated on the fact that it had been children living far away from the 'warfields' of Belfast and Derry, who had been the chief victims of Warrington.[234] Several papers carried a photo of the victims' fathers 'lighting a candle for the boys who died the day evil came to town', whilst the explosion prompted peace marches in Dublin.[235] The *Sunday Times'* Focus on the Warrington blast interestingly featured the comments of UUP secretary Jim Wilson, who 'spoke for many across the political divide' in observing that 'more sympathy and more attention was paid to deaths in England than to deaths in Northern Ireland'.[236] The column proceeded to remind its readers that 'there is a feeling in Ulster that, if terrorism would only be confined to the province, both London and Dublin would be relieved'.[237]

Despite a higher than usual interest in the incident and the similarities in the types of stories relayed by the papers, the more devastating Shankill Road bomb later that year, failed to gain the headlines acquired by the Warrington blast.[238] Again, many of the tabloids responded with their customary venom to both the Shankill blast and the funeral of one of the bombers, Thomas Begley. The *Daily Star* pinpointed the failure of the security forces in preventing the IRA from mounting an armed guard at his funeral as symptomatic of their general inability to guarantee the security of the Northern Irish public. Its leading article demanded:

231 See references to, amongst others, the Enniskillen bombing and the Darkley shootings. 232 Two children were killed and over fifty people injured in explosions in a Warrington shopping centre. 233 A television documentary, Panorama's *An Ordinary Boy*, was an excellent example of how, by Ulster standards, an unexceptional attack, in England was guaranteed more media coverage than more horrendous ones in Ulster (the viewing figures for this edition, which reached 7.5 million, reflect this different level in interest). 234 *Sunday Mirror*, 21 March 1993. The papers exploited the 'human' interest of this story, as they also did for Enniskillen, and, to a lesser extent, the Shankill bombing (where the loss of life was, incidentally, much greater). *The Evening Standard* (22 March 1993) told its readers how a passing nurse had 'cradled the toddler murdered by the IRA', and in typical fashion, the *News of the World*, several weeks after the blast (9 May 1993), featured the resulting strains pre-empted by such a tragedy on the relationship of one of the victims' parents ('Bomb boy's parents split up - Angel's mum quits home'). Incidentally, the circulation figures for the *Sunday Mirror* and *News of the World*, in September 1997 were 2,424,000 and 4,620,415 respectively. 235 *Daily Mail*, 8 April 1993. 236 *Sunday Times*, 28 March 1993. 237 Ibid. 238 11 people were killed in the bombing and nearly 60 were injured.

> Why are terrorists allowed to get away with these repulsive, arrogant gestures time and again in Northern Ireland? ...They (security forces) should be ordered to go in and shoot the bastards ... There can be no negotiating with bloody bombers who murder or maim innocent folk. The only solution is to wipe them off the face of the earth.[239]

Indeed, more space was allotted to castigating the IRA than it was in relaying the sectarian nature of the attack and its effects on the loyalist community.[240] The presence of Gerry Adams at Begley's funeral, carrying his coffin, was to provoke even more rage, with *Today* contrasting the 'hype' associated with the IRA funeral with the 'quiet farewell' given to 'the innocent victims of the bombing'.[241] *Today*'s report observed.

> Thomas Begley's victims went to their graves with no big show. In Belfast and elsewhere across the grief-stricken province, the last 5 of the Shankill Road dead were buried in simple Protestant ceremonies.[242]

The barbaric nature of the Provisionals' attack on a crowded shopping area in a familiar city high street was, as in the case of the Warrington attack, a central theme of press coverage of the incident. The *Observer*'s headline, 'Women and children die in murder of the innocents – revulsion at Bloody Saturday', reflected the horror at the random character of such an outrage, whilst John Hicks' and Graham Brough's vivid reporting of the destruction of a typical shopping area was reminiscent of many previous, albeit mainly mainland, bombs which had secured similar in-depth coverage.[243] The *Mail on Sunday* reporters wrote;

> ... it had started as an ordinary, sunny day – families going about their business like thousands of others across Britain. And then the IRA bombs exploded. In seconds, this busy street was littered with bodies. Mothers lost their children amidst the dust and rubble. Elderly couples struggled to their feet, bloodied and dazed.[244]

As the bombers had donned butcher-style white coats before dropping the bomb in a fish shop, the term 'butchers' was ironically used to describe the IRA incursion.[245] The *Mail on Sunday* had described the perpetrators as the 'Butchers of

239 *Daily Star*, 27 October 1993. The *Star*'s daily circulation in September 1997 was 631,853. **240** The IRA maintained that they were trying to kill a leading loyalist paramilitary who, they had believed, had been in a meeting in a different part of the building earlier in the day. Whilst condemning such an 'excuse' the press tended to accept the rationale behind the attack, labelling it as a 'blunder'. **241** *Today*, 28 October 1993. *Today* folded in 1995. In November 1994 its daily readership was 583,347. **242** Ibid. **243** *Observer*, 24 October 1993 and *Mail on Sunday*, 24 October 1993. **244** *Mail on Sunday*, op. cit. **245** It was ironic in that the term 'butchers' was synomonous with Shankill paramilitaries during the 1970s. For instance, the *News of the World*'s headline, on 24 October 1993, was 'Butchers – meat men drop bomb in chip shop'.

Belfast' and observed that 'only in the twisted minds of the IRA would terrorists dressed as butchers deliver a massive bomb'.[246]

Like the Enniskillen and Warrington bombings, the press focussed on the families of the bereaved. Where Gordon Wilson and Colin Parry had emerged as symbols of hope emanating from the Enniskillen and Warrington blasts respectively, Darren and Lauren Baird, who were orphaned in the Shankill explosion, were soon regarded by the press as symbolising the despair of Ulster. Interest in the children was so high that the *Daily Mail* returned to their plight over two months after the bomb. In a features article, 'The Day our Christmas died', they informed their readers how their grandparents were helping to 'rebuild the lives of the Baird children'.[247] The *Mirror* concentrated on children killed in the blast and their front page story which accompanied photographs of child victims of the attack 'ran' the headline, 'Innocents – the little girls whose young lives were cut short by the bloody bunglers of the IRA'.[248]

Another central theme of press coverage of this bombing was the perception that the response of local people to the blast was considerably more bitter on the Shankill than it has been in Enniskillen.[249] This was probably due to the decline in religious fervour on the Shankill, and the area's reputation as a loyalist hotbed. Nicholas Watt reported in the *Times* that the mood on the Shankill was 'one of revenge with none of the spirit of reconciliation that followed the Enniskillen bombing in 1987', and, tragically too accurately, predicted that the blast 'will set off a chain of reprisals'.[250]

Previously unchallenged, one-dimensional images of loyalism were questioned in the post-Hillsborough period. Features illustrating their triumphalism and bigotry were replaced by references to their betrayal, marginalisation, isolation and insecurity. Robert McCrum, in a *Listener* article, 'Ulster's "chosen people" fear their future', suggested that the picture of loyalists as 'the parochial, aggressive, bigoted figures of legend' needed 'some adjustment', maintaining the reality was that they, 'historical bullies, have also become victims and losers'.[251] Witnessing a Twelfth of July parade McCrum observed:

> For all their boot-faced graveness, these are a war-like, clannish people. Unsure of their future identity, anxious for a secure place, punctilious about the obligations of loyalism, they are always ready to go over the top to protect their territory. They believe they are God's Chosen. Their slogan is 'No Surrender!' The more their cause seems lost, the greater their intransigence.[252]

246 *Mail on Sunday*, 24 October 1993. 247 *Daily Mail*, 30 December 1993. 248 *Daily Mirror*, 25 October 1993. 249 This contrasted with the forgiving mood in Channel Four's *Shankill* programme (see the Channel Four section later). In any case, the Enniskillen mood of forgiveness may have been overstated because of the disproportionate attention paid to the views of one victim, Gordon Wilson. 250 *Times*, 25 October 1993. A number of reports contained references to the hostile reception received by local SDLP MP Joe Hendron when he endeavoured to express sympathy with local people. The response of the loyalist terrorists – they killed seven people at Greysteel inside a week of the Shankill bombing – was not long in coming. 251 The *Listener*, 19 November 1982. 252 Ibid.

Some writers were, therefore, over the duration of the Troubles, to change their attitudes to loyalists and their political predicament. Linda Christmas, a journalist who admitted being initially in favour of Irish unity, described an Apprentice Boys parade as 'a sad day', alleging that the Derry march took place 'without a trace of triumph'.[253] She proceeded to paint a picture of an insecure, alienated community.

> Slamming the gates on King James' men had given them a tenuous supremacy, which they had clung on to at all costs; it had not made them confident, it had made them fearful in the knowledge that at any time they could be toppled. Confident men do not end the day drunk; that is the behaviour of men who are insecure, threatened and defiant.[254]

As was increasingly the case with television coverage of the confict, significant sections of the press were looking more sympathetically at the unionist case in the early 1990s, searching for reasons to help explain their apparent bull-headed intransigence, as well as the increase in the level of military operations on the part of loyalist paramilitaries. This led to an, albeit temporary, expression of sympathy with the unionist community. Such an instance was the press's response to the IRA's 1994 ceasefire. Although the main reaction was one of welcome, and indeed, near-euphoria, several papers warned against complacency and the need to respect unionist opinion. Reports suggested that in accepting the agenda of nationalists and republicans, there was a danger of completely marginalising Protestants and the notion of the Unionists as 'underdogs' emerged in the early post-ceasefire period.[255] The *Sunday Times* was adamant that, in welcoming the ceasefire, the Government should refrain from 'ditching' the unionists. The paper, which had once exposed to the bone the inequitable policies of Unionist Governments now warned against 'betraying' the Protestant community.[256] Its leader, 'Peace – but not at any price', cautioned:

> However intoxicating the so-called peace process becomes, we must never become entangled in a betrayal of the unionist community ... Ulster Unionists have stood by us in times of great peril; we must not betray them now. We owe them more than a shabby sell-out. Mr Major should ensure they do not get one.[257]

The *Sun* and the *Daily Mail* also admonished the Government against 'selling out' unionists. The *Sun*, which had become increasingly sceptical of the Hillsborough Agreement, did acknowledge that the ceasefire signalled 'peace at last' but advised their politicians to approach the future with caution:

253 L. Christmas, *Chopping down the Cherry Trees* (London 1989), p. 100. 254 Ibid. 255 This was the theme of my *Belfast Telegraph* article, 'Loyalists – the new underdogs?' (6 October 1994). 256 The *Sunday Times* Insight team investigated allegations of discrimination and 'misgovernment' by the Stormont authorities and published their findings in 1972. 257 *Sunday Times*, 4 September 1994.

> The slaughter must stop but not at any price ... We must not be fooled by the terrorists' weasel words ... Until the majority votes otherwise it must remain a part of the United Kingdom. There must be no appeasement, no surrender, no sell-out.[258]

In the light of the Government's early 'goodwill' gesture to the IRA – the returning of some of its members to Northern Ireland prisons – a *Mail* leading article spelled out the urgency of assuaging the fears of a vulnerable community:

> The law-abiding majority in Ulster has watched whilst Ministers broke their word not to talk to the men of violence. They have read reports that Britain's sovereignty over Northern Ireland may be weakened. They have seen Dublin win more and more influence over their affairs. They experienced growing pressure from the Americans. Now they see Magee and others like him treated with generosity. Inevitably they are uneasy, no matter how often Ministers tell them that their constitutional position is safer. They need reassurance, they need to be convinced they will never be sold down the river.[259]

The *Independent* too prioritised the need for calming unionist opinion and fears that they were 'powerless to influence events'.[260] Noting their changed role as 'new' victims, the *Independent* suggested that the priority was 'to draw Unionists into discussion' and to convince them that 'their rights will be respected'.[261] The paper cautioned against 'sacrificing' the peace because 'the Protestant community feels overwhelmed by historical foes and abandoned old allies'.[262]

Other editorials forewarned that if this isolation were allowed to continue, the result might well be an even greater increase in the levels of loyalist paramilitary violence. *Today* recognised the importance of 'regaining the confidence of Loyalists' and of the need to 'persuade them to lay down their arms too'.[263] The *Today* editorial proceeded to suggest that a continuation of the loyalist paramilitary campaign on Sinn Fein members and the Catholic community in general could lead to the army being deployed on a much larger scale in Protestant areas, which would, in turn, result in the emergence of a 'new' type of conflict:

> Loyalists have to be convinced that they are in serious danger of falling into a cleverly manipulated trap ... The difference this time would be that the IRA would be sitting it out, claiming it was the peacemaker. It's a trap nobody in Britain can allow the Loyalists to spring.[264]

258 *Sun*, 31 August 1994. The *Sun*'s daily circulation figures in September 1997 were 3,887,097. 259 *Daily Mail*, 2 September 1994. Patrick Magee had been jailed for masterminding the Brighton bombing in 1984. 260 *Independent*, 1 September 1994. 261 Ibid. 262 Ibid. 263 *Today*, 5 September 1994. 264 Ibid. Incidentially, it is intriguing to notice how the term 'loyalism' became increasingly synonymous with Protestant paramilitaries, whereas it has previously been used as an 'umbrella' term to denote an undefined and uncertain political consciousness within the Protestant community.

The calling of the ceasefire by the IRA in 1994 had been another example of republicans calling the agenda in Northern Ireland. However, occasionally Ulster Unionists were perceived by the British media as having the capacity to snatch the political initiative away from their opponents.[265] Such an occasion evolved from John Hume's fiery denunciation of John Major's endorsement of the Unionist Party's idea of an assembly. An *Independent* report suggested that the 'incensed and isolated' Hume provided the 'new' Unionist Party of David Trimble with 'a rare and welcome reversal of roles'.[266] A number of journals maintained that it had been this rare occasion when the Ulster Unionists' parliamentary influence resulted in their agenda being followed that had pre-empted the breakdown of the IRA ceasefire. The *Guardian* argued that the Docklands bomb 'hands Mr Major gift-wrapped into the welcoming arms of Mr Trimble', whilst the *Economist* maintained that it was Major's 'adoption of the Unionist agenda', which had created 'another hurdle in the way of Sinn Fein entering into talks'.[267] Perhaps the most interesting responses to the unionist case came from two papers which were considered left of centre on 'social' or 'human rights' issues, namely the *Independent* and the *Sunday Times.* The latter, as I've already indicated, had been, through its *Insight* team in particular, critical of Unionist administrations in Northern Ireland, and as late as 1981 were calling for 'the releasing of Northern Ireland', arguing that Mrs Thatcher's government should 'face the uncomfortable fact that, historically and actually, the presence of British troops is in itself an encouragement to terrorism'.[268] The *Sunday Times*, like several other papers, grew 'war-weary' and one of a number of leading articles in the early 1990s called for 'selective' internment, suggesting it was time for terrorists on both sides 'to be taken out of circulation for a fixed period of time as long as the emergency lasts'.[269] For a supposedly left of centre paper, the *Independent*'s increasingly reactionary stance on the constitutional question was a particularly interesting feature of its Northern Ireland coverage.

265 The British press continued to reappraise the conventional image of loyalists as the 'bit players' in any 'peace' negotiations. Following the collapse of the 1994 IRA ceasefire and Sinn Fein's eventual political 'acceptance' (epitomised by Tony Blair's government offering them a place at the political negotiations in the autumn of 1997), certain papers reconsidered their views of unionist participation in such negotiations. John Mullin writing in the *Guardian* (25 September 1997), conceded that, at the start of the talks, UUP leader David Trimble was 'the politician that mattered most last week' and he had 'clearly enjoyed his time in the sun'. The *Economist* (20 September 1997) didn't quite affirm the *Guardian's* assessment of Trimble's tactics, but admitted that Ulster Unionists had ' a case which was going by default' due to the 'abdication' of Unionist leadership. More predictably, the *Times* (10 September 1997), argued that it was the Ulster Unionists and not Sinn Fein who would be the 'crucial players' at such talks, maintaining that 'a dialogue conducted without any figures from Ulster's majority community would be an empty exercise'. Others were downright sceptical of Sinn Fein's motives in declaring a second ceasefire in July 1997 and the *Daily Telegraph* relabelled the Blair initiative the 'terror process' and even counselled unionists not to enter talks which would be 'a blackmail process' (*Telegraph*, 26 and 22 September 1997 respectively). 266 *Independent*, 27 January 1996. Matthew D'Ancona also wrote in the *Sunday Telegraph* (28 January 1996) about the 'sweet role-reversal' enjoyed by the Ulster Unionists. 267 *Guardian*, 10 February 1996 and the *Economist*, 17 February 1996. 268 *Sunday Times*, 23 August 1981. 269 *Sunday Times*, 28 March 1993.

Like sections of the tabloid press and broadsheets including the *Daily Telegraph* and *Times*, the *Independent* became increasingly frustrated with the Anglo-Irish Agreement which, like most of Fleet Street, it had initially welcomed. In 1989, a leading article described the Hillsborough Accord as 'an agreement leading nowhere' and the following year its feelings towards the London-Dublin initiative hardened.[270] Following the deaths of four soldiers at Downpatrick, the *Independent* asserted:

> Until the British Government scraps the agreement and rules Northern Ireland as an integral part of the United Kingdom, it will prolong that uncertainty about the province's future which fuels IRA hopes.[271]

There has, therefore, been an increase in the level of the press's awareness of, and sympathy for, the unionist predicament, particularly in the 1990s. This has been reflected not only in the Tory tabloids but also in the leader columns of several broadsheets, even including those to the left of centre in their political outlook. However, it would be disingenuous to overstate the significance of this marginal shift in the tenor of press coverage. Earlier discussion indicated that castigation of mutual 'enemies' and support for mutual 'friends' did not spill over into a massive increase in political sympathy for unionism and 'Fleet Street' consistently supported government initiatives, which were in turn opposed by unionists. Rather what has occurred has been a probing by several broadsheets into what 'loyalism' entails in an attempt to redefine it. Although a number of papers came to rely less heavily on 'violence' stories and stereotypes, and presented a more sophisticated account of what was happening in Northern Ireland, widespread mainland apathy and ignorance about the conflict and the positions involved (notably the unionists) is testimony to the British press's failure to adequately explain the issues involved.

ANALYTICAL TELEVISION COVERAGE OF THE LOYALIST PERSPECTIVE

Introduction

The following section is an investigation into TV analysis of Northern Ireland in general and loyalism in particular, with emphasis on the documentaries and news 'magazine' programmes transmitted by the two leading commercial channels in the south-east, Thames and London Weekend Television (and particularly their respective leading programmes, *This Week* and *Weekend World*), from BBC1's top investigative documentary, *Panorama*, and Channel Four. These programmes and channels were chosen both for their reputation for having investigative tendencies, and also because they had the potential of reaching a considerable audience. Apart from providing the opportunity of gathering some quantitative evidence – I was interested in gauging the number of programmes with a strongly

270 *Independent*, 1 June 1989. 271 *Independent*, 11 April 1990.

'loyalist' input as a proportion of the overall total on Northern Ireland – this also enabled me to assess which aspects of loyalism were deemed to be important enough to be relayed to the nation.

A distinctive pattern emerged from my research into analytical coverage of the loyalist position. Firstly, there was the limited number of programmes devoted to the loyalist agenda, which in each case was roughly half of that afforded to the nationalists. There was also a similarity in their negative presentation of loyalism, with many programmes featuring loyalist intransigence and intimidation, and loyalists being depicted, time after time, as the chief stumbling-block on the road to progress. However, not all documentary coverage confined itself to stereotyping loyalism and the occasional *This Week* or *Panorama* edition attempted to probe deeper into the loyalist psyche.

London Weekend Television

For many years LWT's leading political discussion programme, 'Weekend World', was transmitted on Sunday, and Northern Ireland issues were covered periodically.[272] Like most weekly news programmes, *Weekend World* concentrated on running topical stories and its Northern Ireland news features tended to fall into that category. Therefore, programmes investigated an early IRA bombing campaign in London, the Birmingham bombings, the IRA ceasefire of 1975, the Peace Movement, the H Block hunger strike, the findings of the Irish Forum and the outcome of the Stalker-Sampson enquiry.[273] In the main they focused on factors influencing change in both political and security spheres, though other stories were featured. Between 1 October 1972 and 15 May 1988, 45 *Weekend World* editions relating to Northern Ireland were transmitted, with half of these (23) being relayed in the years of 'peak' violence (October 1972-end 1975).[274] Only 10 of the 45 programmes had a strong 'loyalist' input, compared with 19 which concentrated on the nationalist or republican perspectives, though inevitably there was an overlapping of outlooks in several of these editions. This nationalist dominance of *Weekend World* coverage clearly owed much to the IRA setting the agenda throughout most of the Troubles, a pattern which a weekly news programme would clearly feel obliged to follow. However, on those occasions when loyalists were perceived to be making the running – such as loyalist paramilitary activity in the mid 1970s and the Anglo-Irish Agreement protests during the late 1980s – these were also to be featured in *Weekend World*.

As with other news programmes, *Weekend World* editions stressed the ex-

272 *Weekend World*, whilst keen to probe and analyse issues, was very much a weekly news programme. Therefore, it lacked the scope for investigative documentary-style journalism, adopted by programmes such as *This Week* and *Panorama*. Although the number of features on Northern Ireland might appear large, it should be remembered that this figure encompassed a 16 year period, and most of the slots on Ulster did not constitute whole editions. 273 The transmission dates for these *Weekend World* programmes were 11 March 1973, 24 November 1974, 5 January and 16 February 1975, 28 November 1976, 17 May 1981, 6 May 1984, 25 January 1987 and 7 February 1988. 274 The full list of programme titles, transmission dates and summary of content can be found in my doctoral thesis, 'Loyal Rebels without a Cause?', op. cit.

treme positions adopted by loyalist leaders. One programme conducted a poll to 'test how much the Unionist Party has lost the support of voters' and also to ascertain 'who are the Protestant leaders who command the greatest support?'[275] A majority of loyalist voters (60%) were dissatisfied with the reforming tendencies which Unionist administrations had resorted to in the recent past, and Faulkner, still regarded by many at that time as a 'traditional' Unionist, proved to be the most popular of the Unionist leaders (he was first choice with 48% of the sample).[276] The chilling words of William Craig and the fear that they might precipitate a 'backlash' were also featured on *Weekend World*. Peter Jay based a report around the Vanguard leader's 'controversial' speech to the Monday Club in London and proceeded to discuss the implications of Craig's speech with 'a cross-section of Protestant opinion'.[277] Similar attention was concentrated on another 'extreme' loyalist leader, Ian Paisley, after Robert Bradford's assassination, when a feature entitled 'Paisley's Challenge – Unleashing Chaos', was transmitted.[278]

Expectations of the Protestant 'backlash' grew as the IRA's campaign intensified during the early 1970s and a couple of *Weekend World* editions reflected this concern. One programme highlighting the phenomenal growth of the UDA, profiled a maverick leader of that organisation, Davy Fogel and in the subsequent edition – which followed a week of prolonged rioting – Peter Jay asked 'is this the beginning of the Protestant backlash?'[279] Jay went to St Leonards Street in east Belfast, home of an UDA recruit who had just died in the violence and talked to his friends and neighbours. Jay's report contained the opinions of 37 people from the street who 'talked about the violence and what support there was among ordinary working people for the militant Protestant leaders'.[280] Another edition, thirteen years on, in the midst of loyalist agitation over the Hillsborough Agreement, observed not only the potentially catastrophic repercussions of sustained loyalist street violence, but also its comparative rarity:

> ... the relatively unusual phenomenon of Protestant rioting and intimidation could be of the greatest significance in the future. It is feared that if Protestant violence increases the province could plunge into a deepening spiral of conflict.[281]

Loyalist dissension and frustration over the workings of the Anglo-Irish Agreement were also emphasised in two other LWT programmes. Editions featuring the all-Ireland dimension of the agreement were transmitted towards the end of 1986 and in the second programme, which previewed the initial conference of British and Irish ministers, *Weekend World* interviewed Ian Paisley and assessed 'how far the Unionists would be prepared to go in their campaign and their chances of success'.[282]

275 *Weekend World*, 4 February 1973. **276** Ibid. **277** *Weekend World*, 22 October 1972. **278** *Weekend World*, 22 November 1981. **279** *Weekend World*, 4 February 1973 and 11 February 1973. **280** *Weekend World*, 11 February 1973, op. cit. **281** *Weekend World*, 6 April, 1986. **282** *Weekend World*, 10 November 1986 and 8 December1986.

Yet some positive images of unionism were also disseminated to the British public. The hopes that the 'sensible majority' would eventually replace the existing, stubborn leadership was a constant theme in British media analysis of the loyalist position (which was developed in the press section). Thus, following Ian Paisley's abortive strike in 1977, *Weekend World* adopted a different tack from *This Week*, which had given prominence to the 'depressing' indications that Paisley's popularity was intact, despite the strike debacle. Mary Holland's report from Carrickfergus, where she interviewed members of the local community, saw something 'positive' in the Protestant community's clear reluctance to participate in a 'political' strike.

> Does this apparent reluctance on the part of the Protestant majority to try to force a return to the Stormont system mean that there's a new opportunity for compromise in Northern Ireland?[283]

The following year, in an anniversary edition, 'Northern Ireland – 10 years on', the same reporter noted changes in loyalist thinking, particularly at grassroots level. In her report she interviewed loyalists with reputed paramilitary connections, including John McMichael, Tommy Lyttle and Glen Barr and concluded, 'it seems that there are some people still fighting for ways to reconcile the two communities in a federation or independence'.[284]

Undoubtedly LWT's main contribution to assessing the situation in Northern Ireland was its four part series, *From the Shadow of the Gun – The search for peace in Northern Ireland.*[285] This series focused mainly on attitudes to the conflict and claimed to be the first to test public opinion on hopes for peace in Northern Ireland, not just in the province, but also in Great Britain and the Irish Republic. The core of the series was, indeed, the findings of a MORI survey commissioned by LWT, from which 'some surprising and interesting findings emerged, especially within British opinion'.[286] The main conclusion to be drawn from the survey was that 'public will for a settlement based on compromise exists if the political will can be found'.[287]

In the first programme of the series, the survey's findings were analysed and it was claimed that British public opinion 'now has a more sophisticated grasp of the issues in Northern Ireland and that there is now majority support for co-operation with the Irish Republic in securing constitutional change'.[288] Subsequent programmes examined how attitudes within both communities in Northern Ireland had changed over the years and analysed the political options in favour at the time, and looking at the results of the survey in the Irish Republic, proceeded to argue that 'continuing commitment to Catholic values suggest that

283 *Weekend World*, 15 May 1977. 284 *Weekend World*, 11 June 1978. 285 LWT's *From the Shadow of the Gun* was transmitted during August and September 1984. 286 Fieldwork for the LWT/MORI survey was carried out between 10 and 14 May 1984. It was conducted among a representative quota sample of 1067 in Great Britain, 1028 in Northern Ireland and 1050 in the Irish Republic. 287 LWT, *From the Shadow of the Gun – the search for peace in Northern Ireland*, 1984. 288 *From the Shadow of the Gun*, 26 August 1984.

changes designed to make Protestants more at home in a united Ireland, will only come slowly'.[289] The final programme concentrated on 'exploring the scope for political progress in Northern Ireland' and went on to claim that 'new structures' which would be based on greater Anglo-Irish co-operation' could start 'the long process of reconciling the two communities'.[290]

The series' production team claimed that there were indications from their survey that mainland opinion was becoming 'more complex and sensitive', replacing the previous responses of 'impatience mixed with apathy'.[291] Northern Ireland was placed as the eighth most important national problem (out of a list of fifteen) and LWT argued that 'this finding contradicts what has become a general assumption about British public opinion on Northern Ireland; that it is largely ignored by the electorate and no longer considered of importance'.[292] Emphasising the comparatively high percentage of respondents wishing to see Northern Ireland remain in the United Kingdom (39% compared to 45% in favour of Irish unity), LWT admitted this trend 'might simply arise from a general perception in the population that Northern Ireland has been less troublesome in recent years'.[293] However, they conceded that the findings might also indicate a desire to be 'part of a move away from once-and-for-all measures towards a new preparedness to consider long term solutions based on a compromise between the nationalist and unionist traditions'.[294]

Although respondents were split on the issue of the government talking to Sinn Fein, a majority (61%) 'now believe the Republic should have a say in any constitutional change affecting Northern Ireland'.[295] Interestingly, British governments were not perceived to have been 'even-handed' in the treatment of the two communities. LWT's finding – that 33% felt British policy had favoured Protestants with only 6% believing policy had advantaged Catholics – not only challenged the view of successive governments that they had managed to be even-handed, but also that of the unionists who felt that *they* had been the losers, both in terms of political initiatives and security policy. Other intriguing findings included the increase in British respondents who believed that the border would eventually disappear (from 28% in 1978 to 46% in 1984) and the acceptance of a regional Assembly 'with special guarantees for Catholics' by 80% of Protestants.[296]

Thames Television

Thames, the leading commercial channel in the heavily-populated Home Counties region, made an influential contribution to news coverage of Northern Ireland and quickly earned itself a reputation for investigative journalism. Thames transmitted 67 programmes on the Northern Ireland question between 1969 and 1989 and the majority of these were shown on other ITV channels. Of the 47 Northern Ireland programmes made by the *This Week* team, only 11 were di-

289 *From the Shadow of the Gun*, 2 September 1984 and 9 December 1984. **290** *From the Shadow of the Gun*, 16 September 1984. **291** LWT, *From the Shadow of the Gun*, 1984. **292** Ibid. **293** Ibid. Note that a MORI poll in 1980 had found 50% in favour of breaking the link with Britain, compared with 29% who wished Northern Ireland to remain within the United Kingdom. **294** *From the Shadow of the Gun*, op. cit. **295** Ibid. **296** Ibid.

rectly concerned with the unionist community, with seventeen more related to nationalist/republican issues.[297] Of the thirteen programmes transmitted by the *TV Eye* team, three dealt with loyalist subjects, compared to six which focused on the smaller Catholic community. The programme total seems a large one and compares favourably with other ITV stations, but on closer inspection they illustrate the comparative lack of analytical coverage of Britain's most enduring domestic problem.[298] The total 'running' time for these programmes was under 35 hours, covering a twenty year period. The considerable gap between the volume of coverage devoted to the loyalist case (14 programmes), compared with the nationalist/republican perspective (23 editions) and the restricted range of themes treated in the minority of programmes which concentrated on the loyalist case, is reflected in the coverage of other TV programmes and stations.[299] It is important to investigate the main trends in Thames' coverage of Northern Ireland and to focus not only on the minority of editions dealing with 'loyalism', but also on those which conspicuously avoided unionism, concentrating instead on other dimensions of the conflict.

Thames' programmes on Ulster, produced by the *This Week* and *TV Eye* teams, combined a flair for investigative journalism (as indicated by programmes such as 'Inhuman and Degrading Treatment', 'Death on the Rock' and 'The Guildford Four') with programmes containing either a sprinkling of 'human interest' angles which would reflect the tastes of their targeted social groups. Therefore, the latter included controversial subjects such as the business ventures of the American businessman, John De Lorean ('De Lorean – the missing millions'), 'The Shergar Mystery' and 'Life Behind the Wire' and over half of their programmes on the conflict placed a high reliance on the conflict's backdrop of violence.[300]

Apart from the weekly editions of programmes such as *This Week* and *TV Eye*, Thames produced a major, highly-regarded series on the Northern Ireland conflict. The five part series, 'The Troubles', was transmitted in 1980/81, at a similar time to Robert Kee's series, 'Ireland', the only other in-depth series explaining the background to the conflict.[301] The strength of 'The Troubles', in contrast with the Kee's programmes, was its separate focus on the Ulster (as distinct from the wider Irish) conflict. Both series were attacked in Northern Ireland by the unionist community, and particularly the producers of 'The Trou-

297 The complete list of programmes can be found in my doctoral thesis, 'Loyal Rebels without a Cause?', op. cit. 298 They also indicate the lack of scope for analytical coverage, especially on commercial television, where there is the fundamental and ever-present need to maintain high viewing figures. 299 As with LWT, the number of programmes about 'loyalism' diminished as the Troubles progressed, with the majority (11) of the programmes (14) being transmitted betwen 1969 and 1981. 300 *TV Eye*, 'De Lorean – The Missing Millions', 8 March 1984, *TV Eye*, 'The Shergar Mystery', 3 March 1983 and *This Week*, 'Life Behind the Wire', 22 September 1977. 301 Thames, *The Troubles*, January/February, 1981, The five programmes in this series- produced by Richard Broad and Ian Stuttard – were 'Conquest' 'Partition', 'Legacy', 'Rebellion' and 'Deadlock'. It is an indictment on television production teams that there have only been these two in depth series explaining the historical and political complexities of the Irish conflict over a thirty year period.

bles', for an alleged 'pro-Catholic' bias. Much of the controversy centred on the fourth programme of the series which traced the development of the civil rights movement and the IRA.[302] Another predictably controversial episode was the final one, 'Deadlock', which looked at the post-1972 situation. The producers' depiction of the province was a refreshing change from the misconceptions of many on the mainland. In this edition they decided to portray Northern Ireland 'as it normally is – not erupting in smoke – but quiet, tense, socially deprived and mean – a province in a state of muted insurrection'.[303]

In the early part of the Troubles, *This Week* looked at the various political initiatives and hopes for a solution. This was less a feature of Thames coverage in the latter part of the 1970s and early 1980s when 'solutions' were increasingly regarded as 'remote'. *This Week* reflected the mainland mood of frustration with the Irish question as early as 1971, when they transmitted 'Ulster – what can we do?'[304] Subsequent editions focused on the run-up to the last days of Stormont and the commencement of direct rule, an assessment of the power-sharing period, and the political options on the eve of the Convention.[305] On the fifth anniversary of British military involvement in Northern Ireland, an 'unprecedented' *This Week 'Special'* looked retrospectively at the events of the previous five years and 'attempted to unravel the political and military complexities of the situation, by talking to the men whose decisions have influenced the course of the conflict over the last five years'.[306] The choice of 'influential' figures was an interesting one; those featured on the programme were William Whitelaw, Reginald Maudling, Lord Carrington, Terence O'Neill and Gerry Fitt.[307]

Inevitably, Thames devoted a lot of attention to the role of the army in Northern Ireland, particularly in the early stages of the conflict, when security casualties were mainly army personnel. *This Week's* first programme on the army's role, 'The Army in Ulster – Men in the Middle', was transmitted only weeks after their arrival on the Ulster streets.[308] John Edwards and his crew observed the lives of the army in Belfast and he told his viewers 'this programme is a profile of the work they are doing in this divided city'.[309] *This Week* returned to analysing the soldier's 'lot' towards the end of 1972 when they spoke to a cross-section of army personnel about a plethora of issues, ranging from troops' attitudes to the IRA, towards politicians dealing with the Northern Irish question, British opinion about their presence in the province and their feelings about having to face death on a daily basis.[310] At the end of the decade Thames turned its attention to 'soldier stress', and reported on the relatively low compensation received by injured soldiers.[311]

Public concern over army casualties was the impetus behind a number of

302 *The Troubles*, 'Rebellion', 26 January 1981. 303 *The Troubles*, 'Deadlock', 2 February 1981. 304 *This Week*, 'Ulster – What Can We Do?', 11 November 1971. 305 *This Week* editions covering these themes were 'Ulster - Day of Decision' (29 March 1971), 'The Price of Peace – The Protestants' (24 January 1974), 'The Choices for Ulster' (29 January 1976). 306 *This Week* 'Special, Ulster - Five Long Years', 12 August 1974. 307 Ibid. 308 *This Week*, 'The Army in Ulster – Men in the Middle' 18 September 1969. 309 Ibid. 310 *This Week*,' The Soldiers', 21 December 1972. 311 *TV Eye*, 'Soldiers under Stress', 12 April 1979.

programmes related to the issue of troop withdrawal. Most of this interest occurred in the pre-Ulsterisation period when the majority of casualties were soldiers, and Thames' interest in security force casualties declined in the 1980s (indeed, when attention did turn to attacks on the police, it was in the very different context of loyalist violence against the RUC). A 1972 *This Week* edition discussed an Opinion Research Centre poll which 'indicates for the first time that a majority of Britons feel the army should leave' and Jonathan Dimbleby's report featured Enoch Powell and Richard Crossman putting the case for and against troop involvement.[312] The following summer Peter Taylor put the spotlight on the concerns of relatives of troops serving in Ulster.[313] A soldier's mother, Peggy Charlton, aimed to raise 20,000 signatures requesting the withdrawal of troops from Northern Ireland (one for every soldier serving in the province at that time). In fact she collected more than twice this number and Taylor's report portrayed an interesting contrast between the desire of non-combatants for 'the boys to be brought home' and that of the soldiers themselves (including Peggy Charlton's son), who maintained that such gestures only 'played into the hands of the IRA'.[314]

A criticism of *This Week* and programmes emanating from other commercial television companies (such as Granada and Yorkshire TV) is that their programmes not only concentrated more on one community (also featuring more on 'ordinary' and 'respectable' members of that community), but that the issues which were spotlighted and the language used by reporters tended to be more sympathetic to the nationalist case than the unionist one.[315] Therefore, there was little coverage of Protestant disillusionment at grassroots level and few illustrations of the effects of republican violence on Protestant victims. Indeed, even in a unique case where Protestants had apparently themselves been victims of the legal system, Thames was silent.[316] On the other hand, its treatment of the killing of three IRA members in Gibraltar in 1988 was pivotal in fuelling disquiet in political and media circles.[317] A follow-up programme, taking the form of an 'enquiry' into the findings of the Windlesham Report, was transmitted the following year.[318] Thames looked at other issues which were well up the republican agenda. These included 'critical insights' into the 'supergrass' system, an indictment of the methods used in the RUC holding-centre at Castlereagh, in Belfast and in their programme which followed the acquittal of the Guildford Four, where Thames asked if the result had been 'a triumph or a disgrace for British justice'?[319]

312 *This Week*, 'Should we leave Ireland to the Irish?' 5 October 1972. 313 *This Week*,' Why don't we bring the boys home?', 21 June 1973. 314 Ibid. 315 For instance, several of Yorkshire Television's *First Tuesday* documentaries on Northern Ireland during the 1980s dealt with nationalist issues such as the Guildford Four ('A Case that won't go away', 1 March 1987 and 'The Guildford Time Bomb', 1 July 1986), the Maguire Seven ('Aunt Annie's Bomb Factory'), 6 March 1984 and the use of plastic bullets by the security forces ('Who Killed Norah McCabe?'), 4 December 1984. 316 The case I'm referring to, that of the Armagh Four, has already been examined. 317 *This Week*, 'Death on the Rock', 28 April 1988. In his controversial programme, producer Roger Bolton asked the central questions; 'The deaths of 3 IRA terrorists have created world-wide controversy. Were they gunned down because lives were at risk? Or were the deaths a result of a shoot-to-kill policy?' 318 *This Week*, 'Death on the Rock - The Enquiry', 26 January 1989. 319 *TV Eye*,' The Year of the Informer', 25

One of Thames' best-received programmes on Northern Ireland was 'Creggan', a 1979 insight into the lives of people living on the Catholic Creggan estate in Derry.[320] The documentary adopted a fly-on-the-wall approach and presented external audiences with a fascinating insight into the lives of working class people in that city. The producers' intentions to focus on everyday life were clear.

> Beyond the familiar scenes of violence and the rhetoric of the politicians, what has been happening to the ordinary people who have had to cope with the situation day by day? How do they view their experiences over the past 10 years and more?[321]

An interesting feature of Holland's low-key, non-critical contributions was her almost reverential portrayal of Junoesque, Catholic women. By confining their depiction of the trials and tribulations of Ulster's working class to one community, Thames consolidated the impression that Catholics experienced a monopoly of suffering, both in terms of economic deprivation and the daily threat of violence.[322] Indeed, it had not been the first time that Thames had featured the opinions of Derry Catholics. *This Week* had talked to 'the bitter people of the Bogside' shortly after Bloody Sunday in 1972, and the programme was to return to the same area in 1977, when it observed 'there are few signs of optimism in Derry'.[323] The perspectives of the Catholic community at large (as distinct from those of their political representatives) had also been sought by Thames crews in west Belfast in 1974 when there was a programme on life in the Divis Flats and also in the wake of the particularly gruesome killing of two soldiers in Anderstown.[324] Even the selection of a predominantly nationalist town such as Strabane to illustrate the inter-relationship of economic deprivation and political extremism would have had the effect of reinforcing the impression of 'Catholic-only' deprivation, although an earlier *This Week* had looked at the effect of unemployment on both Catholic and Protestant families in Belfast.[325]

Programmes fostering empathy with Protestants, particularly working class ones were comparatively rare, with most of the Thames editions on the loyalist position concentrating on the harsher images of intransigent unionist politicians and shadowy paramilitary spokesmen. However, there was the occasional effort to foster empathy between the mainland audience and ordinary people in Northern Ireland. *This Week*'s John Edwards, visiting Belfast after the post-internment

November 1982, *This Week*, 'Inhuman and Degrading Treatment', 27 October 1977 and *This Week*, 'The Guildford Four', 19 October 1989. **320** *Thames*, 'Creggan', 1979, (exact date of transmission unavailable). **321** Ibid. **322** Mary Holland belatedly endeavoured to address the balance fifteen years later in her Channel Four documentary, 'Shankill' (see later). **323** *This Week*, 'Aftermath of Bloody Sunday' 3 February 1972 and *This Week*, 'Derry-Time To Remember', 3 February 1977. **324** *This Week*, 'The Price of Peace – the Catholics', 31 January 1974 and *This Week*, 'Weekend in Belfast', 7 April 1988. **325** *This Week*, 'Remember Strabane', 11 April 1974 and *This Week*, 'Unemployment in Northern Ireland', March 1970, (exact date not in records).

riots, tried to place the conflict within the realms of experience of the mainland audience.

> What is life like for the bus driver, the housewife, the OAP – the ordinary decent people – in the middle of the violence? How threatened are the suburbs as the IRA campaign spreads out to the homes of the affluent middle class? And what do families who have decided to emigrate feel about the city they are leaving?[326]

The following year *This Week* took their empathy theme a stage further when they asked the proverbial bus-driver (albeit from Hull and not Clapham!) to experience what life was like on the streets of Belfast. Tom Edmondson and his wife Doris (who had never been further than York on a day trip) visited Belfast for a week in the spring of 1972. Before visiting Belfast, Tom, in conversation with his colleagues at Hull bus depot, had advocated early troop withdrawal.

Peter Taylor and the *This Week* team claimed that the edition asked 'some of the questions that ordinary people always ask about Ulster and films the reaction of Tom and Doris to the conflict in the province'.[327] The Hull couple were exposed to a variety of 'Belfast experiences', as Taylor's report filmed their amazement at the army activity in the streets (Doris, in a disbelieving voice, said 'you've got to see it to believe it!'), their conversation with ardent republicans, and caught on camera their chats with a young soldier, a reticent policeman and a couple of street urchins on the Peace Line. The ultimate experience in empathy was when Tom met a fellow bus-driver on the Turf Lodge route, and Edmondson was astonished to discover that a bus he had recently been driving, had been hijacked. It was the locals' everyday experiences of violence which surprised Tom and Doris the most. Witnessing the cleaning-up after a Co-op store had been bombed Tom observed, 'They're resigned to it these people – they're just wondering where the next one's coming from'.[328]

The Edmondsons' trip to Belfast coincided with the two day strike called by Vanguard in protest at the suspension of Stormont. Although Tom's enquiry 'if you're British why don't you want to be ruled by Britain?' met with a brusque response from a couple of passing Craig supporters, the Edmondsons were visibly impressed by the vast crowd's patriotic singing of the national anthem.[329] Despite their inevitable confusion over loyalists' identity, they felt more sympathetic to the opinions of ordinary, law-abiding citizens and had, by the end of the programme, reversed their position regarding the role of the army in the province. Whilst on the surface a rare propaganda 'victory' for the province's 'silent majority', the programme was more valuable in providing a clear insight into what life was like at a very difficult time, for ordinary people in Northern Ireland.

With the exception of 'No Surrender', virtually all of the *This Week* editions, to varying degrees, presented loyalists in an unfavourable light. By selecting the

326 *This Week*, 'Belfast – Time to Move'? 30 September 1971. 327 *This Week*,' Busman's Holiday', 6 April 1972. 328 Ibid. 329 Ibid.

more melodramatic and easily dismissed images of loyalism – strutting Orangemen, the perenially fiery Ian Paisley and intimidatory strike-organisers, Thames undermined the fears and aspirations of Northern Ireland's majority community.

Intimidatory tactics was another feature of loyalism which caught the attention of Thames journalists.[330] 'Intimidation' focused on 'the new spate of sectarian murder, threats to Ulster's workers and an unprecedented petrol-bomb campaign on homes' and, forecasting a 'stepping-up' of violence in the run-up to the first anniversary of the Anglo-Irish Agreement, asked the question, 'are the politicians of the streets taking over?'[331] *TV Eye* had looked at the intimidatory tactics of some loyalists a few months previously, specifying attacks 'on over 250 police homes'.[332] Peter Gill argued that these assaults were 'part of a campaign to force the British government to abandon the Anglo-Irish Agreement'.[333] Noting that the violence emanated from 'the Protestant community to which most of them (the RUC) belong', Gill posed the basic question, 'will the intimidation campaign work?'[334] Thames had also analysed previous examples of less covertly-organised loyalist violence. In 1972 Peter Taylor watched a group of UDA men drilling and establishing a no-go area in Belfast. Taylor emphasised the new phenomenon of loyalists preparing to 'take on' the British Army and articulated a common British concern at that time.

> It is the first time the Protestants have challenged the British army openly on the streets and it could mean that Mr William Whitelaw will face not only the IRA but military action from Protestants who feel that too many concessions have been given to the Catholics since he took over responsibility for Northern Ireland.[335]

Thames, like other media agencies, reflected the deep divisions within unionism. An early *This Week* edition, 'Ulster: the Power Game', contained interviews with premier Terence O'Neill and the 'two powerful ex-Ministers' Brian Faulkner and William Craig, and Llew Gardner's in-depth report covered 'the activities of the three separate factions of dissident Unionists'.[336] Five years later *This Week* returned to a similar theme when they interviewed loyalist grassroot supporters on the Shankill Road in Belfast. On this occasion the interviewees spoke of Faulkner's 'betrayal' in joining the power-sharing experiment and Peter Taylor, appreciating the irony in Faulkner's unpopularity, posed the question, 'can Brian Faulkner survive the attacks of the Protestant hard-liners, the people from whom he has drawn so much of his support in the past?'[337]

Divisions in the loyalist ranks over the question of a second general strike,

330 Interestingly, this characteristic was less frequently associated with the IRA, who were perceived by many in the media to enjoy at least the acquiescence of many in the Catholic community. 331 *This Week*,' Intimidation', 11 September 1986. 332 *TV Eye*, 'The Thin Green Line', 24 April 1986. 333 Ibid. 334 Ibid. 335 *This Week*, 'Ulster – The Protestants Say No Go!', 25 May 1972. 336 *This Week*, 'Ulster: The Power Game', 6 February 1969. 337 *This Week*, 'The Price of Peace: the Protestants', 24 January 1974.

called by Ian Paisley in 1977, were also featured by *This Week*. 'The Ulster Strike' took the form of a debate on the 'wisdom' in organising such a stoppage.[338] Loyalist lack of unity on the issue was noted by Peter Taylor,

> The strike, now in its third day, has polarised the Protestant community of Ulster, and while its success rests in the balance, this discussion reveals the depth of feeling on both sides.[339]

Another programme was centred around unionist disharmony, though in this case the rationale for doing so was rather suspect. William Craig's personal decision to opt for a 'temporary' sharing of power with Catholic representatives was never likely to get widespread support from his Unionist coalition partners and indeed, led to his comparatively rapid political demise. *This Week* were somewhat optimistic in reporting that there was 'some hope that an agreement could be reached about power-sharing'.[340]

Undoubtedly the Thames programme which came closest to making a fair and accurate assessment of the loyalist predicament was *This Week's* 'No Surrender'.[341] John Taylor's forthright, searching report probed far beyond the stereotypical images of unionist bigotry and intransigence and managed to convey the changing fortunes and predicament of unionists in the post-Hillsborough period. Taylor had in the introduction to his report, emphasised the 'plight' of the Ulster Unionists, and how they earnestly believed their freedom was being 'threatened' by the Anglo-Irish Agreement. In this manner, 'No Surrender' was reassessing loyalism's triumphalist image and was suggesting that feelings of fear and anxiety were now at the heart of loyalist sentiment. In his introduction Taylor noted:

> Today there is a large group of loyal British citizens who claim they're being betrayed by Mrs Thatcher's government, who fear the Prime Minister wants to hand them over to what they regard as a foreign power ... Ulster's largest community feels besieged, under attack from terrorism, ignored by their government.[342]

Taylor highlighted growing loyalist concern over security and noted the increase in terrorist activity since Hillsborough, particularly in the border areas. Observing that the IRA 'had murdered 28 Protestants in Fermanagh and South Tyrone in the past three years', he attempted to explain the rationale behind the IRA's targeting of Protestants in what he called 'the front line'.

> There are many farms along the frontier which have stood empty for years, some long since abandoned by their owners. It's claimed the bombings and the shootings are part of a systematic and deliberate IRA campaign against

338 *This Week*, 'The Ulster Strike', 5 May 1977. 339 Ibid. 340 *This Week*, 'Ulster – The Loyalists Say No!', 18 September 1975. 341 *This Week*, 'No Surrender', 10 November 1988. 342 Ibid.

> the Loyalist community, designed to force them off their land and undermine the significance of the border ... The headstones in the border cemeteries bear grim testimony to the losses that the Protestant community has suffered.[343]

'No Surrender' also pinpointed a fundamental change in the Unionists' political position which had been a direct consequence of the 1985 Agreement. With the emphasis being switched from Belfast and London to Dublin and London, it became apparent to many unionists 'for the first time since the founding of the state' that Protestants 'did not have an effective veto on political change'.[344] Towards the end of the programme Taylor delivered an exposition of the predicament facing unionists. Despite a modicum of sympathy for their dilemma, *This Week* remained in harness with the mainstream media view that unionists were unable or unwilling to make necessary policitical compromises.

> Coming in from the cold presents Unionists with a difficult dilemma. They are unprepared or unable to concede much, yet they are faced with the British Government, which is prepared to hold the line. In reality, what Unionists appear to be offering is more of the same ... There are hard decisions ahead for Ulster's Protestant population, but they say they will never bargain their loyalty to the Crown. That can never be surrendered. In the strength of that belief lies both their triumph and their tragedy.[345]

BBC 1 – Panorama

Perhaps the flagship of all current affairs programmes is 'Panorama' which has been making investigative programmes for transmission on BBC1 for nearly forty years. Northern Ireland has been a perennial subject for *Panorama* editors and its endless nuances in the political and security spheres have provided *Panorama* teams with numerous opportunities for investigative journalism. However, the prolonged tedious nature of the Irish Troubles and their soporific effect on the British viewing public is reflected in the downward spiral trend of *Panorama's* Northern Ireland coverage over the 25 year period investigated. Nearly two thirds of *Panorama* editions on Northern Ireland between December 1968 and February 1995 (47 out of 71) were transmitted in the period between 1968 and 1982, with 24 programmes going out between 1983 and 1995.[346] This decline in coverage is also true of programmes related specifically to the 'loyalist' position, with half of these (7) being transmitted inside the first four years of the Troubles.[347]

Panorama chose not to follow an equal allocation of time approach to its coverage of the perspectives of the two main communities in Northern Ireland. Consequently, of the 71 *Panorama* editions which concentrated on Northern Ire-

343 Ibid. 344 Ibid. 345 Ibid. 346 The high number of programmes is, in part, attributable to the structure of the programme in the 1960s and part of the 1970s, when up to three stories might have been contained in a single edition. *Panorama* has, for a considerable period, offered a single in-depth story. 347 For the full *Panorama* programme summary, see 'Loyal Rebels without a Cause?', op. cit.

land during the 26 year period, only 14 dealt in detail with 'loyalist' issues, whilst 26 programmes had a 'strongly nationalist' focus.[348] In addition to the 26 programmes on the Catholic community, there were a number of other editions which featured issues well up the republican agenda.[349] This was partly a reflection of the fact that for most of the conflict the Catholic community in general and the IRA in particular, dictated the pace of events and the Protestants, particularly after direct rule in 1972, mainly reacted to them. It was inevitable that an investigative, probing programme such as *Panorama* would, by focusing on alleged state 'misdemeanours', bypass loyalists who were unlikely to be involved in such activity. The results of this imbalance of treatment are perhaps even more significant than the justification of such apparent inequity. With politicians and media responding in the main to the grievances and military actions of nationalists and republicans, issues affecting unionists received less attention, both at Westminster and in the British media. Therefore, the issues which were closest to Protestant thinking, such as the undermining of their continued electoral successes and their right to express claims to self-determination, as well as their frustration at, what appeared to them, to be a paucity of concern or sympathy over their suffering at the hands of terrorists, tended either to be ignored or understated on programmes like *Panorama*. A consequence of the media's ignoring the loyalist case was that Protestants retreated further into their bunkers, their marginalisation and intransigence growing at the same time as any hope of the media facilitating an improved understanding of their case, eroded.

Not surprisingly perhaps, a large number of *Panorama* editions focused on the activities of the army in Northern Ireland. There was, however, a distinct change in the nature of their coverage over the years. In the early stages of the conflict, a number of *Panorama* reports empathised, in the main, with the predicament of British soldiers as they patrolled the streets and countryside, endeavouring to defuse bombs and remove barricades.[350] During the last decade in particular, *Panorama* mirrored the concern of other investigative programme-makers over British 'excesses' in Ulster, including the alleged 'shoot-to-kill' policy of the security forces, both in Northern Ireland and elsewhere. By concentrating on incidents allegedly involving security forces members in Northern Ireland, *Panorama*'s editors failed to pay sufficient attention to the inability of those legitmate forces to protect ordinary law-abiding citizens from the attacks of illegitimate forces.[351]

348 The 'strongly nationalist' total did not include a large number of programmes which looked at the position of the government of the Irish Republic. Inevitably, there was a 'cross-over' in coverage with nationalist-unionist issues being covered in lesser detail within the same edition. Indeed, in some of the 'loyalism' programmes, other perspectives were assessed, although the unionist one was the single most important item. 349 This included *Panorama* editions, 'Supergrasses' (24 October 1983) and 'Justice Under Fire', (12 November 1984). 350 *Panorama*, 'British troops in Northern Ireland' (17 November 1969), 'Army in Ulster' (22 March 1971), 'A Weekend spent on patrol with 'D' Company, 2nd Battalion Paratroop Regiment' (16 August 1971),' Belfast Bombs', (11 October 1971) and 'The Invasion of the Bogside' (31 July 1972). 351 *Panorama*, 'Stalker – Coincidence or Conspiracy?' (16 June 1986), 'The position of the SAS and Security Forces under the Law in Northern Ireland in the light of the

Seventeen programmes were based directly around the activities of the IRA.[352] These included two profiles of Gerry Adams, five editions on the hunger strike and 'dirty' protest, the politicisation of the IRA and the government's secret talks with Sinn Fein.[353] Only two programmes looked directly at the effects of the IRA campaign against ordinary people and one of those concentrated on Warrington.[354] The effect of this 'selective rejection' by *Panorama* (and other) editors was that the feelings and frustrations of those exposed to the terrorist campaign were underplayed at the expense of wider human rights issues (though even these were far from multi-faceted in their composition) and consequently misunderstood by the British public.[355] Other *Panorama* 'Irish' angles included the effect of the violence on the region's economy, the attitudes of the Irish government and people to events in the North, and the hopes, futile as they might have seemed, of Northern Irish moderates and peace-lovers.[356]

With the occasional, albeit distinguished, exception, the majority of *Panorama*'s comparatively limited coverage of the loyalist case, has fallen into the mainstream framework of the national media's coverage of events in Northern Ireland. Therefore *Panorama* focused on unionism's violent fringe, the internal divisions within unionism, the possibility of loyalists making political compromise and the way in which they were consistently outmanoeuvred by nationalists.[357] Thus, in a 1972 edition, which followed in the wake of Bloody Sunday and a

Gibraltar Shootings' (17 October 1988), 'Ulster's Regiment – A Question of Loyalty?' (19 February 1990), 'Lethal Force' (22 July 1991) and 'The Trial of Private Clegg' (6 February 1995). **352** This total was, therefore, in itself, greater than the number of programmes afforded to the 'loyalist position. It also doesn't take into account other programmes which had smaller republican input. **353** *Panorama*, 'Gerry Adams – The Provos Politician' (22 November 1982) and 'Gerry Adams: The Man We Love to Hate' (30 January 1995); 'H Blocks – The Propaganda Prison' (12 February 1979), 'The British Government's Attitude to the Hunger Strike in the Maze Prison' (1 June 1981), 'A Time to Compromise – the Hunger Strike' (20 July 1981), 'The Fermanagh by Election' (17 August 1981), 'The Provos Last Card' (21 September 1981), 'Summit in the Shadow of the Gun' (23 September 1985) and 'The Irish Peace Talks' (29 November 1993). **354** *Panorama*, 'The Politics of Violence' (5 December 1983) and 'An Ordinary Boy – Colin and Wendy Parry go on a Journey to Ireland and Boston to try to understand why their child was taken from them' (6 September 1993). **355** BBC1 continues to be selective in its analytical coverage of the Irish situation. Peter Taylor's relatively sympathetic portrait of the IRA ('Provos', shown on BBC1 between 21 September and 12 October 1997, and coinciding with the opening of political negotiations in Belfast) illustrates that broadcasters still believe Sinn Fein/IRA to be the central key to an Irish solution. Thus, there was no corresponding analytical series, or even a 'one-off' documentary on unionism's historical development, or position, on any national channel. **356** *Panorama*, 'Britain's Wasteland' (14 March 1983), 'An Interview with Jack Lynch on the IRA' (1 March 1971), 'A Profile of Jack Lynch' (5 February 1973), 'The Irish Dimension' (interestingly, this specially-commissioned poll cast doubt on Irish premier Lynch's call for the British to withdraw from the North, with only 15% of Irish pollsters thinking that a united Ireland was desirable in the short term (8 May 1978), 'Irish Security – The Role of the Irish Army' (3 September 1979), and 'What are they Talking About?' (30 March 1981); 'Ulster Moderates' (20 April 1970) and 'Ulster Peace People' (11 October 1976). **357** *Panorama* programmes on these themes included editions featuring loyalist paramilitary activity such as 'Northern Ireland Truce' (26 June 1972), 'Events in Northern Ireland Since Bloody Friday' (24 July 1972) and 'The Rising Tension in east Belfast between the Army and the UDA' (23 October 1972); tension within unionism, illustrated

Newry Civil Rights march – 'two rather stunning victories', in propaganda terms, for Catholics who 'are making the running and putting the pressure on London' – reporter Alan Hart noted the increasing marginalisation of unionists who were 'alone in seeing no purpose for any new initiative from London at this time'.[358]

Unfortunately *Panorama* was not above utilising the Protestant community as a convenient scapegoat for the lack of political progress in Northern Ireland. Following the abortive Brooke talks in 1991, John Ware's report, 'No Surrender – No Progress', alleged that it had been the unionists who had 'killed' the talks and had therefore been responsible for scuppering an 'historic opportunity to resolve one of Europe's most ancient quarrels'.[359] Ware rekindled a timeworn mainland perception that loyalists were the chief stumbling-block to progress.

> Many have wearied of trying to comprehend the fixation of Loyalists with their 300 year old triumphs over Catholics and there's exasperation at the defiance of Unionists, whose abiding fear of Catholic domination has led them to undermine talks of a political settlement.[360]

Although he conceded that the SDLP had maintained 'a lofty silence' during the talks, Ware noticed that Unionists 'blame everyone but themselves' for the failure of the talks, in stark contrast to the opinion polls which he suggested demonstrated that 'it is the Unionists that people mostly blame'.[361] Ware's conclusion was that unionism's lack of modernity would relegate Ulster Protestants even further to the political sidelines.

> Older Unionists may choose to go on marching to the sound of former glories, but the longer they refuse to cast themselves in a modern mould, the more likely the future of Northern Ireland will be determined without them.[362]

One of the themes of *Panorama*'s coverage of Ulster loyalism was their portrayal of unionists as 'villains', either as shadowy figures in the terrorist 'underworld', liaising with other undesirable international groups, or as ill-disciplined members of the province's security forces. One such edition was 'Allies in Arms', which presented a fascinating account of loyalist paramilitary links with a sympathetic foreign government.[363] The report concentrated on 'the links between South African arms procurement agency Armscor and the Ulster Resistance Protestant paramilitary group', and investigated both the intricate arms network established by these two diverse groups and also looked at the possible involvement of 'respectable' loyalist agenies in such shady dealings.[364] Early in the programme, reporter Robin Denselow stressed the 'remarkable' nature of this covert liaison

by programmes such as 'Can the Government and Prime Minister Chichester-Clark survive?' (9 February 1970); the possibility of unionist compromise, featured in editions such as 'Belfast Loyalists' (6 October 1975) and 'The Long Peace' (13 June 1988). **358** *Panorama*, 'Mr Heath's Next Move: From the Protestant Point of View' (7 February 1972). **359** *Panorama*, 'No Surrender – No Progress', 21 October 1991. **360** Ibid. **361** Ibid. **362** Ibid. **363** *Panorama*, 'Allies in Arms', 11 December 1989. **364** Ibid.

between a foreign government and 'a shadowy paramilitary organisation in Northern Ireland'.[365] Perhaps in an attempt to make such a liaison appear more feasible, *Panorama* stressed the support of several prominent loyalist leaders (such as the Rev. Ian Paisley) for 'a Protestant people's army' (Ulster Resistance).[366]

An interesting dimension of Denselow's report was his suggestion that the links between the groups were, on reflection, 'not so remarkable' and he proceeded to compare 'the embattled nature of white South Africans' with the siege mentality of Ulster Loyalists.[367] Intermixing footage of Orangemen celebrating in Northern Ireland with that of cattle-driving Boers in the Orange Free State, *Panorama* made a clear parallel between the 'redneck' mentality of white South Africans and the siege mentality of Ulster's Loyalists. In so doing, Denselow's report emphasised the dearth of international support for the latter group, reinforcing the belief that their cause lacked both creditibility and respectability.[368] By overstressing the 'mutual friendship' theme, the programme underestimated the mutual interest factor in such an arms venture. *Panorama* did mention the potential of such a deal for the groups involved but tended to place it within the broader framework of a shared philosophy and fraternity. David McKittrick highlighted the underlying motive of self interest.

> Had the whole conspiracy succeeded South Africa could have obtained the latest in British military technology while extreme loyalists could, for the first time, have come to rival the IRA in terms of weaponry.[369]

Another example of *Panorama* spotlighting unionists as the 'villains' and scapegoating them for the province's problems was their programme on the future of the Ulster Defence Regiment. *Panorama*, in its own synopsis of 'Ulster's Regiment – a question of loyalty', implied that collusion between members of the locally-recruited security forces and loyalist paramilitaries was a significant factor in the increased level of violence,

> Last August Catholic Loughlin Maginn became Northern Ireland's 2744th murder victim. *Panorama* reveals disturbing evidence that it is leaks from within the locally recruited UDR that are the source of such killings.[370]

John Ware's report presented a number of cases where Catholics had been abused by individual UDR members and showed a notebook containing the names and personal details of 281 republican suspects which allegedly had been passed on by a UDR member to the loyalist paramilitaries. 'Ulster's Regiment' also featured an interview with a former UDR member, turned UVF terrorist, who claimed that the organisations were 'the two sides of the same coin', and con-

365 Ibid. 366 Ibid. 367 Ibid. 368 The 'close historical ties between the two countries' was, according to Denselow, personified by the role of Armscor agent, Dick Wright, a native of County Armagh and uncle of leading Ulster Resistance member, Alan Wright. 369 D. McKittrick, *Despatches from Belfast* (Belfast 1989), p. 169. 370 *Panorama*, 'Ulster's Regiment – A Question of Loyalty', 19 February 1990.

tained another claim by Catholic priest Denis Faul that at least 120 UDR men had been involved in 'serious crimes' over a 20 year period.[371]

The effects of the programme were quite profound and far-reaching. As Chris Ryder observed in his book about the regiment, the *Panorama* programme 'contributed more doubts about the internal culture of the UDR and both its willingness and ability to meet the standards of behaviour and impartiality which it publicly proclaimed for itself'.[372] The appearance of Irish Foreign Minister Gerry Collins on the programme, where he called for the 'phasing out' of the regiment, added fuel to the demands for the disbandonment of the force and highlighted the rift between the two governments on the regiment's future.[373] The effects of such a damning indictment of the regiment on an influential TV programme as *Panorama* were immeasurable and certainly contributed to the government's decision in July 1992 to create a new Royal Irish Regiment by amalgamating the Ulster Defence Regiment and the Royal Irish Rangers. The programme also augmented the belief of many unionists that yet again the media was conducting a witch-hunt against them and was enjoying the ready ear of the British government.

Another controversial, 'no punches pulled' investigative *Panorama* edition was John Ware's 'The Dirty War'.[374] The substance of Ware's argument was that British army intelligence failed to pass on to the RUC information from an ex-loyalist terrorist, Brian Nelson, which detailed plans to target Republicans. *Panorama* claimed that 'the activities of the military (in denying the RUC information) amount to the biggest intelligence scandal in two decades of counter terrorism'.[375] Although it had been British military agencies which had been the central target for criticism in the programme, the fact that there was more than a hint of collusion between British military and loyalist terrorists presented a far from accurate picture of British security forces siding with one of the main paramilitary groupings in Northern Ireland. The logical conclusion of such a line of argument was that the two sides (army and loyalist paramilitaries) were fighting a common enemy and that the security forces treated them with 'kid gloves'. However, the opposite was the case, with a far greater proportion of loyalist terrorists being prosecuted than republican ones.

With unionists clearly labelled as 'intransigent' from an early stage in the conflict, any signs of compromise on their part (remote as they might have seemed) were deemed worthy of a documentary feature.[376] Such was the case with *Panorama*'s 1975 edition, 'Belfast Loyalists', in which Michael Charlton asked of unionists' reticence to power-sharing, 'will that hard line hold or is there the chance

371 Ibid. 372 C. Ryder, *The Ulster Defence Regiment – An Instrument of Peace?* (London 1991), p. 240. 373 Ulster's Regiment, op. cit. 374 *Panorama*, 'The Dirty War', 8 June 1992. 375 Ibid. 376 Other programmes which adopted an optimistic approach towards the possibilities of loyalists modifying their attitudes were 'The Long Peace' (13 June 1988) which reported on 'possible signs of a tentative solution to the Troubles as Northern Unionists begin talking to Dublin', whilst David Lomax wrote in the *Listener* (26 March 1987) of 'a breeze of change in the province' (this was a summary of his *Panorama* edition, 'Northern Ireland – The Troubled Peace', which was transmitted on 23 March 1987).

of a Loyalist compromise?'[377] The BBC's timing and cautious optimism are of interest. Curiously they chose to transmit this programme, with its comparatively upbeat mood regarding the possibility of a loyalist compromise, during a time of great unionist division and prior to a Vanguard meeting on the question of power-sharing (at which the party gave support to William Craig's conversion to power-sharing).[378] Michael Charlton detected signs of hope in the working class loyalist areas of Belfast and postulated that this might grow amidst the ongoing 'haemorrhaging' of unionism. Charlton argued:

> There is hope of new initiatives across bitter defences of the sectarian divide, for out of working class Belfast in recent weeks has come a significant gesture – a signal that some sections of the hardline believe they can adapt themselves to the new reality.[379]

Yet Charlton did not underestimate the strength of traditional unionism in their opposition to power-sharing. In his portrait of Alistair Black, a Co. Armagh headmaster and Vanguard member, Charlton admitted that, for many Protestants, the basic values and instincts remained intact. In the shadow of Carson's statue at Stormont, Charlton reiterated the 'no change' dimension of unionism:

> On the lawns of Stormont, Carson – their fanatical violent champion – gestures hypnotically as though commanding the seas to go back. He it was who demonstrated that the strongest weapon Ulster's Loyalists possess is their intransigence ... Now 60 years later with the same blend of defiance and morbid distrust of Westminster's intentions, Alistair Black is one of those organising Protestant Ulster to meet what he sees as the same old challenge and in the same old way.[380]

Perhaps the edition which came closest to unfathoming the esoteric nature of the loyalist psyche was Gavin Hewitt's 1986 report, 'The Loyalist of Ulster'.[381] In emphasising the all-embracing character of unionist resistance, Hewitt noted how the 'high risk strategy' implicit in the Hillsborough Accord 'touches on the Protestants' rawest nerve – betrayal by the English'.[382] The *Panorama* team covered a wide range of loyalist opinion. Hewitt spoke to Ballylumford power workers in Islandmagee, a workforce which had been instrumental in bringing down the Executive in 1974 and observed how they felt 'deeply mistrustful of the Brit-

377 *Panorama*, 'Belfast Loyalists - The Possibilities of a Compromise over Power-Sharing', 6 October 1975. 378 The selection by the media of certain stories (and indeed, their rejection of many others) has not always been easy to understand and it is intriguing that a number of the big stories involving the loyalist community (such as unionist reaction to the abolition of Stormont in 1972 and the UWC Strike in 1974)did not receive the degree of analytical coverage which they warranted, whilst others, including comparatively minor shifts within loyalism (such as the growing support for power-sharing within Vanguard) did receive documentary treatment. 379 *Panorama*, 'Belfast Loyalists', op. cit. 380 Ibid. 381 *Panorama*,' The Loyalists of Ulster – A People in Torment', 10 February 1986. 382 Ibid.

ish government'.[383] He also visited Fermanagh, a county where nearly sixty had been killed since the start of the Troubles, interviewing a part-time soldier and a security force widow who felt that her husband 'had died in vain'.[384] Hewitt noted the great support amongst the Protestant rural working class for the Ulster Clubs which, he argued, envisaged 'a popular uprising', believing that their popularity in such areas as Fermanagh owed much to 'the repressed anger of 17 years of troubles which show no sign of ending'.[385]

The isolation felt by the RUC during this period of loyalist resistance, was also spotlighted in this edition. Hewitt spoke to police representatives who told of the anxiety felt by their members in the wake of the Portadown riots where 53 officers had been injured. He maintained that the marching season later that year would be seen as 'a major test of wills between the Protestants and the government', with the police knowing they would end up 'in the middle'.[386] Hewitt concluded his report by stressing 'the contradiction that tears at the souls' of Protestants.

> The Protestants are on the march, but their destination is unclear. They face a difficult choice; if they rebel they might well weaken what they desire most; if they accept the Irish having a say in their affairs, they believe the door would have been opened to a united Ireland. Either way they lose.[387]

Probably the most pertinent, in-depth analysis of loyalist reaction to the 1994 IRA ceasefire came several weeks after the Provisionals' original announcement. Fergal Keane's *Panorama* report, 'The Uneasy Peace', presented a not unsympathetic portrait of the problems and concerns of unionists, as well as observing change and friction within the loyalist rank and file.[388] The programme looked at the 'new voices' emerging from unionism, especially on the Shankill Road where a community meeting had been in favour of talking to the Provisionals. Keane argued that the greatest shifts in the Protestant community had been in 'the hidden world of loyalist paramilitaries' and maintained that the ceasefire had laid down 'a daunting challenge' for the unionists to carry out 'a searching investigation of their identity'.[389]

Keane's report also discerned differences between rural and urban loyalism. Whilst 'real fears of betrayal' were shared by loyalists in both areas featured in the edition (the Shankill Road and the County Tyrone village of Moy), the latter group were even more sceptical of a peace that 'is too unfamiliar to be trusted'.[390] The item on the Moy community looked sympathetically at the pressures and 'alienation' of Protestants who had seen their Orange hall attacked 29 times and whose loved ones had been victims of republican terrorism. A poignant moment in the report was when the cameras zoomed in on the recently-erected tombstones in the Protestant cemetery, as Keane commented that (for border Protestants) 'life has taught them to be sceptical'.[391] An original feature of this pro-

383 Ibid. 384 Ibid. 385 Ibid. 386 Ibid. 387 Ibid. 388 *Panorama*, 'The Uneasy Peace', 17 October 1994. 389 Ibid. 390 Ibid.

gramme was the editors' decision to 'bus in' a party of Gaelic club members from across the border. The Longford party visited Moy's Orange lodge, with whom they engaged in a tense discussion on the issue of the ceasefire.[392]

Despite its compassionate portrayal of the suffering sustained by border Protestants, *Panorama* asserted that the Moy Orangemen appeared to be 'people without an identity'.[393] 'The Uneasy Peace' like a number of previous programmes, highlighted the confusion loyalists were experiencing over their identity, but in expressing some sympathy for their predicament, Fergal Keane alluded to the strains in their 'loyalty' being exacerbated by the IRA ceasefire. He concluded:

> Ulster Protestantism is on the move but has yet to define its voice ... A moment of decision is approaching for the Ulster Protestants. The unfamiliar peace could prove to be the most fundamental test of their British identity.[394]

Channel Four

Channel Four's decade of coverage of events in Northern Ireland was both comprehensive and controversial.[395] The 'new' commercial channel was, from an early stage, accused of pursuing an anti-state, pro-republican agenda and this was reflected in its choice and content of programmes. The company was involved in a court case in which they defended their right to protect their sources, following a 1991 programme in which they alleged that members of the RUC had been guilty of collusion with loyalist paramilitaries.[396] This *Dispatches* programme had been described as 'a specially extended report into alleged collusion between members of the RUC, UDR and Protestant paramilitaries in murdering Republicans'.[397] Most of the channel's Irish programmes were either critical of state-agencies' handling of the situation or else looked at issues directly involving the Catholic community. Mary Holland's *Dispatches* report was a critical piece on the government's broadcasting ban with particular reference to Sinn Fein and earlier that year the same programme had featured an interview with Sinn Fein President Gerry Adams.[398] Other programmes included a profile of leading IRA member Mairead Farrell, an item based on the shooting of a Catholic child by the security forces and a feature which stressed the 'futility' of the Irish border.[399]

Channel Four's apparent obsession with the nationalist predicament can be further illustrated by its screening of several other programmes which focussed on the Catholic position. These included Michael Grigsby's documentary on a west Belfast Catholic ghetto which maintained that, if similar levels of violence

391 Ibid. 392 In another feature on the loyalist siege mentality, David Lomax made an interesting distinction between 'those border unionists in a minority who maintain that they are happy with their lot and get on with their neighbours' and those living a mere twenty miles away in mixed communities where 'to a man Protestant farmers appears to be united in opposition to the Anglo-Irish Agreement', *Panorama*, 'The Troubled Peace' (23 March 1987 quoted in the *Listener* (26 March 1987). 393 The Uneasy Peace, op. cit. 394 Ibid. 395 The fourth channel on British television was established in 1982. 396 Quoted in the *Sunday Times*, 26 July 1992. 397 Channel Four, *Dispatches*, 2 October 1992. 398 *Dispatches*, 12 November 1990 and 11 April 1990. 399 'Mother Ireland', 11 April 1991, 'Unfinished Business', 7 June 1993.

had been experienced by the citizens of Tunbridge Wells, 'it would have been resolved many years ago' and proceeded to argue, with some justification, that 'Northern Ireland is out of sight, out of mind'.[400] However, as with most programmes, the squalor and suffering tended to be confined to one community. This emphasis on the nationalist experience was epitomised by Channel Four's *Long War* series in 1994 (coinciding with the 25th anniversary of British military involvement), when the majority of programmes looked at the situation from a Catholic perspective. These included an investigation of the effect of the early phase of the conflict on the Catholic population, a repeated showing of the Thames production, 'Creggan', Malachi O'Doherty's 'Frontline' which suggested that the Northern Ireland problem 'might eventually solve itself when Roman Catholics become the majority', and Moira Sweeney's description of her experiences as a Catholic girl growing up in Northern Ireland.[401]

This is not to say that Channel Four desisted from from featuring a range of 'different' Irish stories. These included 'fillers' such as 'Belfast Lessons', which provided a fly-on-the-wall account of life in Belfast's Hazelwood College, an integrated school, 'An Astonished Eye' which looked at the attempts of four Derrymen from different backgrounds who, over a 18-month-period, 'tried to bridge the Catholic and Protestant divide', another fly-on-the-wall documentary about paramedics in post-ceasefire Belfast, 'A Love Divided', which looked at the problems facing couples in mixed marriages, a passion play involving Catholic and Protestant participants in a Belfast cathedral and a profile of socialist playwright, Sam Thompson.[402]

As was the case with other television companies, Channel Four, on the rare occasion when it did turn its attention to loyalism, tended to focus on its negative characteristics. The connections between shady political groups on the extreme right in Great Britain and loyalist paramilitaries was examined in a *Dispatches* edition and, failing to fill in the background to loyalist caution and reticence in the wake of the ceasefire, another programme portrayed unionists as the 'peace blockers', highlighting their 'mixed hopes for the future'.[403] However, a number of other programmes did allow more eloquent unionists the comparatively rare opportunity of expressing their opinions. Thus Robert McCartney was able to express his 'novel approach to the Northern Ireland problem' in 'New Voices' and Tony Stewart was adept in expressing the unionist viewpoint in 'Opinions – Ulster Misunderstood'.[404]

Furthermore Channel Four featured the case of the Armagh Four which other

400 'The Silent War', 8 February 1990. **401** 'The Last Colony', 2 July 1994,' Creggan', 5 July 1994, 'Frontline'; 6 July 1994 and 'Out of the Blue – Coming Home', 15 August 1994. **402** 'Belfast Lessons'; (transmitted throughout much of 1994) , 'An Astonished Eye', 14 February 1994, 'Cutting Edge – Healing Wounds', 14 November 1994, 'A Love Divided', 17 June 1991, UTV's production for C4 'A People's Passion', 24 March 1989 and 'Sam Thompson – Voice of Many Men', another UTV production transmitted by C4, 4 November 1986. **403** *Dispatches*, 26 October 1994 and 'The Trouble with Peace', 31 August 1995. **404** 'New Voices', 31 July 1983 and 'Opinions - Ulster Misunderstood', 3 August, 1983. Tony Stewart was also featured in the' Divided Kingdom – Ulster's Clash of Identities', 8 November 1988 (referred to in the political section).

leading television companies, in stark contrast with other 'miscarriage of justice' stories, chose to ignore.[405] Channel Four made a conscious effort to redress the balance with their transmission of a *Granada Special*, 'Here we Stand' in 1984.[406] The aim of this programme was to present 'a cross-section of unionist opinion' in the border areas of Northern Ireland, and to probe behind the stereotype of Protestants as 'sectarian bigots'.[407] A number of reasoned contributions came from a clergyman, border farmer and RUC widow, but these were overshadowed by the strident bigotry which emanated from a couple of Free Presbyterians and a shop steward whose words, 'It's worth fighting for ... to be a Britisher', ended the programme.[408] Therefore, despite the documentary's declared intentions, the lasting impression is one of illogical, aggressive nationalism.

The whole question of Channel Four's impartiality in its reporting of the Northern Irish situation was raised by A.A. Gill in his *Sunday Times* column at the end of Channel Four's 'Long War' week.[409] Accusing Channel Four of 'Sooty and Sweep journalism', Gill attacked their selection and presentation of programmes for their 'Irish' season. He made an intriguing comparison between the company's coverage of the nationalist position and its presentation of the Shankill community.

> The whole week was decidedly pro-republican – this being Channel Four that was about as big a surprise as Monday morning ... It was at its worst in Creggan, a film about a Catholic estate where the women were portrayed as Mother Courage; gritty, stoical, quiet heroines, nurturing freedom fighters. And in the Shankill, its Unionist counterpart, where the Protestants were spoken for by confused apologists shamed by their past, uncertain and divided about their future.[410]

This dismissal of what was Channel Four's most evocative and sympathetic depiction of the Protestant community is not consummately fair. Though he agrees that Michael Whyte and Mary Holland's film 'concurs with conventional diagnoses of the conflict' and that the essential 'voice of Shankill' is one of defeatism, David Butler does concede that 'the film breaks with the monolithic projection of unionism-loyalism' and that in so doing 'it goes some way to counter the unwitting bias of most British reporting in favour of a liberal-nationalist epistemology'.[411] Certainly the documentary was different in that all its subjects appeared reasonable people who were prepared to compromise.[412] This decision to combine a utilisation of articulate, moderate working-class Protestant voices with

405 'Armagh Four – Free for All', 6 March 1991 (this was discussed earlier in the chapter). **406** *Granada Special* for Channel 4, 'Here We Stand – A Protestant View of Ulster', 9 February 1984. **407** Ibid. **408** 'Here We Stand', quoted in D. Butler, *The Trouble with Reporting Northern Ireland* (Aldershot 1995) p129. **409** *Sunday Times*, 10 July 1994. **410** Ibid. **411** D. Butler, op. cit., p. 130–1. **412** The fact that they were so reasonable bemused some critics who clearly believed in the stereotype. An *Independent* review of 'Shankill' (8 September 1994) could not take the film seriously because of 'a unrealistic absence of hate'.

panoramic film footage of the Shankill wastelands devoid of soundtrack, resulted in a characterisation of a Protestant community which was infinitely more sympathetic in tone than anything Channel Four had previously attempted.

The loyalists interviewed in the programme enounced a number of perspectives previously underplayed in the media. Progressive Unionist Party member Billy Hutchinson reminded the Channel Four audience that Protestants too had been discriminated against, although perhaps in a different way to Catholics. Referring to the poor quality of Shankill housing, Hutchinson made light of the oft-cited 'labour aristocracy' thesis, with his wry comment that 'because you're a Protestant you can get a slum quicker'.[413] Although the documentary included footage of an Orange parade, the notion of triumphalism was rejected by Jackie Redpath who argued that the Shankill was 'a community in retreat on almost every front', and Mary Holland proceeded to outline its economic decline (up to 40% were unemployed in some Shankill wards), low educational standards – 'only a handful of children on the Shankill pass the 11+ every year' – and the great population 'leakage' in the Shankill and its surrounding areas in the course of the Troubles (from an estimated 120,000 to 56,000).[414] A couple of contributors spoke of the effects of the religious fragmentation in the area (the cameras panned in on many of the Shankill's 23 churches), on community development in the Shankill and its tendency towards individualism, although some evidence of community cohesion was evident.[415] Much of the final strand of the programme looked at the effects of the fish shop bombing on the Shankill the previous year and instead of the media's predictable accentuation of the anticipated vitriolic loyalist response, Michael Whyte and Mary Holland elected to end with Charlie Butler's dignified response to his deep personal loss.[416]

BRITISH PUBLIC OPINION AND LOYALIST ISSUES

There is much to suggest that the restricted and analytically-weak media coverage of the unionist position has contributed to the mainly negative mainland response to such a case and issues directly related to it. How much each dictates the other, is, of course, a broader and complex issue, which I will be unable to delve into here. However, it's pertinent to note that public opinion findings have not been entirely damning for unionists, as survey findings on troop withdrawal and Irish unity indicate.

Over the years opinion polls have been, according to David Miller, emphatically in favour of military withdrawal.[417] Miller claims that he could find no trace

413 The argument was that in return for their political support, the Protestant working class received superior economic and social benefits. Many Shankill Protestants contested the degree of 'privilege' they were supposed to have received from the Unionist establishment. 414 *The Long War* – 'Shankill' 7 July 1994. 415 Such an example was the Hummingbird women's educational group. 416 In the course of endeavouring to dig out the injured from the rubble, Charlie Butler was to stumble across the bodies of his niece, her husband and their daughter. 417 D. Miller, *Don't Mention the War – Northern Ireland, Propaganda and the Media* (London 1994), p. 279.

of evidence which suggested that those in favour of troop disengagement from Northern Ireland had ever dropped below 50% between 1974 and 1986.[418] However, this conceals the fact with withdrawal figures had dropped significantly below the 50% figure earlier in the conflict and, as Miller himself points out, also reflected the correlation between high levels of IRA violence and support for British military commitment to Northern Ireland.[419] In 1972, when violence was at its peak, only 34% were in favour of withdrawal, but this had risen to 55% in December 1974 and 64% in December 1975, by which time the loyalist paramilitary campaign had picked up momentum.[420] By the end of 1975 only 13% thought troop levels should be maintained, contrasting with 22% in 1974 and 29% in 1972 and only 11% called for an increase in troop levels (compared to 10% in 1974 and 28% in 1972). Later in the conflict respondents were required to verify their strength of feeling on the issue of military disengagement. In 1989 over a quarter of those questioned in a MORI poll (27%) 'strongly' agreed with 'immediate' troop withdrawal while another 20% merely 'agreed' with such a measure (of the 30% who opposed the proposal, only 13% 'strongly' disagreed).[421]

A distinction also emerged between short and long term military withdrawal and this, to some extent, reflected the difference between those mainly motivated by frustration with the deadlock in Northern Ireland and those with deeper political reasons for supporting disengagement. Thus, polls in the late 1980s and early 1990s indicated a preference for phased withdrawal of troops. An *Economist*/MORI poll in March 1988 showed that, of the 50% who favoured withdrawal, 29% wanted it over a longer period of time.[422] Also, in a 1991 MORI poll there was an increase both in the overall numbers of favour of disengagement and those who preferred the phased option.[423] In this MORI poll, 23% wanted an immediate withdrawal of troops and 38% requested it in a pre-set period (31% wanted troops kept there indefinitely).

The numbers interested in withdrawal tended to be higher than those attracted by Irish unity. This mirrors the distinction between mainland frustration with events in Ireland and the wish to disengage, and the more politically motivated desire to change the constitutional status of the region, which was mainly the aim of those, particularly on the political left, as well as republican sympathisers in Great Britain. This is reflected in various survey findings. Although there was a consensus that Great Britain should be absolved from ultimate political responsibility for Northern Ireland, the numbers in favour of unity were normally (but not always) in a minority. Surveys such as LWT's 'From the Shadow of the Gun' (1984) and a 1991 MORI poll suggested that there was a substantial amount of support for maintaining the union (39% in the first case and 33% in

418 Ibid. 419 As Miller pointed out, the Enniskillen bombing in 1987 is a good example of how exceptionally violent tactics could mitigate against the republican cause on the British mainland. I refer to a *Marplan/C4* poll which reflects this antipathy in the Enniskillen case study. 420 *Daily Telegraph/Gallup*, 6 December 1975. 421 MORI, *We British – Britain under the Microscope* (London, 1989). 422 Quoted in the *Independent*, 25 March 1988. 423 MORI, *British Attitudes to Northern Ireland*, 21/24 March 1991.

the second), and 4 MORI polls between 1980 and 1991 showed that support was greater for maintaining the British link.[424]

There was an interesting contrast between those who supported the constitutional guarantee in Northern Ireland (64% in favour, compared to 23% against in a 1987 MORI poll) and many (including some who probably believed in the first option) who believed that Irish unity would eventually happen.[425] Therefore, 41% anticipated Irish unification within a comparatively short-term period (20–30 years).[426] This, aligned to the belief that Dublin should have a real involvement in the affairs of Northern Ireland, illustrates that it was more out of a 'sense of duty' and fear of the unionist response rather than unequivocal support for the cause of the union, which prevented the British public from being more vociferous in demanding short-term unity. Therefore, support for Dublin involvement from 48% in favour of its Hillsborough role (compared to 30% against), in the overwhelming support for the Framework Document (92%) and a substantial majority of British voters (68%) feeling that unionists would be 'unjust in refusing to take part in talks'.[427]

As public opinion polls in Great Britain have, therefore, been directed towards gauging mainland attitudes to troop withdrawal and the question of Irish unity – both of which, whilst giving some insight into attitudes pertaining to the unionist predicament, fall far short in terms of explaining attitudes to unionists in Northern Ireland – I thought it would be appropriate, given the stated 'brief' of this research, to probe further into mainland responses to a variety of images associated with Ulster loyalism. I therefore compiled a 10 question survey which aimed to produce a mixture of quantitative and qualitative evidence. Nearly half of the space for answers was devoted to eliciting respondents' opinions and I was particularly pleased with the detailed and informed explanations I received from several groups. Apart from ascertaining respondents' views of familiar images associated with loyalism, for example, the Orange Order, Ian Paisley, Stormont and hooded terrorists, and other important factors in the wider Northern Irish conflict, such as improved relations between the London and Dublin governments, Gerry Adams and the IRA ceasefire, victims of IRA terrorism and media coverage of the Troubles, my intention was to assess the extent to which these and other extreme manifestations of loyalism affected their perception and degree of sympathy towards the demands of unionists. I anticipated that these questions would provide greater insight for my own analysis of such manifestations of loyalism, as well as illustrating the dichotomy between their composition and intent and the manner in which they were presented within the national media. I deliberately chose what I believed to be instantly recognisable images to initiate a reflective process.[428]

424 This poll is referred to in greater detail in the LWT section. I also refer to the MORI 1991 poll (op. cit.). **425** MORI/*Daily Express*, 19/24 January, 1987. **426** Ibid. **427** Ibid. and the *Daily Telegraph*, 24 February 1995. **428** Therefore, 'visual context' material accompanied the questions. It must be said, however, that these images were not immediately recognisable in every case, with a number of respondents failing to recognise the unionist leaders (particularly Jim Molyneaux).

The practicalities of time and money, meant that my survey would be comparatively small-scale in its nature and, as I was unable, for the aforementioned reasons, to draw on external professional agencies, the conducting of the survey would have to be carried out by myself or contacts in other parts of the country. I had already decided that at least half of my respondents would be students in two of the 'new' London universities. Apart from easy access (I work in the first and have a contact in the second), I was particularly interested in enticing what I hoped would be informed comments of relatively young voters.[429] I decided to test opinion in other parts of the country because I was aware of the pitfalls involved in focussing on possibly distorted or skewed impressions emanating from the responses of a single region. By seeking the opinions of people in Lancashire, Strathclyde, Devon, South Wales and Surrey/Berkshire, I was able to get a more even age and gender balance, as well as making provision for any differences of opinion between inner city, suburbs and countryside. Respondents proved to be a mixture of university students (young and not so young!), teachers and lecturers, doctors, barristers, printers, electricians, engineers, housewives and pensioners. Although I was not able to achieve the 'spread' I desired (particularly in terms of class and age), I felt that there was a reasonable 'mix' which certainly provided me with reams of information for analysis.[430]

Nearly 250 survey forms were distributed in six main areas mainly between March and June 1995.[431] Apart from the two London universities, South Bank (where 43 students, and staff completed forms) and Guildhall (44 student responses), 'semi-stratified' samples were arranged in Burnley (centred round a general surgery in the town), a Glasgow suburb, Post Office workers in a Surrey town, Exeter and the surrounding area and members of a University of Wales extra-mural class.[432] The short-fall between the number of despatched questionnaires and completed forms – 160 were returned to me – indicates some apathy, although I was reasonably satisfied with the number and particularly the quality of responses which I received.[433]

The respondents came from a variety of backgrounds, not only in terms of area, but social environment and experiences of Northern Ireland. Over half of the respondents (81) had never visited Ireland or had links with it, whilst 27 (just over 17%) had 'close' affinity with Northern Ireland and another 17 (just under 11%) had links with the Irish Republic (half of the Scottish group were in either

429 Yet it would be incorrect to create the impression that these were 'typical' students, certainly, in terms of their age. Many of the South Bank students in particular, were 'mature learners'. 430 I also strove to avoid selecting people from Northern Ireland, as my main aim was to gauge mainland opinion and I was relatively (but not totally!) successful in achieving this. 431 The exceptions were Glasgow and Exeter where the forms were completed in September/October 1995. 432 There were also 28 responses from Lancashire, 18 from Glasgow, 15 from Surrey/Berkshire and 12 from Devon/Wales. The samples were 'semi-stratified' in that there were suggested criteria for potential respondents (in terms of gender membership, age and occupational categories). 433 Apathy was most apparent in the western group, where only 12 out of 45 forms were returned and in Surrey where 15 out of the 30 despatched were completed.

of the latter two categories). A disproportionate number of the survey group were in their 20s or 30s (over 60%, or 97 respondents), with only 14% (or 22 respondents) being over 50 years of age. This was, to a degree, inevitable, given that the two largest groups were composed of university students. Although the number of male and female respondents was virtually the same, this was not the case with individual groups, with women predominating at South Bank University (30 to 13) and men outnumbering women, particularly in Glasgow (12 to 6) and Surrey (12 to 3). Only 47% (75 respondents) identified themselves as 'Christian', with the number of Catholics (27) just over half the number of Protestants (48).[434] There were also over twice as many people from a middle class background as there were from working class backgrounds.[435] I accepted that this would probably happen given that over half of the respondents were attending university courses, but whilst there might have been a slight imbalance in class terms, the quality of evidence was probably better as a result.

Forty-five per cent of the respondents admitted having 'little knowledge' of events in Northern Ireland, with 19% (30 respondents) maintaining they possessed a 'great' deal of knowledge of the situation.[436] Their interest levels were higher than their knowledge ones. Although a high number (27% or 43 respondents) had little interest in Northern Ireland, more people had a 'high' interest level (28% or 46 respondents) with the largest number (under 32% or 53 respondents) having 'medium' levels of interest.[437] Over half of the respondents had 'limited' knowledge of the unionist case (81), with only 31 or nearly 20% saying they had 'great' knowledge. Support for the unionist case was even less, with only 19 people (less than 12%) saying they had a 'great' deal of sympathy for unionists, whereas nearly 46% had 'limited' support for them.

The findings

The intention behind the first question was to gauge the effect Ian Paisley had on the formulation of mainland public response to the unionist case. Only 7 respondents (4%) though he had 'strengthened' support for the loyalist position, whereas 85 people (53%) felt he had 'weakened' it.[438] The results were, therefore, given the one-dimensional nature of British media coverage produced by the Paisley stereotype, and unionists' difficulty in improving the quality of the British publicity material, rather predictable. What was of more interest were the opinions of respondents regarding his success and their own attitudes to his in-

434 Again, there were regional differences, with nearly twice as many Catholics as Protestants in the Glasgow group and the reverse trend occurring in the case of the Lancashire group. 435 The occupations of students' parents were used where necessary. 435 This is substantiated by the findings of a NOP Research Group survey, reported in the *Daily Express*, 4 September 1997, in which 75% of the British population considered that they did not 'fully understand' the Irish situation. Interestingly enough, there was a significant difference between the numbers of women and men who admitted their confusion over the situation (57% and 43% respectively). 437 Proportionately, the highest interest levels were in the west and Surrey. 438 Indeed, many of those who felt that he had 'little effect' on changing their attitudes to the unionist position, were also critical of his contributions.

fluence on Northern Irish, and indeed, British politics.[439] A Belfast-born clerk, living in Devon, suggested that it was the DUP leader's 'force of personality' and his ability to maintain 'a high-profiled support of issues affecting his community which explained his great support in the province. Although others also mentioned his important role in 'voicing the opinions of his community', a significant number of respondents suggested that he was 'playing on Protestant fears and prejudices'. A Liverpool-born process worker suggested that Paisley was 'exploiting loyalist fears of uncertainty' whilst a Lancashire barrister argued that, in 'preying upon the historical insecurity of his community', Ian Paisley had been highly successful in 'mixing a dangerous cocktail of religion and politics'.

A variety of responses were given for the predominantly critical response to Ian Paisley's contribution to Northern Irish politics. Several stressed his 'bigotry' and 'arrogance' and a Burnley engineer was not alone in suggesting that, for Paisley, compromise 'seems to be out of the question'. Although a South Bank University student conceded he was 'a brilliant mob orator' it was precisely his forthright delivery of the loyalist 'message' which she and many other repondents found so off-putting. Therefore, in recognising Paisley's 'charisma and forceful personality', another South Bank student suggested his 'portrayal in the press greatly weakens his credibility as an opinion former'. This view was mirrored by a Burnley housewife who suggested that 'when someone shouts, no matter how good the cause, one finally doesn't listen to the message, just the noise'.[440]

There was also, however, voluble, if restricted, support for the DUP leader. A Burnley Methodist pointed out that most of his predictions had been 'correct' and that 'he is respected in the Protestant community for his integrity' and a Surrey manager spoke of his 'good reasoned arguments'. The most fulsome praise came from a Glasgow salesman who described Ian Paisley as 'the Winston Churchill of Ulster', arguing that, 'without his leadership, resolve for the loyalist case may have crumbled' and that the loyalist community 'recognises his dedication and commitment to their just cause'. Predictably the Glasgow community was divided, largely along religious lines, on their interpretation of the DUP leader. In contrast with the last comment which came from a Glaswegian whose father had been a Church of Scotland minister, a retired Catholic builder argued that Ian Paisley was 'blinkered in his opinions and has no interest in listening to other opinions'.

439 The impression of Paisley as a religious bigot and intransigent politician had been formed early in the conflict and, unfortunately both for Paisley and the wider unionist community, was rarely challenged in the subsequent quarter century. The consequence was unionism's loss of 'important allies in Britain and abroad where a more rational experience of its case might have evolved great sympathy' and a resigned response from the British public following Paisley's periodic, predictably excessive outbursts (E. Moloney and A. Pollak, *Paisley* (Dublin, 1986), p. 439). This is reflected in a Simon Hoggart article in the *Guardian*, 30 November 1993, when he wrote of Paisley's removal from the Commons; 'Like the Changing of the Guard, the ejection of Mr. Paisley is a fine spectacle but you don't need to see it twice'. For a more detailed analysis of the effects of the Paisley stereotype on the presentation of the unionist case in Great Britain, see 'Loyal Rebels without a Cause?' op. cit. 440 Another Lancashire respondent suggested that when Ian Paisley 'opens his mouth his brains fall out!'

Diverse interpretations of Paisley's high standing in unionist politics were revealed by the survey. A Derby-born doctor believed that dearth in political talent amongst the unionist ranks – 'there is no other leader to represent the loyalist view' – explained Paisley's predominant position in unionist politics, whilst a South Bank University student suggested that Paisley 'does not represent the majority of the unionists and has no apparent desire to see the peace process work'. A Guildhall University student suggested that Revd Paisley's 'right wing ideals appeal to many Protestants', whilst a South Bank University student queried whether the British public was getting the 'full picture' on Ian Paisley ('I am sure he has a different side that we don't see here'). Others contributed Paisley's electoral success to his 'consistency', the fact that he was 'a well-known figurehead who says what Protestants want to hear', whilst an Aldershot-born Guildhall University student argued that Ian Paisley was 'a strong character, who speaks his mind and is the very loud voice of the silent few who do not have the personality to speak out for themselves'. This survey illustrated the distinction beween the perception of Ian Paisley in Great Britain and amongst Northern Ireland's Protestant population, but there was some evidence of a significant minority of respondents being aware (despite its understated treatment in the British media) of a number of reasons for his success amongst the loyalist community.

Depicting the resolute James Molyneaux and Ian Paisley outside Stormont, the second question was designed to test respondents' attitudes to the degree of plausibility which unionism had as a political doctrine, as well as providing an opportunity to hear their views on why loyalists were seemingly so opposed to compromise.[441] Perhaps surprisingly, the numbers which thought unionism a 'reasonable' and 'acceptable' political doctrine were exactly the same as those who perceived it to be 'negative' and 'irrational' (68 respondents). Despite this apparent acceptance of unionism's 'legitimacy', there was a distinctive feeling among many that unionists were unwilling to compromise (57 believed they were, compared to 22 who felt that republicans were more so). Several felt that this was due to the fact that unionists, on account of their 'representing the status quo', actually had 'more to lose' than nationalists. Unionist 'caution' was interpreted by some as an indication of their view that 'any compromise would be seen as weakening the union' and this was exacerbated by their 'growing isolation' from Britain and their 'weakening political case'.

Others took a harsher approach to unionist reluctance to compromise. A South Bank University student felt that unionists were 'more concerned about party politics, than peace in Ireland'. Unionist stubborness and intransigence were cited by several respondents, with a Glasgow nursing auxiliary saying that 'Unionists think only they are right and they don't listen to any opposition'. Some believed that such intransigence was inevitable considering 'the historical Protestant perspective' which had conditioned them into the politics of entrenchment, 'blinkering them into believing that they are above democratic principles.'

441 For most of the respondents, Jim Molyneaux was still the UUP's leader at the time they completed the survey.

Others probed more deeply into the unionist position and whilst many remained critical of their lack of political mobility, the tone of their responses was marginally more sympathetic. Several explained that unionists were reluctant to compromise because they felt 'they had no where to go'. The ultimate 'bogey' of Irish unity was pinpointed by a Guildhall University student who suggested that unionists shunned political compromise because they believed it 'involved influence being allowed from the Irish Republic which they do not want', perceiving 'any change to the current situation as a threat to their way of life'. One respondent felt that the all-pervading stereotype of Ian Paisley 'shadowed' other more 'reasonable' unionists. Referring to Ken Maginnis, a Guildford-born South Bank University student said that the DUP leader's 'presence and reputation have been such a turn-off so that perhaps the issues and aspirations of unionists do not get proper media interpretation in Great Britain'.

Fifty per cent of the total number of respondents (80) felt that the Orange Order were 'a negative influence on events in Northern Ireland', with another 17% (26) dismissing them as having 'little influence' over such events. The number of those who felt that Orangeism was a 'negative' influence was nearly four times as many as those who thought Orangemen to be a 'positive' influence (21 respondents). A variety of responses were given to the question, 'Why do Orangemen want to march?'[442] These included 'a demonstration of power', a chance to 'show solidarity against forces in favour of Irish unity', an opportunity to demonstrate they were 'the defenders of the Protestant faith' and an occasion 'to reinforce their tribal culture'. The traditional, or cultural emphasis was stressed by a Welsh legal secretary who claimed that Orangemen marched to 'cling on to their roots', whilst a Crawley-born manager argued that they saw it 'as part of their heritage'. Linked to this explanation was the perception that marching 'maintained their separate identity' and afforded loyalists the opportunity of strengthening 'their sense of belonging'. Others saw a more sinister side to their apparent obsession with marching. A retired Exeter police officer suggested that they paraded 'purely to cock a snook at the Catholic community', whilst a South Bank University student also emphasised the triumphalist nature of a march which 'keeps alive the victory of Protestant over Catholic'. Others underline the political motives of an ostensibly 'religious' pressure group. A Lancashire headteacher said that they walked to 'demonstrate their total opposition to a united Ireland', whilst a Guildhall University student suggested that Orangemen desired 'to be seen and heard, and to remember days in the past when they had control'. Others saw more than a hint of desperation in the actions of Orangemen. A South Bank University student described their marching as 'a gesture of defiance' and another suggested that their message was 'this is our land and we won't give it up'. A retired Welshman thought their behaviour indicated feelings of confusion and despair. He asked the question 'why do people whistle in the dark?' and suggested that it was 'because they fear what might be out there'.

442 This 'obsession' with marching was seen by many to be 'alien' to the British way of life and fitted the 'Irish' stereotype.

'The question 'What are Orangemen trying to demonstrate?' provided a similar response. A South Bank University student suggested that Orangemen were trying to 'express their religion, their power, their allegiance to Britain and their basic right to march', whilst a Lancashire health professional suggested they were striving to demonstrate 'their loyalty to the Crown and their history, as well as their superiority over Catholics'. The triumphalist nature of Orangeism was criticised by several respondents. A Glasgow teacher argued that Orangemen, in demanding their 'so-called right to walk on any street at any time, no matter who they were offending', were exhibiting 'their reluctance to live in the late 20th century'. Others deplored the 'secret society' aspect of Orangeism. A South Bank University student conceded that the Order's marching was 'a traditional honouring of historical events in Northern Ireland', but maintained that it was also 'a very sensitive issue for Catholics to witness or even acknowledge'. She added that there was something 'eerie', or 'mason-like' about Orangemen. A smaller number of respondents proferred 'excuses' for Orangemen, ranging from their 'simple desire to maintain the status quo', to their 'feeling threatened' by events and a basic need 'to reassure themselves about their own status and where they belong'. These responses reflected the generally accepted impression of the Order being an antediluvian organisation, the existence of which symbolised the resistance of Ulster Protestants to progress. However, a surprising feature of the survey was the informed replies of a sizeable minority of respondents who, although unsympathetic towards their position, were cognissant of their motives and fears.

The fourth question looked at the effect IRA bombing of civilian targets in Northern Ireland had had on British public opinion. It was intended to ascertain if respondents differentiated between such attacks and those on the army and whether they increased sympathy for the unionist position. The majority of respondents saw no political or moral justification for such attacks on any section of the population, but a significant number (48) reported feeling 'more sympathetic' to the victims of such an attack as the Shankill than for military victims (13 respondents said they had more sympathy for army or police casualties than they did for Northern Irish civilian victims).

However, such attacks did not lead to an increase in sympathy for the unionist position, with half of the respondents declaring that the Shankill bombing had left their attitudes 'unchanged', and a smaller number (62) equally divided in their sympathies to the unionist plight. Forty-five per cent (72 respondents) cited the IRA as their chief reason for prompting their responses, with a lesser number (25) criticising the Westminster government and Unionist 'intransigence' (19). As has already been indicated, the main response was a condemnation of such explosions, with the qualification that attacks on military targets were 'more acceptable' than those of civilian targets. However this condemnation didn't automatically lead to an increase in sympathy for loyalists. A part-time tutor at Swansea University felt that such attacks made him 'more critical of security arrangements in Northern Ireland', rather than force him into questioning his overall views of the problem. Many made the point that *all* bomb attacks were 'abhorrent' and a Lancashire housewife stressed she had 'sympathy for any bomb victims, providing they had not themselves been involved in violence'. Other suggestions that the involvement of loyalist paramilitaries in violence had made it more difficult to empathise with Protestant grief, were expressed, with a Burnley teacher admitting such attacks on the Shankill did not change her attitudes because she regarded such blasts as being motivated by 'revenge'.

Seventy-six % of the respondents (121) expressed their support for improved liaison between the London and Dublin governments and of the 15% (24 respondents) 'sceptical' of initiatives such as the Downing Street Declaration and the Framework Document, party political reasons and a general distrust of politicians, rather than a concern for unionists, was the central motivating factor.[443] This support for an increased 'Irish' dimension was reflected in respondents' attitudes towards a political settlement, with nearly 79% (125 respondents) believing that Irish unity was a likely future development. However, 59% (95 respondents) believed that practicality of community division would prevent such unity occurring within the specified 'short term' (25 year) period, and only 11% (17 people) felt that the British Government was against Irish unity under any circumstances and had a clear interest in protecting the interests of unionists'.

Yet this belief in the ultimate 'solution' of unity was not the prime reason for their support of increased liaison between the two governments. Rather than express a genuine preference for the political option of an all-Ireland state, the majority of respondents either said that an increased role for Dublin would help to maintain the peace process or that, in the absence of any other workable alternative, it would be necessary if negotiations were to proceed successfully. In reaching these conclusions, few considered the right of the Irish government to be involved in such negotiations. What was all-important was ensuring that 'the fighting does not return'. A Lancashire respondent suggested 'anything that stops the bombing has to be favourable' and a South Bank University student suggested that the government was merely reflecting the feelings of many that there was 'a fundamental need to change the situation – for better or worse'. The primacy of a 'centralised' solution, with the main decisions taken by the two governments was unchallenged by most respondents. Therefore, a Lancashire administrative officer believed that 'discussion at government level is the best way of achieving a settlement which is acceptable to all interested parties' and a South Wales legal secretary maintained that 'in order to achieve any progress the two governments must liaise'.

Many were aware of the potential effect such liaison would have on unionist confidence. Several respondents conceded that loyalist fears of being 'sold out' would increase as a result of joint initiatives. An Exeter manager suggested that this fostered 'the same fears as Falkland Islanders' – a belief that Britain 'would eventually sell them out' and other pointed to their 'growing isolation' and, 'increased fears of discrimination in a projected Irish union'. This was an acknowledgement that such developments as the Downing Street Declaration and the

443 One Lancashire respondent refused to 'trust our politicians to be concerned with anything other than their own image'.

Framework Document would 'confirm the views Unionists have taken of the British Government since the Anglo-Irish Agreement'. Others maintained that unionists exhibited 'business and cultural fears' about possible unity and were aware that 'loyalist wishes are being ignored by the British government'. A Surrey clerk said that she was 'far from convinced that either party (London and Dublin Governments) has the Unionists' interests at heart – the British are selling them out and the Dublin government is trying to steal what was never theirs'. Yet this surprising appreciation of loyalist fears did not manifest itself in increased political support, largely because many felt there was no real substance in such fears. A South Bank University student argued that unionists displayed 'stubbornness for the sake of it', whilst a Reading-born telephone engineer felt that unionist fears over Irish unity would have 'very little effect' on Northern Ireland's population, 'the majority of whom want peace'. A retired Glasgow salesman sensed that their fear of being 'pushed into a united Ireland' was 'unjustified' and a South Bank University student sardonically suggested that '100 years would be long enough (for unionists) to get used to the idea'. To many, however, the bottom line was the interests of the nation at large, rather than those of one of its regions. A Surrey printer said that loyalists 'might think they're being sold out but people in Great Britain don't care – we just want peace and so should they'.

Around 47% of those questioned in the survey (76 respondents) considered loyalist paramilitaries to be 'terrorists', but more interestingly, an impressive 19% (31 respondents) saw the reactive tendencies of groups such as the UUF and UVF as forming their most prominent attribute.[444] However, a similar-sized number thought loyalist paramilitaries were 'criminals and sectarian bigots with no political cause' (27 respondents, or nearly 17% of the total number questioned) and only a derisory 7% (12 respondents) believed them to be 'freedom fighters with a genuine political cause'.

Many stressed that they saw no difference between the actions of loyalist and republican paramilitaries. A Swansea local government officer felt that 'both are equally guilty and misguided in their practices' and a Devon resident suggested that both groups had 'sectarian bigotry at their core'. However, a noteworthy number of respondents differentiated between the nature of their respective political philosophies and the quality of their respective personnel. A South Bank University student suggested that the IRA had 'a stronger political case' and a Glasgow architect referred to studies which (in contrast to republican paramilitaries)' indicate that loyalist terrorists tend to come from a history of criminal activity, prior to their paramilitary involvement'. Other respondents alluded to the 'purely reactive' and 'less professional' essence of loyalist paramilitary activity. A Guildhall University student said that 'loyalists seem to pick solely on Catholic civilians which is petty retaliation' and others described the loyalist paramilitaries as 'acting in revenge'. Some respondents advocated that loyalist terrorists were 'superfluous' and had no place in a conflict where 'the army fights for their (Protestant) cause'.

444 This response may well have been consolidated in some respondents' minds by the loyalist paramilitaries' declaration of a ceasefire in October 1994.

The next question endeavoured to test respondents' views of the British army's attitudes to republican and loyalist paramilitaries. Over half of the survey group (81 respondents) thought the army was even-handed in their approach, but a considerable minority (over 35% or 57 respondents) believed them to be 'more aggressive' towards republican terrorists (only 4 respondents, or just over 2% of the total, believed that the army was tougher on loyalist paramilitaries than they were on republicans). Some believed that this was on account of the British army 'taking sides' in Northern Ireland. A South Bank University student intimated that because 'loyalists support Britain and adopt British symbols such as the Royal Family and the Union Jack, the army has developed a kindred spirit towards them'. Others suggested possible 'collusion' between the security forces and loyalist paramilitaries and a Guildhall University student argued it was inevitable that the army would be more aggressive towards nationalists because they were 'accountable for the loss of their comrades'. Many maintained that the fact the IRA, unlike loyalist paramilitaries, targetted them inevitably meant they would become more hostile to such terrorism. A Surrey printer pointed out that 'the IRA kill more soldiers than the UDA' whilst a Devon respondent suggested that as 'both organisations carry the same flag', loyalist paramilitaries were 'no threat' to the the British army.

The majority of respondents (106, or approximately 65% of the total) maintained that their attitudes to Gerry Adams and Sinn Fein had not changed on account of the ceasefire, although the numbers who expressed more sympathy (28 respondents, or just under 18% of the total) were double those who were less sympathetic to Sinn Fein's view (14 respondents, or just under 9%). Whilst there was not a widespread shift of support towards Gerry Adam's viewpoint, the majority of respondents (82, which constituted just over 51% of the total number) believed that he was a 'more significant' political figure than Ian Paisley or Jim Molyneaux, with only 11% (18 respondents) believing that the elected unionist leaders were 'more significant' than the then unelected President of Sinn Fein.

Perhaps the most popular interpretation of Adam's success was the manner in which the media had been 'manipulated' by Sinn Fein. This was borne out by its leader's 'high profile' and the widespread impression that 'events were moving in its direction'. The importance of such thinking outside the United Kingdom was underlined by a Glasgow sales consultant who argued that Adams, unlike the unionist leaders, 'had the ear of America'. Sinn Fein's success in this area was also stressed by a Lancashire student who said that its 'media manipulation' had 'highlighted the party to such a degree that it has, in effect, been elevated from minority party status to having the power of a much larger one'. Others believed that this had resulted in Adams being perceived as someone who was 'more prepared to compromise than the unionist leaders' and as someone who 'comes across as a fair man with a just cause'.

A significant number of respondents, whilst condemning the methods of Adams and his colleagues, conceded their successful use of the media. An unemployed Lancashire personnel manager described Gerry Adams as 'a very skilled and articulate leader who always appears to be a jump ahead of the British government in matters of publicity'. The propaganda success of the ceasefire was acknowledged by many people. A South Wales local government officer asserted that Adams was 'a worm but an astute one and Sinn Fein have now seen the benefits of embracing constitutional means and grabbing all the glory for themselves'. Several respondents believed that Adams's burgeoning reputation as the 'winner of the ceasefire' was a serious factor in explaining his increased status. A Glasgow plasterer pointed out that the Sinn Fein leader 'had worked hard to get the ceasefire', whilst a Burnley headteacher attributed his higher status to the fact that he 'had taken the initiative' in trying to bring the conflict to an end. Others pointed to his close associations with the IRA. An Exeter scientist believed these were regarded 'by many as being crucial in sustaining peace'.

However, many respondents were not convinced by such propaganda. A Guildhall University student was 'sickened by Mr Adams tapping the Yanks for sympathy and money. After Oklahoma, perhaps Noraid will not seem so attractive. Glorious causes kill!' Others suggested that he was the subject of too much media attention. Thus, a Burnley accountant argued that Adams's views should be 'heard in their proper context, as representing a small group of extremists'. He was not alone in suggesting that Adams, at the time an unelected politician (and indeed, one who was, in the end, 'answerable to the IRA') should be considered less important than politicians who had been elected. However, this did not unhinge the general opinion of respondents that unionist leaders were peripheral to events. A Glasgow student remarked that 'Ian Paisley appears dated, Jim Molyneaux has little charisma or authority whilst Gerry Adams is more in the public eye and knows how to handle the media'.

Respondents had some problems deciding whether the everyday experience of people in Belfast were 'fundamentally the same' or 'fundamentally different' from those living in other British cities. Forty-six per cent (75 respondents) felt that life was 'fundamentally the same' for Belfast citizens, whilst 43% (71 respondents) perceived it to be 'fundamentally different'. This uncertainty was reflected in the more detailed accounts of their impressions of life in Belfast. Several admitted to thinking of Belfast as a 'war zone' in which the conflict was 'an intrinsic part of their lives'. A Burnley doctor thought that the volume of security measures and 'the fear of terrorist attack' contributed to 'a definite diminuition of citizens' quality of life', and a South Bank University student said that life was 'not normal' in Belfast because 'the people there live in fear of bombs and have soldiers patrolling their streets'. A number of respondents believed that people in Northern Ireland had become accustomed to violence, and that, for many, it was simply a matter of 'business as usual'. Another South Bank student believed 'people go about their daily lives in spite of the threat of death as best they can', whilst a Surrey engineer caught the dilemma of a population 'trying to lead an ordinary life but constantly looking over their shoulders'.

Respondents questioned the quality of television coverage of events in Northern Ireland, querying whether they were getting the 'full picture'. One wondered if the emphasis on violence 'had been blown out of all proportion to the everyday experiences of ordinary people', whilst a Guildhall University student suggested that, as television didn't always 'accurately report what is going on in Northern Ireland', people in Britain 'are given a limited view of the conflict'. There were profound differences in opinion between the interpretations of respondents regarding the degree to which the fear of violence affected the lives of people in Northern Ireland, with those most sympathetic to the unionist cause stressing its importance and those with nationalist sympathies under-playing it. Hence a Glasgow Protestant salesman, writing about Belfast's 'state of suspense, if not fear', maintained that television had 'not emphasised this enough', whilst a Catholic Glasgow management consultant suggested that TV was responsible for depicting 'disruption and tragedy on a scale which appears more widespread than it is in reality'. Others felt that the media 'exaggerates' the impact of violence in Northern Ireland. A Swansea University tutor argued, 'I wouldn't have thought life there (in Belfast) in the main, was like life in Beirut or Sarajevo', whilst another respondent believed that 'the media deliberately endeavoured to 'make life in Belfast appear the same as life in London', while in reality, 'in many places it is very different'. Therefore, respondents were divided in their attitudes to the degree of 'normality' of life in Belfast, with a significant number of people stating that they felt television had failed to provide them with a multi-dimensional view of life in that city.

A wide range of sources were utilised by the respondents in their gathering of information about the conflict.[445] Many cited newspapers as their chief source of information, the majority of which were broadsheets,[446] However, the most common source of information was *BBC1 News* (110 respondents). Approximately 64% (103) of the total group said they were 'interested and concerned' about events in Northern Ireland, compared to 20% (32 respondents) who admitted to being 'bored and apathetic'. Although this reflects considerable antipathy towards Northern Ireland, it also illustrates that the majority of respondents felt concerned about what was going on there. Others expressed their concern over the quality of the media coverage. A Guildhall University student complained that the media 'never ask the important questions or get them answered properly – everybody flannels!' whilst a South Bank University student demanded 'a detailed, "This is Your Life, Northern Ireland-style" programme on prime time telly on a Saturday night!'

Many respondents mentioned how the 'repetitive' nature of news stories from Ulster had dampened their interest in the subject. A South Bank University student said that because of 'the "Catch 22" situation in Ireland, because the problem has been going on for so long, when you read a report on the problem or watch TV news, you think, oh no, not again!' A Lancashire student said that 'constant exposure to the problems of Northern Ireland precipitated a personal response of switching off to some degree as the interest level wanes after such

445 These ranged from discussions with friends and personal experiences of Northern Ireland to listening to *Radio Eireann*, *Sky TV News* and reading journals as diverse as the *Scottish Daily Record* and *New Statesman/Society*. **446** In order, the most popular papers were the *Guardian*, *Times*, *Independent*, *Daily Telegraph*, *Daily Mail* and the *Observer*.

exposure'. Many respondents admitted that it was a combination of the gravity of the situation in Ulster and concerns over personal safety which sustained their interest. A South Bank University student cited personal reasons for 'wanting to see peace in Ireland in my lifetime', arguing that she was disillusioned by 'bad news on TV bulletins, cancelled trains and the threat of bombs in London'. Others said that their concern over events in Northern Ireland were prompted either by family – a Surrey clerk with 'relatives of both religions' in Northern Ireland was concerned at 'their (unionists') treatment by the British Parliament, Dublin and the IRA' – or because of historical links between their own city and Belfast (a Glasgow management consultant observed that 'many Scots are of Irish origin and share the Celtic culture, so we are naturally concerned that the conflict might spread to Great Britain').

'Indifference' to the loyalist plight proved to be the most common response (36% or 59 respondents). Surprisingly, a higher proportion of respondents expressed 'sympathy' for the unionist position than 'hostility' (over 26% or 42 respondents, compared with under 20% or 31 respondents). The preferences and comments reflected an increased awareness of the loyalist case but the tone tended to be dispassionate rather than sympathetic, with a significant number stressing the antiquated nature of unionism and concluding that their increasing marginalisation was their own fault. A number also considered loyalists to be the chief threat to the all-important peace process. One South Bank University student considered loyalists' 'fears of Catholic power to be damaging prospects for peace', whilst a Surrey engineer believed that unionists 'are only marginalised because of their own doing, by placing obstacles in the way of talks'. This notion that regrettable though their marginalisation might be, it was largely their own fault, was reflected in the comments of a Glasgow architect who suggested that 'as you sow so shall ye reap', maintaining that 'a (loyalist) willingness to examine basic principles and to have respect for others would have prevented the present conflict'. Other sources of antipathy to unionists were their perceived 'hatred of Catholics' (a Glasgow electrician) or that their fears 'lacked foundation'. A number acknowledged that unionists had lost ground and had become increasingly marginalised, particularly since the ceasefire. A South Bank University student was wary of 'the peace at any price stance of the British Government' and had some sympathy for loyalists whom she felt would 'lose out in the end', while another South Bank University student felt that Protestants were beginning to adopt the mantle of 'victims', which had been 'so long claimed by Catholics'. An unemployed personnel manager from Lancashire believed that there was a discrepancy between the quality of the unionist case which was 'a good one' and the reception of that case which was 'poor' because they 'have never been able to project an image which is anything other than defensive'. Other respondents, including a Glasgow housewife, felt 'some sympathy for Protestants who fought in the wars and are now probably feeling betrayed' but prioritised the peace process which was 'the only way forward'. A Glasgow plasterer agreed with this viewpoint, arguing that unionists had 'allowed themselves to become marginalised' and 'desperately needed to show their willingness to become deeply involved in the peace process'. The outdated nature of their case was mentioned by several respondents. A Lancashire housewife criticised loyalists for 'looking back', admitting she had 'no patience with them whatsoever', whilst others pointed out unionists' disregard for the wider, 'European' dimension. A South Bank lecturer argued:

> Part of the problem may well relate to the difficulty which many on mainland Britain now have in identifying with or even recognising the political entity to which unionism appeals ... That said, the Ulster Protestants are as a minority with a strong identity and we need to devise a political solution to accommodate them.

For many an increased affinity with the unionist predicament was tempered by continuing criticism of their notional political intransigence and religious bigotry. A Lancashire training advisor said he could 'begin to understand their fears for the future of their culture but I have no time for the religious intolerance upon which that culture is based'. Another South Bank University lecturer conceded that loyalists have 'probably become marginalised in recent years', but qualified his remark by suggesting that unionists 'haven't presented themselves as forward-looking or able to negotiate'. Those who did express empathy towards the unionist position were occcasionally prompted by the activities of others, most notably Gerry Adams (a Guildhall University student talked of the latter's 'Greatest Hits Tour' which had increased her sympathy for the loyalist position). However, others were more open in their expressions of agreement with the 'legitimacy' of the unionist case ('a simple desire to remain part of the British community'), whilst a retired Exeter police officer suggested that what had occurred in South Africa was in stark contrast with Northern Ireland, where 'the majority are very pressurised by the minority which is counter to the wishes shown by the ballot-box'.

Therefore despite substantial, self admitted ignorance of the Northern Ireland situation in general and loyalism in particular, there was some evidence of an increasing awareness of change in the unionist predicament, particularly reflected in the answers to questions on Ian Paisley, the Orange Order, loyalist paramilitaries and unionists' marginalisation. This did not lead to an increased sympathy for the unionist position and indeed, despite an expression by the majority of an interest and concern for Ulster's problems, this did not extend to unionists, to whom the main response was one of indifference rather than sympathy or even hostility. Their answers indicated that this was a result of unionism's negative portrayal in the media over a period of many years and the prevalent perception that loyalists were mere 'spectators' on the political and military scene. A constant theme of the findings was that unionists were 'losing out' in a variety of ways to nationalists. Therefore, although Gerry Adams failed to make any impression on his already dented reputation as a result of his role in the ceasefire, he was regarded by many to be more significant than the two unionist leaders.

Unionists were also unable to capitalise in the area of human suffering, with most respondents interpreting attacks such as the bombing on the Shankill Road as onslaughts on 'civilians' rather than attacks on 'Protestants'. This was in stark contrast with the Catholic community, which had, over a period of many years, claimed its own 'victims' of British military aggression. Another conclusion to be drawn from the survey findings is that, on the whole, the British public has not been partisan to one particular side (a trend, indeed, which is mirrored in the 'honest broker' role of its government). This is illustrated by their endorsement of increasing Dublin involvement in the affairs of Northern Ireland, not because people on the mainland necessarily agree with the notion of Irish unity per se, but rather that it was felt this could strengthen the all-important peace process.

CHAPTER FOUR

Conclusion

A constant theme of this book has been unionism's failure to project its case and elicit sympathy either at political level or in the national media. Therefore, their own propaganda and political pressure activity had little effect on influencing the policy of the main British political parties (most notably in the case of their protests against the Anglo-Irish Agreement) and, with the odd exception, unionists' political demands have not met with an enthusiastic response from the British press. Consequently public opinion has constantly supported the ultimate withdrawal of British troops and a diminuition of British political control over Northern Ireland. My own research not only showed respondents' desire for eventual Irish unity but also illustrated their broad indifference to the political wishes of loyalists. Why then have unionists so clearly lost the all-important propaganda 'war' in Northern Ireland?

As I have attempted to show there are a number of possible explanations. Firstly, it is fair to argue that much damage was self-inflicted. The chasms and divisions which were widening within unionism at the start of the conflict were capitalised upon by unionists' opponents who also intensified Unionism's problems in the late 1960s and early 1970s in disseminating its message to a wider audience. These internecine bickerings and the resulting instability produced an even greater reluctance on the part of loyalists to compromise during a period of intense terrorist activity and political change. Early opportunities to differentiate between 'constitutional' and 'political' issues were not taken and loyalists' genuine concern about their right for self-determination was shrouded by an apparent mean-mindedness over the granting of comparatively basic social and political rights. The consequence of this was the early formulation of a belief that the loyalist community, with its multiplicity of political and paramilitary groups, particularly in the early and mid 1970s, was a squabbling, boisterous and belligerent one, which was stubbornly hanging on to the remaining vestiges of power. The monotone political message which emanated from, what appeared to an external audience, a sterile political leadership which failed, both in terms of its personnel and its policy, to change over the years, combined with unionism's own weakness in the area of propaganda to ensure that their case rarely got the response its numbers deserved. Failing to recover from early propaganda setbacks, Unionists were unable to persuade the mainland audience of the veracity of their case (despite publishing some effective 'enemy' propaganda booklets in the early 1970s, which targetted Bernadette Devlin and the IRA in particular). Unionists, indeed, appeared resigned to perpetual frustration in this sphere and only established a permanent 'propaganda' department with its own regularly-produced newsletter in 1988, and a public relations department in London during 1996.

The initial labelling of unionists as the 'baddies' and the early stereotyping of some loyalist leaders and organisations stigmatised unionism and resulted in loyalists' failure to capture the political initiative. Therefore the tendency to focus on the negative images of loyalism – bigotry, intolerance, intransigence, the 'blockers' of progress – at the expense of other, more revealing, facets (including the populist nature of the political success of Ian Paisley, the Ulster Workers Council strike and the anti-Hillsborough campaign, as well as Orangeism's cultural dimension) was understated in the British media. As I have already illustrated, the most enduring of these images were those of Ian Paisley and the Orange Order. Even significant changes in the loyalist predicament and the widespread feeling within the Protestant community of their increased vulnerability did not persuade most sections of the British media into doubting the notion that Orange marchers were primarily 'bigots in bowler hats'. Ian Paisley was the inveterate pariah as far as the national media was concerned and the chief obstacle in the path to political progress in Northern Ireland. Thus he was considered to be a convenient scapegoat for explaining events with which he had no obvious connection (such as the Enniskillen bombing) as well as providing a ready safety-valve for erring British Secretaries of State. The early stereotyping by the media of a complex political ideology solidified and over the period of the Troubles mitigated against Ulster Unionists' endeavours to present themselves as a 'reasonable' political party.

Another factor which prevailed against unionism was the manner in which the media's early contextualisation of the Irish problem, along with the broad consensus of support for a similar parliamentary response, was to remain in place for the duration of the Troubles. For unionists, the contrast with the great volume of support which they had enjoyed in the Edwardian period, was hard to bear. Ironically they enjoyed more success from Labour administrations than they did from Conservative ones. In the latter case, it was particularly painful for loyalists to see their erstwhile partners opting for a political 'separation', if not a 'divorce'. The decision of Tory administrations, started by Margaret Thatcher and continued by John Major, to foster closer liaison with Dublin and to pursue a 'non-persuading' role as far as the issue of the union was concerned, was a great blow to unionist confidence. Despite the polarisation on the political extremes, the unusual cross-party consensus on Northern Ireland resulted in an early acceptance of the need for governments to adopt a 'neutral' position, thus making it difficult for unionists to make political inroads (indeed, the prospect of this occurring was only apparent during occasional periods of political tension and uncertainty, especially when Unionists' parliamentary support was sought after). This 'middle of the road' approach was also, albeit to a lesser extent, prevalent in media coverage of Northern Ireland. Although they were to reconsider their initial perceptions of the conflict and were to become increasingly critical of the emerging republican paramilitary threat, this did not lead to an increased sympathy for political loyalism. Television companies, despite their requirement to be politically 'neutral', gave more exposure to other viewpoints on Ulster and even Tory papers, despite their condemnation of the IRA, tended to concur with the major policy decisions of their governments, rather than lending their support to unionists.

In a sense it was inevitable that unionists would fare badly in the propaganda 'war'. With a few exceptions, it was nationalists and republicans who set the military and political agenda. Thus, as loyalist paramilitaries restricted their activities to Northern Ireland, their actions gained fewer headlines in the Press and they were also in a weaker position to influence political developments. Consequently, the British media conveyed the inevitability of the loyalist announcement of their ceasefire in October 1994 and it was republican issues such as the release of prisoners, demilitarisation and a guaranteed place at the conference table for all factions, as well as Gerry Adams's visits to America, which dominated the headlines. Since the mid 1980s the 'Irish' dimension had not only predominated British political discourse, but had also been central to its media coverage of Northern Ireland. Accordingly, loyalists' political wishes, such as the speedy restoration of meaningful devolved government to the province, have received far less attention than joint governmental initiatives. Nationalists even managed to gain the moral high ground in judicial matters, when a series of miscarriages of justice received enormous media coverage in Britain, assisting in no small way the reversal of the initial judicial decisions. The media's selectivity of news stories certainly mitigated against loyalists. Investigative programmes tended to focus on the government's errors of judgement and the alleged excesses of the security forces, issues with which loyalists were less likely to concur. Therefore, apart from being largely bypassed by the broadcasting of stories related to miscarriages of justice, the use of plastic bullets and media censorship, they were unable to ensure that their own issues received comparable coverage. As a result, unionists were unsuccessful in pre-empting an alteration in the media's contextualisation of the conflict which had, from its earliest stages, mitigated against their position.

The importance which Liz Curtis rightly gives to 'quality' coverage of events occurring in a region, of which most British citizens had little first-hand experience, is not reflected in the actual coverage which tends, in the main, to be factual, rather than analytical.[1] There has been little 'prime' time analytical coverage of Northern Ireland's historical development and its political problems and those programmes which did adopt an analytical approach tended to be in the 'quizzical of the government' category referred to above. As loyalists were, technically at least, supporters of the status quo, they were less likely to be chosen as the subjects for such programmes, even though they felt they had, as a community, equally significant, grievances. This failure on the part of the national media to probe behind the headlines was not just on account of unionists being less likely to have set those headlines by their political or military actions, but also

1 L. Curtis, *Ireland - The Propaganda War*, op. cit.

because the complex nature of their political ideology meant there would inevitably be problems disseminating this to an already frustrated audience who were used to seeing the conflict and particularly the unionists in stereotypes.[2] My research has illustrated the disproportionate attention given to the republican or nationalist perspective in the minority of those programmes which were analytical and showed how those featured images of loyalism were inclined to be mainly negative and, with the occasional distinguished exception, simply had the effect of reinforcing existing stereotypes. This was also largely true of the tabloid press which tended to focus their attention on covering the conflict's violent backdrop, and, in the main, affording their support to government initiatives.

In assessing the degree of sympathy for the unionist position emanating from British politicians and media, it is important to note both a fluctuation in the degree of support over the years and a clear distinction between maintaining a genuine regard for the 'innocent' victims of violence, the 'silent majority', and a comparative indifference to the political desires of Northern Ireland's majority. The initial 'blanket' criticism of unionist leaders and a lack of commiseration for their declining political fortunes at the start of the current conflict was modified, particularly as the IRA campaign escalated and the 'intrusion' of the Irish Government increased. However, this should not be seen as constituting an overnight conversion to a unionist agenda. Rather, it was that a new 'enemy' or 'enemies', had been identified and those in power in Great Britain became increasingly disgruntled, both with their own inability to solve Northern Ireland's security and political problem and more especially, with the mounting criticism of 'external' commentators for their failure to do so. Nor was it solely a matter of ignoring the unionists will because they weren't seen to dominate the pace of events. Hence, on those few occasions when unionists did, like the UWC strike in 1974, and, albeit with less success, the anti-Hillsborough protests, there was little evidence of an increase in mainland sympathy for their case. Therefore,even when they were marginalised, unionists did not enjoy widespread, sustained support. However, this probably owed more to the perceived stridency of the unionist response. Thus when this rejoinder was deemed to be belligerent, as in the case of Hillsborough, or towards the Executive in 1974, political and media treatment tended to be sharply critical. However, when unionist reactions were subdued, as in the case of the Ulster Unionists' initial response to the Downing Street Declaration, or in the loyalist reaction to the IRA ceasefire, there was a modicum of commiseration for the predicament of the new 'underdogs'.

Despite the perennial presence of a small but voluble 'rump' of parliamentary support for the Ulster Unionist case, there was a gradual 'distancing' between the latter group and their erstwhile friends in the Conservative Party. This political 'separation' was more apparent to unionists in the mid 1990s as their opponents managed to bury their political differences in their endeavours to promote the 'Irish' dimension. Arguably unionists got more support from the conservative press than they did from a Conservative government. Several leading

2 This was even more evident in American television coverage of Northern Ireland, which was reliant on easily dissected news items.

articles in tabloids such as the *Sun*, *Daily Mail* and the *Daily Express*, were increasingly critical of the government's security policy and their 'concessions' to Dublin, and conservative broadsheets like the *Daily Telegraph* and the *Times* were increasingly outspoken in their demands for the introduction of alternative political measures, such as integration and the return of devolved government to the province. Yet, even during a period when several of these conservative papers were backing a rival, 'rookie' candidate to John Major for the Conservative leadership, they rallied behind the premier over his Irish policy, supporting initiatives such as the Downing Street Declaration and the Framework Document (just as they had backed Mrs Thatcher's signing of the Anglo-Irish Agreement in 1985).[3] Indeed, the Tory press were more critical of unionist 'enemies' and supportive of their 'friends' than they were in siding with the political demands of unionist representatives. Therefore, they were more vociferous in their condemnation of IRA attacks, Dublin's 'interference', and supportive, to varying degrees, of the army and RUC in the province, than they were in backing unionist demands for the restoration of devolved government and the adoption of a clear 'persuading' role as far as the Union was concerned. By pursuing the agenda and issues dictated by republican paramilitaries (no matter how vigorously their condemnation of it actually was), the press further marginalised a political group with whom they were supposed to enjoy close fraternal relationships. In any case, even the conservative press were inclined to criticise the unionist leadership, lamenting their intransigence, as well as castigating the more pronounced presence of the loyalist paramilitaries. Arguably by portraying loyalist paramilitary attacks as politically 'senseless' (in contrast with the more clearly motivated actions of Sinn Fein and the IRA), the media was reinforcing an impression that such loyalist organisations lacked the political credibility of their opponents. In general, the media played mainly on unionism's negative features and by selecting certain features of the Irish conflict at the expense of others which might have created greater understanding of the unionist position, a one-dimensional portrait of the Irish conflict was painted for an undiscerning British public. These included 'border genocide', the sectarian nature of attacks on the RUC and UDR, occasional instances of cohesion within the loyalist community and the populist nature both of the UWC and anti Anglo-Irish Agreement protests and the leadership of Ian Paisley.

My investigation into the nature of loyalism highlighted the scale of change occurring within unionism since 1968. Apart from noting the break-down in monolithic unionism and the success of the DUP, I observed some differences between the media's interpretation of the traits of loyalism and those components which modern unionists think most important. Unionists are also concerned by the way their political case still fails to be taken seriously in Great Britain. I concluded that this was a combination of loyalists being unable to dismantle the communication barriers imposed by the initial stereotyping of their position and a result of their poor propaganda. The upshot of this has been their

3 John Redwood, whom Major defeated in a 1995 leadership contest, enjoyed the support of several Tory tabloids.

increasing political marginalisation. In terms of achieving its objectives, republican propaganda has been noticeably more successful. Perhaps the latter's greatest achievement has been to ensure that most of the British public are either unable or unwilling to differentiate between representatives of terrorist organisations and leaders of constitutional parties. Confused by the intricacies of an interminable conflict, they refuse to distinguish between Gerry Adams and Ian Paisley and indeed, as my survey indicated, consider the former, at the time an unelected, politician to be a more significant figure than the latter, an elected representative for both British and European Parliaments. In some ways, this illustrates a perception that some people in Britain have that intransigent unionists almost deserve the IRA. Unionist propaganda has been unsuccessful, both in terms of preparing material which has the potential for persuading large numbers of the veracity of their case, and its inability to reach a significant proportion of the Great British public.

Contemporary unionists are, in practice, more dependent on the media's output on Northern Ireland than they were in the past. Thus, the scale and success of the anti-Home Rule propaganda campaign of 1910-14 far exceeded that of contemporary unionist propaganda which has reached a far smaller audience and has over-relied on appealing to the already-committed. The fact that this media coverage was generally poor in its quality and tended, on balance, to portray loyalism in one-dimensional terms, made unionists' own propaganda failures even more apparent. The leading TV programmes which I investigated featured unionist issues less frequently than republican or nationalist ones and much of the tone of the coverage of the loyalist case was critical. More sympathetic portrayal of the unionist position was given in sections of the conservative press but the monotony of the news stories and the complex political background which was rarely explained adequately in the press and on television resulted in the stereotyping of loyalist viewpoints, and the early spread of apathy within Great Britain. After a quarter of a century, the majority of the British public are unable to make informed comments about the situation in Northern Ireland which, in itself, speaks volumes about the quality of the media coverage. This affected the loyalist case more than the nationalists whose 'friends' (the Irish government and Irish-Americans) remained 'constant' and whose mindset was focussed on the long-term. The British public, desensitised by the enduring nature of the conflict, are largely indifferent to unionists' political plight, as my survey showed. Although many are better informed about unionist fears, this has not increased their degree of sympathy for their political cause. Occasionally terrorist outrages, such as the Enniskillen bomb in 1987, could result in an outpouring of sympathy and understanding which had, from the unionist viewpoint, positive repercussions in the area of public opinion, although this was neither overtly political in its nature nor was it to be sustained.

Central to this research has been the testing of the premise that the enormous chasm between unionist interpretations of the moral rectitude of their case and mainland scepticism towards such attitudes, could not be breached. This was due to the presence of differing perceptions about what 'loyalism' actually entailed, as well as diverse analyses of its political message. Unionists have expressed peevishness at the manner in which they have been portrayed in the media and by the aloof response of British politicians to their increasingly marginalised political predicament. Another principal theme of this work was the combined effect of inadequate unionist propaganda and analytical media coverage on the British public's understanding of the conflict. The consequence was diminished appreciation of the loyalist case in Great Britain which meant that the British public were less likely to align itself with unionists. Indeed, it was this direct correlation between the low calibre of information available to the British public and the subsequent dearth of support for unionism which was the kernel of my argument. It has also raised the wider issue of the quality of the media's analytical coverage of the conflict and how select coverage of specific concerns at the expense of others has mitigated against proper understanding of the longest-running problem in British politics.

Since the social, cultural and political manifestations of their loyalism are reported within the long-established mainstream contextualisation of the Northern Irish problem, unionists are rarely able to enjoy the satisfaction of seeing their case presented in anything other than stereotypical terms. On account of the predominance of investigative programmes into allegations of state transgressions in Northern Ireland, as well as the complex nature of their political philosophy (not to mention their own presentational shortcomings), loyalism has been especially susceptible to simplistic one-dimensional media coverage and has been the subject of significantly fewer programmes than nationalism or republicanism. Despite press condemnation of unionist 'enemies' such as the IRA or successive Irish governments, unionism has rarely received sustained press support when it was urgently required and there has been a marked distinction between media condemnation of republican terrorism and overt sympathy for loyalists' political plight. Due to the dearth of analytical coverage and the media's insistence on presenting the Irish problem in a simplistic fashion, unionists continue to be misunderstood in Great Britain. If one accepts that there is a 'British' as well as an 'Irish' problem and that British understanding of the most enduring domestic problem over their last thirty years has barely improved, then one should be disturbed by continuing intolerance in Great Britain towards both traditions in Northern Ireland, and especially the unionist one. Or perhaps after all, such a characteristic is not confined to the 'bigots in the bowler hats' ...

Bibliography

PRIMARY SOURCES

Newspapers and magazines (mainly the period between late 1968 and early 1996)

Belfast NewsLetter
Belfast Telegraph
Birmingham Post
Daily Express
Daily Mail
Daily Mirror
Daily Star
Daily Telegraph
Economist
Evening Standard (London)
Financial Times
Fortnight
Guardian
Hibernia
Independent
Independent on Sunday
Irish News
Irish Times
Listener
Mail on Sunday
News of the World
Newsweek
New Statesman/Society
Observer
Orange Standard
People
Protestant Telegraph
Radio Times
Spectator
Sun
Sunday Express
Sunday Mirror
Sunday News
Sunday Telegraph
Sunday Times
Times
Times Educational Supplement
Today

TELEVISION PROGRAMMES

The main focus for this study was on investigative programmes relating to Northern Ireland. The four programmes or TV stations featured in depth in the third chapter were supplemented by programmes bearing on the case studies. Research tended to concentrated on BBC1's 'Panorama' (the records are housed at the BBC Archives Library, near Reading), London Weekend Television, Thames Television and Channel Four. Thames and LWT have their own records on programmes relating to Northern Ireland, held at their respective headquarters in London; Channel Four provided an (incomplete) list of such programmes. Where the records were available, complete programme scripts were consulted.

OFFICIAL PUBLICATIONS

Northern Ireland reports

The Cameron Report (1969), *Disturbances in Northern Ireland*, Cmnd 532 (HMSO, Belfast).

The Scarman Report (1972), *Violence and Civil Disturbances in Northern Ireland in 1969*, Cmd 566 (HMSO, Belfast)

United Kingdom reports, papers and constitutional agreements

The Anglo-Irish Agreement (1985), Cmnd 9690 (HMSO, London).
The Downing Street Declaration (1993), (HMSO, Belfast).
Framework for the Future (1995), (HMSO, Belfast).
The Windlesham/Rampton Report on Death on the Rock (London 1989).
Hansard Parliamentary Debates (mainly the 5th and 6th series 1968-92, HMSO, London).

Local Government

GLC (1984), *Report on the Prevention of Terrorism Act in London*, London.

Republic of Ireland

Report of the New Ireland Forum (1984, Dublin).

ARCHIVES OF POLITICAL PARTIES

CONSERVATIVE

Manifestos

1970 Manifesto, *A Better Tomorrow*
Feb. 1974 manifesto, *Firm Action for a Fairer Britain*
Oct. 1974 manifesto, *Putting Britain First*
The 1979 Conservative Manifesto
1987 manifesto, *The Next Moves Forward*
1992 manifesto, *The Best Future for Britain*

Party literature

Biggs-Davison, J. (undated), *Catholics and the Union*, Friends of the Union.
Cooke, A.B. (1988), *Ulster – The Origins of the Problem*, Conservative Political Centre
Gow, I. (ed.) (1987), *Hope for Peace – A New Anglo-Irish Agreement*, Friends of the Union.
Gow, I. (undated), *After the Agreement*, Friends of the Union.
Storey, D. (1988), *Wanted – a Positive Policy for Ulster*, Monday Club

LABOUR PARTY

Most of these documents can be found in Section 329 LAB A1 of the Labour Party Archives Library in London.

Manifestos

All of the Labour manifestos between 1964 and 1992, including:
February 1974 manifesto, *Let us Work Together – Labour's Way out of the Crisis.*
October 1974 manifesto, *Britain Will Win*
1979 manifesto, *The Labour Way Is the Better Way*
1983 manifesto, *The New Hope for Britain*
1987 manifesto, *Labour Will Win*
1992 manifesto, *It's Time to Get Britain Working Again.*

Policy documents/conference statements

National Executive *Statement to the Conference* 1974
Labour's *Programme for Britain Conference* statement 1976
NEC's *Conference Statement to the Conference* 1981

Reports

Reports of Labour Commission to Ireland 1921
National Executive Council of the British Anti-Partition League, *Labour and Ireland – Then and Now,* 1950

LIBERALS

Including not only Liberal Party material but also that belonging to the Alliance and the Liberal Democrats

Manifestos

February 1974 manifesto, *Changing the Face of Britain*
1979 manifesto, *The Real Fight Is for Britain*
1983 SDP/Liberal Alliance manifesto, *Work Together for Britain*
1987 SDP/Liberal Alliance manifesto, *Britain United – The Time Has Come*
1992 Liberal Democrats manifesto, *Changing Britain for Good*

Policy documents

Liberal Democrats, *A New Deal for Northern Ireland*, 1994

Unionist party documents

Brownless, W., Ulster Monday Club (undated), *It has all happened before – the Munich Agreement and the Hillsborough Deal.*
Clark, G.A./UUC (1969), *This is the Real Ulster – The Facts*
Gillies, D./Scottish Unionists Group (undated probably 1973), *In Place of Truth – Ulster the Victim.*
Queen's University Ulster Unionists Association (1988), *3 Years After – The Anglo-Irish Process Reviewed*
Reynolds, L./UUC (1995), 'Provo Think', in *Ulster Review*
Smith, P. (1984), *Opportunity Lost – A Unionist View of the Report of the Forum for a New Ireland*

Unionist Party (undated, probably 1971), *The Right of a Free People to Live without fear*
Unionist Party (1973), Assembly Manifesto, *Peace, Order and Good Government*
Unionist Party (1984), *The Way Forward*
Unionist Research Department (undated), *Northern Ireland – The Hidden Truth*
Unionist Research Department (1972), *Continuing the Terror and the Tears – More Facts about the Inhumanity of the IRA*
UUC (1969), *Bernadette's Millions*
Ulster Unionist Information Institute Newsletter; particularly nos 1–5, (1988–90) and no. 10 (1993).
UUII (1995), *Blueprint for Stability*
UUP (1985), *Framed – A Critical Analysis of the Framework Document.*
UUP (1985), Local Government Manifesto, *Keep Ulster British*
UUP (1980), *Northern Ireland – The Truth*
UUP (1995), *A Practical Approach to Problem-Solving in Northern Ireland*

DEMOCRATIC UNIONIST PARTY

Allister, I. (undated, believed to be 1986), *Irish Unification – A Anathema*
Calvert, D. (1973), *A Decade of the DUP*
DUP (1973), *Assembly Manifesto*
DUP (1981), *The Future Assured*
DUP (1982), *The Voice of Ulster*
DUP (1984), *The Unionist Case - the Forum Report Answered*
DUP (1985), *Local Election Manifesto*
DUP (1993), *Breaking the Logjam*
DUP (1995), *Formula for Political Progress*
Paisley, I. (1974), *An Enemy has done this – Terror and Treachery in Northern Ireland*

Other Loyalist publications

Joint Unionist Working Party (1986), *The Anglo-Irish Agreement – A Legacy of Violence*
Joint Unionist Working Party (undated, probably 1986), *Why Ulster Unionists Say No.*
Meredith, I. (1989), *England's Orange Evangelicals: A Personal Testimony, in The Twelfth* (Orange Order).
New Ulster Political Research Group (1979), *Beyond the Religious Divide*
New Ulster Political Research Group (1987), *Common Sense*
Porter, W.W. (1990), *A Celebration – 1690–1990 – The Orange Institution*
Shankill Road Conference Report (1995), *Beyond the Fife and Drum*
Ulster Vanguard Progressive Party (1972), *Ulster – A Nation*
Ulster Vanguard Progressive Party (1973), *Assembly Manifesto*
Ulster Workers Council Strike Bulletins (1974)

DIARIES AND MEMOIRS

Baker, K. (1993), *The Turbulent Years – My Life in Politics*, London
Benn, T. (1989), *Tony Benn – Against the Tide Diaries 1973–76*, London
Bloomfield, K. (1994), *Stormont in Crisis – Memoir*, Belfast
Callaghan, J. (1973), *A House Divided – The Dilemma of Northern Ireland*, London
Carrington, P. (1988), *Reflect on Things Past – The Memoirs of Lord Carrington*, London
Castle, B. (1986), *The Castle Diaries 1964–67*, London
Cole, J. (1995), *As it seemed to me – Political Memoirs*, London
Crossman, R. (1977), *The Diaries of a Cabinet Minister*, Volume 3, London
Devlin, B. (1969), *The Price of my Soul*, London
Faulkner, B. (1978), *Memoirs of a Statesman*, London
Fitzgerald, G. (1991), *All in a Life*, Dublin
Gilmour, I. (1992), *Dancing with Dogma – Britain under Thatcherism*, London
Ingham, B. (1991), *Kill the Messenger*, London
King, C. (1975), *The Cecil King Diary, 1970–74*, London
Lawson, N. (1992), *The View from No. 11: Memoirs of a Tory Radical*, London
Milne, A. (1988), *D.G. – The Memoirs of a British Broadcaster*, London
O'Neill, T. (1969), *Ulster at the Crossroads*, London
Owen, D. (1991), *Time to Declare*, London
Prior, J. 1986), *A Balance of Power*, London
Rees, M. (1985), *Northern Ireland – A Personal Perspective*, London
Steel, D. & Owen D. (1987), *The Time Has Come – Partnership for Progress*, London
Tebbit, N. (1988), *Upwardly Mobile*, London
Thatcher, M. (1993), *The Downing Street Years*, London
Whitelaw, W. (1989), *The Whitelaw Memoirs*, London

SECONDARY SOURCES

Adamson, I. (1982), *The Identity of Ulster – The Land, the Language and the People*, Belfast
Alexander ,Y. & O'Day, A. (eds) (1989), *Ireland's Terrorist Trauma*, London
Anderson, D. (1994), *14 May Days – The Inside Story of the Loyalist Strike of 1974*, Dublin
Arthur, P. (ed) (1987), *Government and Politics of Northern Ireland*, London

Arthur, P. & Jeffery, K. (1988), *Northern Ireland Since 1968*, Oxford
Aughey, A. (1989), *Under Siege – Ulster Unionism and the Anglo-Irish Agreement*, Belfast
Barritt, D.P. & Carter, C.I. (1962), *The Northern Ireland Problem: A Study in Group Relations*, Oxford
Bardon, J. (1992), *A History of Ulster*, Belfast

Barton, B. & Roche, P.J. (1994), *The Northern Ireland Question – Perspectives and and Policies*, Aldershot
Beattie, G. (1992), *We Are the People – Journeys through the Heart of Protestant Ulster*, London
Belfrage, S. (1987), *The Crack – A Belfast Year*, London
Bell, D. (1990), *Acts of Union – Youth Culture and Sectarianism in Northern Ireland*, Basingstoke
Bell, G. (1976), *The Protestants of Ulster*, London
——(1982), *The Labour Party and the Irish Question – Troublesome Business*, London
Bew, P. and Gillespie, G. (1993), *Northern Ireland – A Chronology of the Troubles 1968–93*, Dublin
Bew, P. & Patterson, H. (1985), *The British State and the Ulster Crisis from Wilson to Thatcher*, London
Bolton, R. (1990), *Death on the Rock and Other Stories*, London
Boulton, D. (1973), *The UVF 1966–73 – An Anatomy of Loyalist Rebellion*, Dublin
Boyce, D.G. (1989), 'The Irish Connection' in *The Thatcher Effect – A Decade of Changes*, ed. by D. Kavanagh and A Seldon, Oxford
——(1988), *The Irish Question and British Politics 1868–1986*, London
Boyle, K. & Hadden, T., (1985), *Ireland – A Positive Proposal*, London
Bruce, S. 1986), *God Save Ulster! The Religion and Politics of Paisleyism*, Oxford
——(1992), *The Red Hand – Protestant Paramilitaries in Northern Ireland*, Oxford
——(1994), *At the Edge of the Union – The Ulster Loyalist Political Vision*, Oxford
Buckland, P. (1993), *Irish Unionism 1885–1923*, Belfast
——(1981), *A History of Northern Ireland*, Dublin
Butler, D. (1995), *The Trouble with Reporting Northern Ireland*, Aldershot
Cathcart, R. (1984), *The Most Contrary Region – The BBC in Northern Ireland 1924–84*, Belfast
Christmas L. (1989), *Chopping down the Cherry Trees*, London
Cooke, A. (ed.) (1989), *Margaret Thatcher and the Revival of Britain – Speeches on Home and European Affairs 1975–88*, London
Cooke, D. (1996), *Persecution Zeal – A portrait of Ian Paisley*, Cork
Cosgrave, P. (1989), *The Lives of Enoch Powell*, London
Crawford, R.G. (1987), *Loyal to King Billy – A Portrait of the Ulster Protestants*, Dublin
Cunningham, M.J. (1991), *British Government Policy in Northern Ireland 1969–89) – Its Nature and Execution*, Manchester
Curtis, L. (1983), *Ireland – The Propaganda War*, London
Darby, J. (1983), *Northern Ireland – Background to the Conflict*, Belfast/New York
——(1984), *Dressed to Kill – Cartoonists and the Northern Ireland Conflict*, Belfast
de Paor, L. (1990), *Unfinished Business – Ireland Today and Tomorrow*, London
Dillon, M. (1988), *The Dirty War*, London
——(1989), *The Shankill Butchers*, London

——(1992), *Stone Cold – The True Story of Michael Stone and the Milltown Massacre*, London
Downey, J. (1983), *Them and Us – Britain, Ireland and the Northern Question 1969–82*, Dublin
Elliot, P. (1976), *Reporting Northern Ireland: A Study of News in Britain, Ulster and the Irish Republic*, Leicester
Ellul, J. (1973), *Propaganda: The Formation of Men's Attitudes*, New York
English, R. & Walker, G (eds) (1996), *Unionism in Modern Ireland – new perspectives on Politics and Culture*, Dublin
Fairweather, E., McDonough R. & McFadyean, M. (1984), *Only the Rivers Run Free – Northern Ireland and the Women's War*, London
Farrell, M. (1976), *Northern Ireland – The Orange State*, London
Fisk, R. (1975), *The Point of No Return – The Strike Which Broke theBritish in Ulster*, London
Flackes, W. & Elliott, S. (1989), *Northern Ireland – A Political Directory 1968–1988*, Belfast
Foster, R. (1988) *Modern Ireland – 1600–1972*, London
Gaffikin, F. & Morissey, M. (1990), *Northern Ireland – The Thatcher Years*, London & New Jersey
Gebler, C. (1991), *The Glass Curtain – Inside an Ulster Community*, London
Glasgow University Media Group (1985), *War and Peace News*, Milton Keynes
Goldring, M. (1991), *Belfast – From Loyalty to Rebellion*, London
Guelke, A. (1988), *Northern Ireland – The International Perspective*, Dublin
Hall, M. (1986), *Ulster – The Hidden History*, Belfast
Harbinson, J. (1973), *The Ulster Unionist Party 1882–1973*, Belfast
Hastings, M. (1969), *Ulster*, London
Holland, J. (1989), *The American Connection: US Guns, Money and Influence in Northern Ireland*, Dublin
Holmes, M. (1985), *The Labour Government 1974–9 – Political Aims and Economic Reality*, London
Hume, D. (1996), *The Ulster Unionist Party 1972–92 – a Political Movement in an era of Conflict and Change*, Belfast.
Jowett, G. & O'Donnell, V. (1986),*Propaganda and Persuasion*, Beverley Hills
Kee, R. (1980), *Ireland – A History*, London
——(1986), *Trial and Error – The Guildford Pub Bombings and British Justice*, London
Kennedy, D. (1988), *The Widening Gulf – Northern Attitudes to the Independent Irish State 1919–49*, Belfast.
Kenny, A. (1986) *The Road to Hillsborough – The Shaping of the Anglo-Irish Agreement*, Oxford
Kingsley, P. (1989), *Londonderry Revisited – A Loyalist Analysis of the Civil Rights Controversy*, Belfast
Lee, J. (1989), *Ireland 1912–85 – Politics and Society*, Cambridge
Longford, F. & McHardy, A. (1981), *Ulster*, London
Lucy, G. (1996), *Stand-off! – Drumcree, July 1995 and 1996*, Lurgan

McCann, E. (1974), *War and an Irish Town*, London
McCreary, A. (1990), *Marie – A Story from Enniskillen*, London
MacDonald, M. (1986). *Children of Wrath – Political Violence in Northern Ireland*, Cambridge
McKittrick, D. (1989), *Despatches from Belfast*, Belfast
——(1994), *Endgame – the Search for Peace in Northern Ireland*,
Miller, D. (1994), *Don't Mention the War – Northern Ireland, Propaganda and the Media*, London
Miller, D.W. (1978), *Queen's Rebels: Ulster Loyalism in Historical Perspective*, Dublin/New York
Moloney, E. & Pollack, A. (1986), *Paisley*, Dublin
Moore, C. & Heffer, S. (1989), *A Tory Seer – The Selected Journalism of T.E. Utley*, London
MORI (1989), *We British – Britain Under the Microscope*, London
——(1991), *British Attitudes to Northern Ireland*, research conducted on behalf of Northside Productions, 21–4 March 1991, London
Mullin, C. (1986), *Error of Judgement – The Truth About the Birmingham Bombings*, London
Murphy, D. (1991), *The Stalker Affair and the Press*, London
Negrine, R. (ed) (1994), *Politics and the Mass Media in Britain*, London
Nelson, S. (1984), *Ulster's Uncertain Defenders – Loyalists and the Northern Ireland Conflict*, Belfast
O'Malley, P. (1983), *The Uncivil War – Ireland Today*, Belfast
——(1990), *Biting at the Grave – The Irish Hunger Strike and the Politics of Despair*, Belfast
Osmond, J. (1988), *The Divided Kingdom*, London
Owen, A.E. (1994), *The Anglo-Irish Agreement – The first three years*, Cardiff
Paisley, I. Jnr. (1991), *Beyond Reasonable Doubt – The Case for the UDR Four*, Cork
Porter, N. (1996), *Rethinking Unionism – An Alternative Vision for Northern Ireland*, Belfast
Purdy, A. (1989), *Molyneaux – The Long View*, Antrim
Rolstron, B. (ed)(1991), *The Media and Northern Ireland – Covering the Troubles*, London
Rose, R. (1971), *Governing without Consensus*, London
Rowan, B. (1995), *Behind the Lines – The Story of the IRA and the Loyalist Ceasefires*, Belfast
Ryder, C. (1989), *The RUC — A Force under Fire*, London
——(1991), *The UDR – An Instrument of Peace*, London
Schlesinger P. (1978), *Putting Reality Together, BBC News*, London
Seymour-Ure, C. (1991), *The British Press and Broadcasting Since 1945*, London
Stewart, A.T.Q. (1977), *The Narrow Ground – Aspects of Ulster 1609–1969*, London
Sunday Times Insight Team (1972), *Ulster*, London
Taylor, G. (1993), *Changing Faces – A History of the Guardian 1956–88*, London
Taylor, P. (1989), *Families at War – Voices from the Troubles*, London

Turner, M. (1995), *Pack Up Your Troubles – 25 Years of Northern Ireland Cartoons*, Belfast
Wichert, S. (1991), *Northern Ireland since 1945*, Harlow
Wilkinson, P. (1977), *Terrorism and the Liberal State*, London
—— (ed)(1981), *British Perspectives on Terrorism*, London
Wilson, T. (1989), *Ulster – Conflict and Consent*, Oxford
Winchester, S. (1974), *The Holy Terror – Reporting the Ulster Troubles*, London
Woodman, K. (1985), *Media Control in Ireland 1923–83*, Galway
Wright, F. (1987), *Northern Ireland – A Comparative Analysis,* Dublin
Utley, T.E. (1975), *Lessons of Ulster*, London

DISSERTATIONS/THESES

Butler, D. (1994), 'The Representation of Northern Ireland and the Crisis in British Broadcasting' DPhil, University of Ulster.
Campbell, N B. (1978), 'The Unionist Party and the Protestant Working Class 1918–26', MA, University of Ulster
Foldi, P.S. (1989), 'Ulster (still) Says No!, The Anglo-Irish Agreement and Unionist Reactions 1985–87', MSc, LSE
Hamilton-Tweedale, B. (1986), 'The British Press and Northern Ireland: A Case Study in the Reporting of Violent Conflict', PhD, Sheffield University
Miller, D. (1994), 'The Struggle Over, and the Impact of Media Portrayals of Northern Ireland', PhD, Glasgow University
Parkinson, A.F. (1989), 'Ulster will Fight and Ulster Will be Right! – The Presentation of the Anti Home Rule Case in Great Britain 1912–14', MA, University of Westminster
——(1996), 'Loyal Rebels Without a Cause? The Presentation and Reception of the Loyalist Case in Great Britain 1968-1996', PhD, Swansea University

ARTICLES, PAMPHLETS, CHAPTERS

Aughey, A. (1994), 'Contemporary Unionist Politics' (Chapter 2) and 'Conservative Party Policy and Northern Ireland' (Chapter 5) in B. Barton & P.J. Roche (ed.), *The Northern Ireland Question: Perspectives and Politics* (Aldershot).
Clifton, T. (1982), 'Northern Ireland - An Exercise in Futility' in *Newsweek*, 25 January 1982
Francis, R. (1977), *The BBC in Northern Ireland*, 3 March 1977
Kirkaldy, J. (1984), 'Northern Ireland and Fleet Street: Misreporting a Continuing Tragedy' in Y. Alexander & A. O'Day (eds), *Terrorism in Ireland*, (London)
Kyle, K. (1979), *The Irish Dimension in Political Quarterly*, 50, No. 1, Jan-March 1979, 24–35.
Lomax, D. (1987), 'The Troubled Peace' in the *Listener*, 26 March 1987

Lyons, F.S.L. (1978), *The Burden of Our History* (Queen's University, Belfast).
Parkinson, A.F. (1982), 'Yer Man about the Bush – Northern Irish Studies in Britain', in *Irish Studies in Britain*, No.11 (London)
Stewart, A.T.Q. (1986), 'The Siege of Ulster' in the *Spectator*, 11 January 1986
Wright, F. (1973), 'Protestant Ideology and Politics in Ulster', in *European Journal of Sociology*, XIV, 2, 213–80.

Index

Also from Four Courts Press

An Ascendancy Army
The Irish Yeomanry, 1796-1834

ALLAN BLACKSTOCK

In mid-1796 the Irish government faced the threat of domestic insurrection and the likelihood of an invasion by the forces of revolutionary France. The spreading power of the United Irishmen was paralyzing the law and order system and threatening to overwhelm wavering, unorganized loyalists. The Irish Yeomanry, a voluntary, part-time, local defence force, was formed in September 1796 in response to this deepening crisis. Using a wide range of primary sources this book reconstructs Irish Yeomanry's organizational system and provides a membership profile in social and religious terms. The Yeomanry's origins are located in the tradition of Protestant self-defence stretching back to the plantations. Its linkages with the old Irish Volunteers and the recently formed Orange Order are investigated to shed new light on the critical years leading up to the 1798 rebellion.

Allan Blackstock is a graduate of Queen's University Belfast and works at the Institute of Irish Studies, Queen's University Belfast.

ISBN 1-85182-329-8

The Uniforms of 1798-1803

F. GLENN THOMPSON

This book details (in full colour) the uniforms of soldiers and regiments who fought in Ireland during the period 1796 to 1803. Its 26 full colour plates show the dress and arms of the Insurgents, the French, the Regulars, Yeomanry, Militia, Fencibles, Artillery, etc.

ISBN 1-85182-393-X cloth
ISBN 1-85182-396-4 pbk

Also from Four Courts Press

The Williamite War in Ireland, 1688-1691

RICHARD DOHERTY

This book is an account of the war that convulsed Ireland from 1688 to 1691, the echoes of which can be heard to this day. This is a military historian's view of that war which describes the major battles and sieges, including the Boyne, Aughrim, Derry and Limerick, as well as actions that are not so well known such as the sieges of Carrickfergus, Charlemont and Athlone. In these pages we also meet some of the principal commanders, including the two kings who fought at the Boyne and men such as Tyrconnell, Ginkel, Kirke and Solms. Above them all tower the names of Marlborough and Sarsfield, while the talent of the duke of Berwick begins to flower during the war.

The author challenges some of the accepted myths of the Williamite war, including those surrounding the siege of Derry, and he also analyses why the final victory went to the Williamites rather than to the Jacobites, concluding that the reasons were entirely military and political rather than as a result of any moral superiority of the victors.

Richard Doherty is a writer and broadcaster and has presented both radio and TV programmes for the BBC and RTE. His books include Clear the Way! A History of the 38th (Irish) Brigade, 1941-47.

ISBN 1-85182-374-3 cloth;
ISBN 1-85182-375-1 pbk

Also from Four Courts Press

The Royal Irish Constabulary
A Short History and Genealogical Guide with a Select List of Medal Awards and Casualities

JIM HERLIHY

In the period 1816 to 1922 some 85,000 men served in the RIC and its predecessor force. Information on all these policemen is available, constituting a quarry for their hundreds of thousands of descendants in Ireland, USA and elsewhere.

This book consists of introductory chapters about the history of policing in Ireland (to illustrate the type of men in the Force, their background and lifestyle etc.) followed by a core chapter on 'Tracing your ancestors in the RIC'. This is followed by useful appendices which point the way to the RIC lists as a genealogical source; these appendices include a select list giving names of men who were casualties in 1916-22, men who volunteered for and joined the British Army in WWI, and men who were awarded the Constabulary Medal, the King's Police Medal, as well as those who joined the Garda Síochána after they were disbanded from the RIC. Dr Kevin B. Nowlan provides a foreword.

Jim Herlihy, a member of the Garda Síochána and a founder member of the Garda Síochána Historical Society, Dublin Castle, has worked on these sources for a number of years.

ISBN 1-85182-337-9 cloth
ISBN 1-85182-343-3 pbk

The Siege of Derry in Ulster Protestant Mythology

IAN MAC BRIDE

The Siege of Derry (1688-9) is the key political myth in Loyalist culture. This study looks at the Siege, reconstructing the ways in which the defence of Derry has been commemorated and interpreted over the last 300 years. Celebrated by historians, artists, poets and preachers, re-enacted in anniversary demonstrations and parades, the Siege provides a unique insight into the mixture of triumphalism and insecurity that lies behind the slogan 'No Surrender!'

The story of the Siege embodies in dramatic form a series of timeless lessons regarding the relationship between Ulster Protestants and their ancestral enemies, and the book shows how each generation has emphasised or suppressed different components according to its ideological needs. At various times the emblematic events of 1688-1689 have been represented as a providential deliverance from popery, the restoration of the ancient constitution, a blow struck for the rights of man, and the original act of loyalist rebellion. The memory of the Siege has been a source of discord as well as an agent of union, exposing tensions between Liberals and Conservatives, Anglicans and Presbyterians, the social elite and the common people. A fuller understanding of its role in the Loyalist imagination affirms the complexity and diversity of the Protestant tradition.

Ian McBride is a lecturer in history at the University of Durham. He is the author of Scripture Politics: Ulster Presbyterians and Irish Radicalism in the Late Eighteenth Century *(Oxford, 1997).*

ISBN 1-85182-299-2